SIMPSON'S
1-2-3 MACRO
LIBRARY

SIMPSON'S
1-2-3™ MACRO
LIBRARY

Alan Simpson

Berkeley • Paris • Düsseldorf • London

Cover art by Thomas Ingalls + Associates
Book design by Lorrie Fink Graphic Design

Library of Congress Card Number: 86-61062
ISBN 0-89588-314-7
Printed by Haddon Craftsmen
Manufactured in the United States of America
10 9 8 7 6 5 4 3 2 1

To Susita and The Boys

Acknowledgments

I am indebted to everyone at SYBEX who helped bring this book from the idea stage into your hands. Starting with Rodnay Zaks, who first approached me with the idea, and Carole Alden, who got the project going. Many thanks to Valerie Robbins, manuscript editor; Ray Keefer, technical reviewer; David Clark and Olivia Shinomoto, word processing; Donna Scanlon, typesetting; and Laura Hurd, proofreading.

Many thanks to Bill and Cynthia Gladstone, my literary agents at Waterside Productions, for helping me get 15 books written and published.

And many thanks to my wife Susan, who took care of me through some pretty frantic schedules.

Table of Contents

Introduction

Are you starting to get a little tired of selecting the same old options from the same old menus to get a task done in 1-2-3? Are you starting to find that 1-2-3 cannot accomplish a job you want done? Do you have some great worksheets that you would like to share with computer novices? Are you looking for a lot less typing and a little more automation, customization, and power? If you can answer yes to any of the above questions, then you're ready to start mastering Lotus 1-2-3 macros.

Macros often scare away occasional 1-2-3 users because they sound like they belong to advanced users or programmers. But macros actually have something for everyone. For the occasional user, macros can take the drudgery out of repetitive keystrokes. For the more advanced user, macros can extend 1-2-3 beyond its off-the-shelf capabilities. For the power user and programmer, macros can bypass the 1-2-3 menus altogether so you can develop user-friendly, custom applications that anyone can use.

Who Should Read This Book

This book is not intended for the 1-2-3 novice, though prior experience with macros or programming is not at all necessary. As long as you have a basic feel for 1-2-3 worksheets, menus, and functions, you should have no problem understanding and creating macros. In fact, if you just create and try the first macro (in Chapter 1), you'll get a good idea of what a macro is. By the time you get to the last chapter in this book, you'll have made 1-2-3 perform tricks you may have never thought possible.

The New 1-2-3 (Version 2.0)

This book uses version 2.0 of 1-2-3 for all macros. Those of you who have recently upgraded to version 2.0, or are contemplating doing so, should read Appendix A of this book for a complete description of new features. (If you are still using version 1A, you're missing out on a lot of powerful new features and capabilities.)

Structure of the Book

This book is designed as both a tutorial and a reference. As a tutorial, the book begins with the basics and works towards more complex macros. As a reference, the book contains a collection of macros that you can type in (or purchase) and use for your particular applications.

The first three chapters take an easy walk through 1-2-3's *typing-alternative* macros. These are the easiest macros to create and use and are also some of the handiest!

Chapter 4 discusses *macro commands* that add the power of a computer programming language to your macros. Chapters 5 through 10 present many macros for automating and expanding upon the 1-2-3 worksheet, graphics, and database management capabilities. Chapters 11 and 12 discuss *custom menus,* which you can develop to temporarily replace the built-in 1-2-3 menus. Chapter 13 discusses interfacing with other software systems. Appendix A discusses features new to version 2.0 of 1-2-3.

Purchasing the Macros on Disk

If you wish to purchase copies of the macros in this book on disk, please see the last page of the book for a coupon. The macros are delivered on 5¼ inch IBM double-sided, double-density disks, using PC-DOS Version 2.1 format.

1

YOUR FIRST
MACRO

THIS CHAPTER BEGINS with the basics of creating and playing (or *executing*) macros. If you've never created a macro in your life (or if you're not sure whether you've ever created a macro), this is the place to start. This chapter begins with a discussion of what a macro is and some other fundamentals. Then you'll load up 1-2-3, create a simple macro, play it, and save it.

What Is a 1-2-3 Macro?

In its simplest form, a 1-2-3 macro is a collection of keystrokes stored on the 1-2-3 worksheet. The entire collection of keystrokes can be "typed" simply by pressing a couple of keys. For example, to turn global protection on, you need to type /WGPE (slash Worksheet Global Protection Enable)—five keystrokes. Optionally, you can store the characters '/WGPE in a cell, and give that cell a macro name, such as \p. Then, you can just type Alt-p (hold down the Alt key and type the letter p) to turn on global protection. This way, two keystrokes take the place of five.

Saving three keystrokes is hardly something to get excited about. But then again, a single macro could just as easily store and repeat a thousand keystrokes. Macros can do much more than save keystrokes, though. With the aid of *programming commands,* macros can ask questions, make decisions, and perform tasks that extend beyond the built-in capabilities of 1-2-3.

For example, in this book there are macros that can print mailing labels and form letters, present graphic "slide shows," memorize keystrokes to build macros, and much more. Such tasks would not even be possible in 1-2-3 without the aid of macros.

Macros also allow you to replace the menus that appear at the top of the worksheet with your own menus. This extremely powerful technique allows you to create fully customized and automated worksheets that can be used by people with no 1-2-3 experience whatsoever. In essence, you can "hide" 1-2-3 from the user, and allow them to interact only with your customized accounting, inventory, database, or other custom application.

Macro Keystrokes

Many keystrokes stored in a macro will be identical to the keystrokes you type in at the keyboard. For example, to save a 1-2-3 worksheet, you call up the menu and select the File and Save options by typing a slash, then the letters FS. In a macro, you would simply store the exact keystrokes, /FS.

Some of the special keys on the keyboard, such as those for moving the cell pointer, have special names in macros. These keystrokes have curly braces ({}) around the key names (except for the Return—or Enter—key). Table 1.1 shows the *macro keywords* for these special keys.

You can have a macro repeat a keystroke several times by placing a blank space and a number after the keyword (but inside the braces). For example, the keyword

   {RIGHT 7}

presses the → key seven times. The keyword

   {DOWN 4}

is the same as

   {DOWN}{DOWN}{DOWN}{DOWN}

Macro Names

A macro can have any single letter from A to Z as its name and must begin with a backslash (\) character. Upper- and lowercase

MACRO KEYWORD	DESCRIPTION
	Return or Enter key (⏎) (called a tilde)
{UP}	Up-arrow key (↑)
{DOWN}	Down-arrow key (↓)
{LEFT}	Left-arrow key (←)
{RIGHT}	Right-arrow key (→)
{HOME}	Home key
{END}	End key
{PGUP}	PgUp key
{PGDN}	PgDn key
{BIGLEFT}	(Page left) Ctrl-←
{BIGRIGHT}	(Page right) Ctrl-→
{EDIT}	Edit key (F2)
{NAME}	Name key (F3)
{ABS}	Absolute Value key (F4)
{GOTO}	GoTo key (F5)
{WINDOW}	Window key (F6)
{QUERY}	Database Query key (F7)
{TABLE}	Database Table key (F8)
{CALC}	Calculate key (F9)
{GRAPH}	Graph key (F10)
{ESC} or {ESCAPE}	Escape key
{BS} or {BACKSPACE}	Backspace key
{INSERT}	Insert key (Ins)
{DEL} or {DELETE}	Delete key (used only in Edit mode)
{{}	Left curly brace
{}}	Right curly brace
{~}	Tilde
{?}	Pause until Return is pressed

Table 1.1: Macro keywords

are equivalent, so \A is the same as \a. This means that you can have up to 26 macros in a single worksheet. The two columns below show both valid and invalid macro names:

VALID	INVALID
\a	\cat
\m	\1
\Z	/Z
\t	\F1
\j	\Artichoke

Since 1-2-3 interprets the backslash as a "repeat" symbol, the macro name must be entered with a label prefix. Therefore, the macro name

   \a

is actually typed into a cell as

   '\a

(though, of course, it appears as \a on the worksheet).

A Simple Macro

Generally speaking, the process of creating and using a macro can be broken down into these four steps:

1. Enter the macro name
2. Enter the macro keystrokes
3. Assign the macro name using Range Name Labels Right
4. Play the macro using the Alt key and macro name

The following simple and amusing macro will cause the cell pointer to run a lap around the screen whenever you type Alt-t.

If you have 1-2-3 handy, start it up in the usual fashion so you have a blank worksheet on your screen. Type in this macro using these steps:

1. Enter the macro name. Move the cell pointer to cell A1, type in '\t and then press Return. You should see \t appear in cell A1.

2. Enter the macro keystrokes. Move the cell pointer one row to the right (to cell B1) and type in these macro keystrokes:

   {HOME}
   {RIGHT 7}
   {DOWN 19}
   {LEFT 7}
   {UP 19}

   Your screen should look exactly like the screen in Figure 1.1.

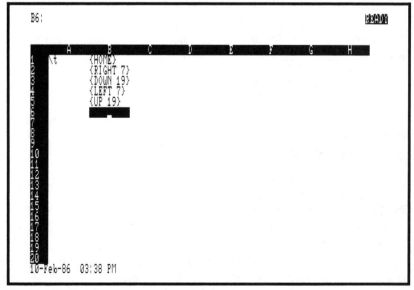

Figure 1.1: Simple macro on the worksheet

3. Assign the macro name using the Range Name Labels Right options. Highlight cell A1, type /RNLR, and press Return. Assign the name \t to the cell on the right (cell B1).

4. Play the macro using the Alt key and macro name. Type Alt-t (hold down the Alt key and type the letter t). You'll see the cell pointer run a quick lap around the screen. If you hold down the Alt key and type the letter t repeatedly, you'll see the cell pointer take several laps around the screen.

The cell pointer took a lap around the screen because the Alt-t (\t) macro told 1-2-3 to put the cell pointer in cell A1 ({HOME}), to press → seven times ({RIGHT 7}), to press ↓ 19 times ({DOWN 19}), to press ← seven times ({LEFT 7}), and finally to press ↑ 19 times ({UP 19}). The macro stopped playing when it encountered the blank cell beneath the {UP 19} command.

It is not essential that each keyword in a macro be on a separate line. For example, you could have entered the keywords in this macro as

{HOME}{RIGHT 7}{DOWN 19}{LEFT 7}{UP 19}

But there are other reasons for breaking macros into several separate lines, as you'll see in the next chapter.

Saving a Macro

You save a macro as you would any other worksheet. To save everything, call up the menu and select the File and Save options. Enter the file name and press Return. To retrieve a macro, use the usual File Retrieve options.

You can also use the File Xtract and File Combine options, discussed in the next chapter, to save and retrieve macros. These are useful for passing macros from worksheet to worksheet.

Summary

Take a moment to review what has been discussed so far. In this chapter you've created your first macro and learned a few fundamentals, as summarized below:

- A macro can be a simple typing alternative, a way of extending 1-2-3's built-in capabilities, or a custom application designed for novice computerists.

- Keystrokes are stored in macros either exactly as they appear on the keyboard, or as special keywords enclosed in curly braces.

- Macro names begin with a backslash character (\) followed by a single letter, A–Z. Upper- and lowercase are the same.

- To create a simple macro, enter the macro name, enter the macro keystrokes, and assign the macro name using Range Name Labels Right.

- To execute a macro, hold down the Alt key and type the letter name of the macro.

- To save and retrieve a macro, use the usual File Save and File Retrieve options from the menu.

The next chapter discusses some finer details of macro creation and management.

2

BUILDING MACROS

THE SIMPLE MACRO presented in the last chapter gave you an idea of what a macro is and how to create one. But when you begin building your own collection of macros, a little planning is advised. This chapter discusses the factors involved in building a collection of useful macros.

Placing a Macro

Generally, the first step in creating a macro is deciding where to put it. Even though, technically, you can put a macro anywhere on a worksheet, there are several reasons why some places are better than others.

First, the /WDR (Worksheet Delete Row) options are a powerful enemy to the macro. For example, suppose you have a worksheet model like the one shown in Figure 2.1. Notice that the model is stored in the upper-left corner of the worksheet.

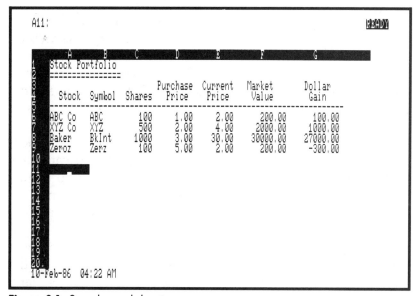

Figure 2.1: Sample worksheet

Now suppose you place a macro over in column Z on this worksheet, as shown in Figure 2.2.

Figure 2.2: Sample macro in column Z

If you use the Worksheet Delete Row (/WDR) options to delete the third row from the worksheet model, you will unfortunately also delete the third row from the macro in column Z. That's because the /WDR command reaches across the entire worksheet to column IV. The chances are that when you attempt to use your macro again, it will not work properly because of the missing row.

The same problem can happen with /WDC (Worksheet Delete Column). Similarly, inserting a row or column can place blank lines in a macro, which will cause a macro to stop prematurely. (Macros end as soon as they encounter a blank line.)

To avoid potential problems with deletions and insertions, store your macros below and to the right of your worksheet (or above and to the left). The advantage of below and to the right over above and to the left is that the worksheet stays in the home position, while the macros stay relatively out of sight. Figure 2.3 shows how you might want to position a range of macros in relation to a worksheet.

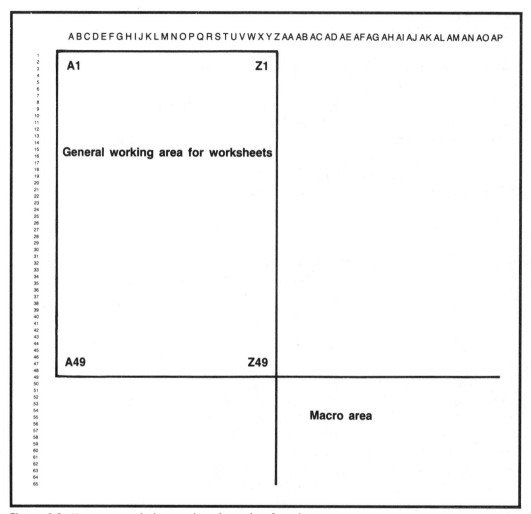

Figure 2.3: Macro range below and to the right of work area

In this book, most macros will be placed in the range beginning at cell Z50, leaving the range A1..Z49 open for data. Use the GOTO (FS) key to move quickly to cell Z50. Depending on the available memory in your computer and the size of your worksheets, you may want to use a different range. However, do try to keep your macros below and to the right of your main work area.

Named Ranges

Another problem that can occur with macros is the repositioning of information with any of the Delete, Move, or Copy commands. To avoid errors caused by relocation, you should try to use range names, rather than specific addresses, as much as possible. (Unlike formulas, cell references inside macros are not updated during Move or Copy.)

For example, suppose your macro contains a command to move to a particular cell:

   {GOTO}A22 ~

When data in the worksheet are moved even slightly, the contents of cell A22 may no longer be what they were when you created the macro.

A better technique is to use a range name in the macro:

   {GOTO}Target ~

Then, move the cell pointer to cell A22 and use the Range Name Create options to name the cell. For example, you could name the cell "Target." Any Delete, Copy, or Move commands that move the worksheet in the future will also update the Target range name; therefore, your macro won't send the cell pointer to the old cell location when the {GOTO} command is executed.

If you haven't used range names in your worksheets before, this discussion will seem a little abstract to you right now. Don't worry about it. You'll see many examples of using range names with macros throughout the book.

Planning a Macro

For simple macros, planning is as easy as performing the tasks that your macro is to perform and writing down your keystrokes as you type them. For example, suppose you want to write a macro to save a worksheet you use often. To save a worksheet that has been saved before with a particular file name, you need to call up the menu (/), select File and Save (FS), and press Return (~) to use the previously assigned file name. Then you need to select Replace from the Cancel and Replace options (R). Hence, your keystrokes are

/FS ~ R

If your macro involves cursor-positioning or special keys, you'll need to use the proper macro keywords (listed in Table 1.1) in your macro. But while jotting down your keystrokes, you can use abbreviations. For example, I often jot my keystrokes down on paper as below:

Home End → ↓ ↓

then later use the proper keynames in the macro, as below:

{HOME}{END}{RIGHT}{DOWN}{DOWN}

(Actually, I often use a macro that simply records my keystrokes as I type them, so I don't have to remember macro keywords at all. This macro is in Chapter 8 of this book.)

Entering a Macro

Technically speaking, you can enter your macro in just about any format. However, these rules must be obeyed:

1. Do not use spaces between menu options. For example, /FS ~ R is acceptable, while / F S ~ R is not. There are some exceptions to this rule, such as {RIGHT 4}, but generally, you should avoid blank spaces in macros.

2. No single macro line can be over 240 characters long.

3. When macro keystrokes begin with a / character, a number, or a formula character, you need to use a label prefix. For example, to enter the keystrokes /FS ˜ R into a macro, you need to actually type '/FS ˜ R. Otherwise, 1-2-3 will simply perform the /FS ˜ R as you enter them.

4. Make sure that the macro has at least one blank row beneath it. Hence, two macros must be stored as below:

\a   /FS ˜ R

\t   {HOME}{LEFT}/QY

and not as below:

\a   /FS ˜ R
\t   {HOME}{LEFT}/QY

The technical rules for macros really do not place many constraints on the macro maker. However, there are a few constraints you might want to put upon yourself as a creator of macros, to make your work easier and more productive in the long run. These constraints are discussed next.

Structuring a Macro

The techniques of *structured programming* were developed in the 1960s to standardize programming techniques in programming teams, and to make everyone's work easier and more productive. You can use these same techniques to build *structured macros* to make your work with macros easier and more productive as well. Some of these techniques, modified slightly for 1-2-3 macros, are discussed below:

- Identify macro names. Put the macro name at the top row of the macro, one column to the left of the macro keystrokes. This allows you to use the Range Names Labels Right options to name the macros; it also lets you see macro names at a glance.

- Keep it simple. Break each macro into short lines on contiguous rows to make them easier to change in the future and easier to debug (correct) should you make an error.

- Use upper/lowercase consistently. Develop an upper- and lowercase scheme for macro commands, keystrokes, and special key names.

- Use comments. Put plain English comments in your macro to interpret abstract lines and commands. These will allow you to readily locate specific portions of a macro and to make changes quickly and easily.

A couple of examples will serve to demonstrate these techniques. Take a look at the macro in Figure 2.4. Although it is a perfectly legitimate macro, there is no way of knowing what keystrokes execute it, or what is the purpose of the macro. Furthermore, you need to scroll around to see the entire macro. Now, suppose you want to change the portion of the macro that saves the file. Where is that portion of the macro?

Now take a look at the very same macro in Figure 2.5. Even though this macro performs the same task, it looks completely

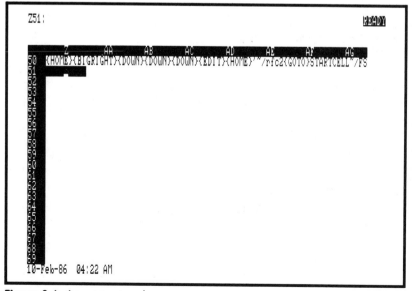

Figure 2.4: An unstructured macro

different. For one thing, the macro name and a description of the macro are included near the top of the macro. For another, the macro is broken into several short lines. Within the macro, key names in curly braces consistently use uppercase, menu options use uppercase, and range names (such as StartCell) use both upper- and lowercase.

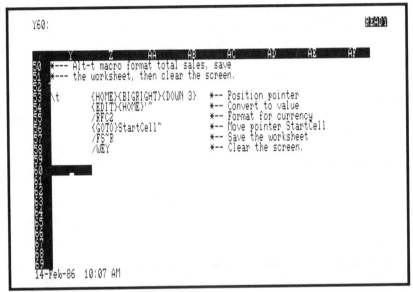

Figure 2.5: A structured macro

Next to each line, a *programmer comment* describes the purpose of the line. It's easy to locate the portion of the macro that saves the file. Just read down the comments column (column AC).

In larger macros, you may find that you cannot really place a comment on every row; or, you may prefer not to clutter up the screen with too many comments. In that case, you might want to place at least a description of the macro above the macro name. Using leading characters in the figure (such as *--) helps make the comments more visible even on a cluttered screen.

As you'll see in later chapters, it is also useful to break larger macros into separate, reusable *subroutines* and *procedures,* which allow you to build new macros more quickly and to avoid repeating old errors.

Playing a Macro

As you saw in the last chapter, you can play (or *execute,* or *invoke,* or *run*) a macro by holding down the Alt key (or MACRO key on some keyboards), and typing in the name of the macro. While a macro is running, the indicator at the bottom of the screen reads CMD.

A macro *always* begins by performing the keystrokes in the upper-left corner of the macro and continues in a left-to-right, top-to-bottom manner from there. (Note that this is the same as the order in which you're reading the words on this page.) The macro quits when it encounters a blank row. (Chapter 4 discusses macro commands that can alter the strict top-to-bottom execution of a macro.)

Interrupting a Macro

To interrupt a macro at any time while it is running, press the BREAK key. (On the IBM keyboard, hold down the Ctrl key and press Scroll Lock.) You may need to press the Escape key after the BREAK key to get back to the worksheet READY mode.

Sometimes, a macro will not perform quite as you expect. Therefore, it is always a good idea to save your entire worksheet just after entering a macro, but before playing it. That way, if the macro seems to be wreaking havoc on your worksheet, just press BREAK to stop the macro. Then use File Retrieve to retrieve the latest copy of the worksheet with the macro in it; then you can correct the macro.

Editing a Macro

Editing the contents of a macro is the same as editing any other cell in a worksheet. Move the cell pointer to the macro keystrokes that you want to modify and press the EDIT key (F2). The macro keystrokes will appear at the top of the screen ready for editing. You can use the usual keys for editing; they are listed in Table 2.1.

KEY	EDITING FUNCTION
←	Move cursor one space left
→	Move cursor one space right
Home	Move cursor to the far left
End	Move cursor to the far right
Backspace	Erase character to the left
Del	Delete character over cursor
Ins	Toggle Insert/Overwrite mode
↵, ↑, or ↓	Finish editing and return to READY mode

Table 2.1: Keys to use for editing a macro

After editing a macro, press Return, ↓, or ↑ to return to READY mode. You need not use the Range Name Labels Right options to rename the macro, unless you've moved either the macro name or the macro keystrokes.

Debugging a Macro

Once you execute a macro, things start happening very quickly. If your macro fails, it is not always easy to pinpoint the exact location of the problem. Therefore, 1-2-3 includes a single-step feature that will execute your macro a single keystroke at a time. This makes it much easier to locate and debug (correct) problems embedded in macros.

To activate the single-step feature, press the STEP key (Alt-F2 on the IBM keyboard). You'll see the word STEP at the bottom of the screen. Then run your macro in the usual fashion.

To proceed through the macro in single-step mode, just press the space bar (or any key) to execute the macro one keystroke at a time. (If the macro contains the {?} command, you'll need to press Return to proceed beyond it.)

When you locate a possible error in your macro, you'll need to stop the macro to fix it. Just press the BREAK key to interrupt the macro. (If you get an error message at the point of the error, you can just press Return to interrupt the error and fix the macro.) Use the usual EDIT key (F2) to modify the macro.

To leave single-step mode and return to normal macro execution, press the STEP key (Alt-F2) again. You will probably not need the single-step feature until you start developing very large macros. But keep it in mind, because it is a very useful tool at the right time and place.

One potentially frustrating error to watch out for is blank spaces at the end of a line in a macro. Since the blank spaces are invisible to the eye, the problem isn't easy to spot. To check to see if there are blank spaces at the end of a line, move the cell pointer to the line and press the Edit (F2) key. If there are no blank spaces, the cursor will appear at the end of the line in the control panel like this:

'/WGCS4 ˜ _

If there are blank spaces, the cursor will appear to the right of the spaces instead, like this:

'/WGCS4 ˜   _

You can use the Backspace key to remove the blank spaces, so that the cursor lines up just past the last character in the line.

Summary

This chapter discussed general techniques for creating and using macros, including the following examples.

- You should always place your macros below and to the right of existing worksheet entries, so that commands that insert and delete columns and rows do not affect the macros.

- Use named ranges in macros, rather than specific cell locations, to avoid problems caused by commands that move data on the worksheet.

- The easiest way to plan a macro is simply to perform the keystrokes that you want the macro to perform and jot them down on a piece of paper.

- When entering macros, use techniques of *structured programming* to structure your macros and make them easier to manage.

- To interrupt a macro while it is running, press the BREAK key (Ctrl-Scroll Lock on IBM keyboards).

- To edit a macro, move the cell pointer to the cell that needs to be changed and press the EDIT key (F2). Press Return after making your changes.

- To help debug a macro, press the STEP key (Alt-F2) to begin single-step mode.

The next chapter will put these techniques to work, developing some macros that will come in handy in a variety of situations.

3

SOME HANDY
LITTLE MACROS

IN THIS CHAPTER WE'LL present a number of useful "typing alternative" macros that can save you time and keystrokes in any worksheet project. We'll store these macros in a range beginning at cell Z50. Memory restrictions or large worksheets may require that you place these macros elsewhere. However, for all the examples in this book, we'll use cell Z50 as the upper-left corner of the macro's range.

Macro to Blank a Cell

To erase (blank) a single cell on a worksheet, you need to position the cell pointer on the cell, call up the menu, select the Range and Erase options, and press Return. Our first simple macro will replace this series of keystrokes with the keys Alt-e.

```
Z69:                                                              READY

         Z        AA       AB       AC       AD       AE      AF       AG
  50 \e    /RE~                          *-- Erase a cell
  51
  52 \d    @DATE(86,{?},{?})~/RFD4~       *-- Enter a date
  53
  54 \t    /RFD2~@TODAY~                 *-- Enter today's date
  55
  56 \p    /PPR{?}~GQ                     *-- Highlight and print a range
  57
  58 \l    {EDIT}{HOME}'~                 *-- Convert a formula to a label
  59
  60 \f    {EDIT}{HOME}{DEL}~             *-- Convert a label to a formula
  61
  62 \v    {EDIT}{CALC}~                  *-- Convert a formula to a value
  63
  64 \b    /FLW                           *-- Display worksheet file names
  65
  66 \k    ^!~/C~{DOWN}.                  *-- Enter column divider
  67
  68 \s    {GOTO}Menu~                    *-- Show menu of options
```

Figure 3.1: Handy macros on the worksheet

The macro is shown below:

    \e   /RE ˜   *-- Erase a cell

To put this macro on your worksheet, move the cell pointer to cell Z50 and enter the macro name

    '\e

into the cell. Move the cell pointer to cell AA50 and enter the keystrokes (with the label prefix) shown below:

    '/RE ˜

Move the cell pointer to cell AD50 and type in the comment

    *-- Erase a cell

To name the macro, move the cell pointer back to the macro label (cell Z50) and select the Range Name Labels Right options (type /RNLR). Press Return to select cell Z50 as the cell containing the macro name.

To test the macro, press the Home key to move up to a blank part of the worksheet. Enter anything into the cell. To erase the cell, just type Alt-e.

This is indeed a simple macro, but it saves you a couple of keystrokes when you need to erase a single cell.

Macro to Enter a Date

Entering dates in 1-2-3 can be a bit troublesome because of all the date functions and formats. Here is a handy macro that can simplify entering a date:

    \d   @DATE(86,{?},{?}) ˜ /RFD4 ˜ *-- Enter a date

The macro name (\d) is in cell Z52; the macro keystrokes are in cell AA52; and the macro comment is in cell AD52. Once you've entered this macro, move the highlighter to cell Z52 and select the Range Name Labels Right options from the menu. Press Return to select cell Z52 as the cell containing the range label (macro name).

To test the macro, press Home to move to an out-of-the-way place on the worksheet. Then, type Alt-d to start entering a date. The control panel will show

@DATE(86,

You type in the month (e.g., 12) and press Return. Next the control panel shows

@DATE(86,12,

You type in the day (e.g., 31) and press Return. The macro fills in the rest and displays the date as below:

12/31/86

Let's take a moment to discuss how this macro works. First, the macro types in the @DATE function and the year followed by a comma. Then the {?} macro keyword waits for you to type in some data. It keeps waiting until you press Return.

After you enter a month, the macro types in another comma, and the {?} portion of the macro waits for you to type in the day, followed by a press on the Return key. After you enter the day, the macro puts the closing parenthesis on the @DATE function and enters it into the cell by pressing Return (˜).

Next, the macro calls up the menu and formats the cell as Date-4 (/RFD4), and presses Return (˜) to specify the currently highlighted cell.

This macro can easily be modified to display the date in another format. For example, to display the date in 31-Dec-86 format, use date format 1, rather than 4:

@DATE(86,{?},{?}) ˜ /RFD1 ˜

The only problem with this format is that it requires more than the default width of nine spaces to display the full date. To compensate for this, you can have the macro also set the column width to 10, by adding the menu option Worksheet Column Set-Width 10, as shown below:

@DATE(86,{?},{?}) ˜ /RFD1 ˜ /WCS10 ˜

Formats for displaying dates are all under the Range Format Date options. In version 2.0 of 1-2-3, your options are

FORMAT	EXAMPLE
DD-MMM-YY	31-Dec-86
DD-MMM	31-Dec
MMM-YY	Dec-86
Long International	12/31/86
Short International	12/31

Dates data can also be displayed in these time formats, using the Range Format Date Time options from the menu:

FORMAT	EXAMPLE
HH:MM:SS AM/PM	02:55:46 PM
HH:MM AM/PM	02:55 PM
Long International	14:55:56
Short International	14:55

Note that International date and time formats can be modified using the Worksheet Global Default Other International Date options.

Macro to Enter Today's Date

If you need to enter today's date into a worksheet, you might prefer to use this macro:

\t   /RFD2 ˜ @TODAY ˜   *-- Enter today's date

Cell Z54 contains the macro name \t. Cell AA54 contains the macro keystrokes, and cell AD54 contains the comment. Move the cell pointer to cell Z54 and select the Range Name Labels Right options to name the macro. Press Return to specify cell Z54 as the range label.

To test the macro, move to an empty cell and type Alt-t. The macro will fill the cell with the current date and format the cell as Date-2. As with the previous date macro, you can modify this macro to use a different date format.

Macro to Highlight and Print a Range

By using this macro, you can reduce the task of printing a worksheet to a few keystrokes:

\p	/PPR{?} ˜ GQ	*-- Highlight and print a range

Before using this macro, use the Print Printer Range options once to highlight the area that you want to print. That way, when you use the macro in the future, it will "remember" the range you printed last (because 1-2-3 remembers print ranges). This makes the macro even easier to use.

In this example, cell Z56 contains the macro name \p. Cell AA56 contains the macro keystrokes, and cell AD56 contains the comment. Put the cell pointer in cell Z56 and use the Range Name Labels Right options to specify cell Z56 as the range label.

To test the macro, first make sure your printer is ready. Then, move the cell pointer to the upper-left corner of the range you want to print (perhaps cell Z50 in this example), and type Alt-p.

You'll be given an opportunity to highlight the range that you want to print using the usual arrow keys. Press Return after highlighting, and the macro will print the highlighted range.

The macro performs this feat by calling up the menu and selecting the Print Printer Range options (/PPR). The {?} causes the macro to wait while you highlight the range and press

Return. The ˜ portion of the macro presses Return again to define the range (your press on the Return key only terminated the {?} keyword). Then the macro selects the Go and Quit (GQ) options from the Print menu.

This macro will "remember" previously defined ranges, and therefore is particularly useful for printing a worksheet that doesn't vary in size. If you prefer to redefine the range each time you use the macro, you can add a Backspace keystroke (you can use either the {BACKSPACE} or {BS} keywords for the Backspace key):

/PPR{BACKSPACE}{?} ˜ GQ

The Backspace causes the macro to erase any suggested range before requesting that a new range be defined.

Macro to Convert
a Formula to a Label

Occasionally, it is handy to convert a formula to a label. For example, you might want to copy a formula such as

@DATE(A3,A2,A1)-@DATE(B3,B2,B1)

to a new cell, but not change the cell references. One way to do this is to make all the cell references absolute, as below:

@DATE(A3,A2,A1)-@DATE(B3,B2,B1)

But this can be pretty tedious if you just want to make a quick copy.

The second method is simply to change the formula to a label, make the copy, then change it back to a formula. Here is a macro to change the formula to a label:

\I   {EDIT}{HOME}'˜   *-- Convert a formula to a
                                   label

Cell Z58 contains the macro name \l, and cell AA58 contains the macro keystrokes {EDIT}{HOME}' ~. Cell AD58 contains the comment. Use Range Name Labels Right to specify cell Z58 as the range label.

The macro performs the conversion by bringing the formula to the control panel for editing ({EDIT}), moving the cursor to the start of the formula ({HOME}), typing in a label prefix ('), and pressing Return to finish the job (~). To test the macro, press Home to home the cell pointer, and type -64 into the cell. Move the cell pointer to cell A2 and type in the formula

@SQRT(@ABS(A1))

The cell will display the result, 8 (the square root of the absolute value of − 64). To change the formula to a label, simply type Alt-l, and the cell will contain the formula itself, rather than the results:

@SQRT(@ABS(A1))

You can Move or Copy this formula without the cell reference changing. Then, you can use the next macro to convert it back to a formula.

Macro to Convert a Label to a Formula

This macro turns a label into a formula or a number:

\f   {EDIT}{HOME}{DEL} ~   *-- Convert a label to a
                                         formula

Cell Z60 contains the macro name \f, and cell AA60 contains the macro keystrokes. Cell AD60 contains the comment. Use the Range Name Labels Right options to specify cell Z60 as the range label.

To test the macro, put the cell pointer on the formula you just copied in the last example and type Alt-f. The macro will remove the leading label prefix, thereby converting the label back to a formula.

Macro to Convert a Formula to a Value

The Alt-v macro, shown below, can change any formula into a value. For example, if a cell contains the formula @SQRT(100), that cell displays the number 10. However, after using this macro on the cell, the formula will disappear and the cell will contain the number 10 only. This is the Alt-v macro:

\v	{EDIT}{CALC} ~	*-- Convert a formula to a value

In this sample worksheet, cell Z62 contains the macro name, cell AA62 the macro keystrokes, and cell AD62 the comments. The macro name was assigned using the Range Name Labels Right options with cell Z62 as the range label.

To test the macro, put a formula such as 10+10 in a cell. You'll see the result, 20, on the worksheet, but the formula 10+10 up in the control panel while the cell is highlighted. If you type Alt-v while the cell is highlighted, you'll see the formula, 10+10, disappear from the cell, leaving only the result, 20, in the cell. Note: The Range Values options from the Main menu (in version 2.0) allow you to convert a range of formulas to values.

Macro to Display Worksheet File Names

The Alt-b macro displays the names of previously stored worksheets on drive B (or your hard disk if you have one). To use the macro, simply type Alt-b at any time, and you'll see file names displayed on the screen, as shown in Figure 3.2.

You can move the highlighter around to see additional information about each file, as displayed on the screen above the file names. When done viewing the file names, press Return to return to the worksheet.

The simple Alt-b macro merely selects the File List Worksheet options. Cell Z64 contains the macro name, \b; cell AA64 contains the macro keystrokes, /FLW; and cell AD64 contains the comment:

\b   **/FLW**   ***-- Display worksheet file**
                                                          names

Use the usual Range Name Labels Right options to assign the name \b to the macro. To test the macro, simply type Alt-b. After viewing the file names, press Return to return to the worksheet.

Incidentally, you can modify this macro to view other types of files. /FLP will display print (.PRN) files, /FLG will display graph (.PIC) files, and /FLO will display all (*.*) files. Of course, you must create a separate macro for each display.

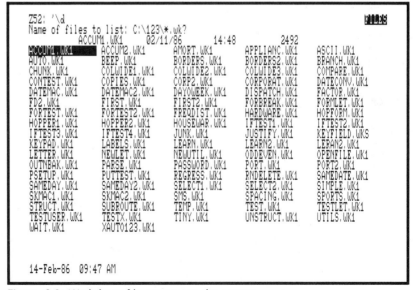

Figure 3.2: Worksheet file names on the screen

Macro to Enter Column Dividers

Entering column dividers into a worksheet can be a bit tedious. This macro lets you highlight a range of rows, then fills in the ¦ symbol, centered, as a divider:

\k   ^¦~/C~{DOWN}.   ***-- Enter column divider**

Cell Z66 contains the macro name \k. Cell AA66 contains the macro keystrokes ^¦~/C~{DOWN}., and cell AD66 contains the comment. Of course, cell Z66 was assigned as the range label using the Range Name Labels Right options.

To test the macro, move the cell pointer to any empty area on the worksheet. Type Alt-k, and the macro will allow you to highlight the column that needs cell dividers. Use ↓ or PgDn to highlight a range, as shown in the example in Figure 3.3.

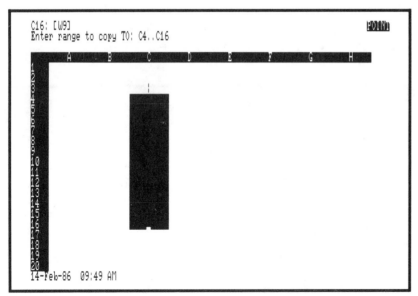

Figure 3.3: Range for cell dividers highlighted

Press Return after highlighting the range of cell dividers. The ¦ character will fill in the cells, as shown in Figure 3.4.

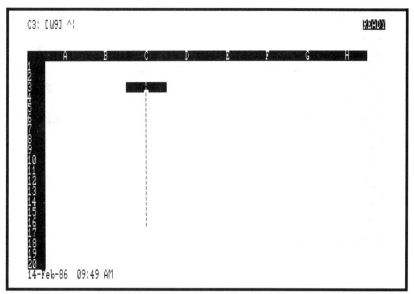

Figure 3.4: Cell dividers entered on the worksheet

The macro works by entering the ¦ character into the cell preceded by the centering label prefix (^¦~). Then the macro selects the Copy option, moves the cell pointer down a cell, and enters a period to draw a range (/C~{DOWN}.). You complete the copy by drawing the range and pressing Return.

You might want to change the column width after entering the divider, or have the macro do it for you. For example, this macro enters the cell divider, then narrows the column to three spaces using the Worksheet Column Set-Width options:

^¦~ **/C**~{**DOWN**}.{**?**}~**/WCS3**~

The {?} portion of the modified macro waits for you to highlight the range, then completes the copy (~) and sets the column width to three spaces (/WCS3~).

Macro to Display a Menu of Macros

When your worksheet has many macros, it's nice to be able to see a quick list of macro names and functions as a reminder of which macros do which jobs. You can create a macro that displays a menu of macro names, as shown in Figure 3.5.

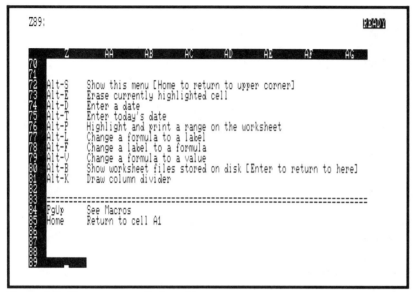

Figure 3.5: Macro names displayed in a menu

To display a menu for these macros, find an out-of-the-way area of the worksheet (such as cell Z70 in this example), and assign a name to the upper-right corner of the menu. (In this example, put the cell pointer in cell Z70, select the Range Name Create options from the menu, type in the name Menu, press Return, and specify Z70 as the range.)

Next, type in the menu as it appears in Figure 3.5. Use this table to help you determine the exact contents of each cell:

Z72:	'Alt-s
AA72:	'Show this menu [Home to return to upper corner]
Z73:	'Alt-e
AA73:	'Erase currently highlighted cell
Z74:	'Alt-d
AA74:	'Enter a date
Z75:	'Alt-t
AA75:	'Enter today's date

Z76:	**'Alt-p**
AA76:	**'Highlight and print a range on the worksheet**
Z77:	**'Alt-l**
AA77:	**'Change a formula to a label**
Z78:	**'Alt-f**
AA78:	**'Change a label to a formula**
Z79:	**'Alt-v**
AA79:	**'Change a formula to a value**
Z80:	**'Alt-b**
AA80:	**'Show worksheet files stored on disk [Enter to return to here]**
Z81:	**'Alt-k**
AA81:	**'Draw column divider**
Z83:	**\ =**
AA83:	**\ =**
AB83:	**\ =**
AC83:	**\ =**
AD83:	**\ =**
AE83:	**\ =**
AF83:	**\ =**
AG83:	**\ =**
Z84:	**'PgUp**
AA84:	**'See Macros**
Z85:	**'Home**
AA85:	**'Return to cell A1**

Once you've created the menu, you need to put a macro for displaying it on the worksheet. Row 68 contains the Alt-s macro for showing the menu:

\s   **{GOTO}Menu ~**   ***-- Show menu of options**

Put the macro name \s in cell Z68 and use Range Name Labels Right to make it the macro name. Put the macro keystrokes in cell AA68 and the comment in cell AD68.

Note the use of the named range within the macro. Since the menu itself might move around slightly as rows and columns are added to or deleted from the worksheet, we've assigned the range name Menu to the upper-left corner of the menu (cell Z70). The macro simply moves the cell pointer to the Menu range using the GOTO key [F5] and the named range.

To test the macro, first press Home to move the cell pointer to an out-of-the-way cell. Then type Alt-s to see the menu. Press Home again to return to the home position after viewing the menu.

Saving the Macros

Be sure to save your work after entering the macros in this chapter. You might want to name the worksheet UTILS, because these macros act as small *utilities*. Under version 2.0 of 1-2-3, the file will be stored as UTILS.WK1.

Moving the Macros

If you want to use some (or all) of these macros in an existing worksheet, use the usual File Retrieve options to call up the existing worksheet. Then, use the File Combine Copy Entire-File options to read in a copy of the UTILS worksheet. If you perform the File Combine with the cell pointer in cell A1, the macros will be stored in the range starting at cell Z50 in your existing worksheet.

The only disadvantage to using File Combine to read in the macros is that the range names are lost in the process. You'll need to reassign range names in the new worksheet. The next section describes a quick and easy way to do that.

Naming Groups of Macros

When you use File Combine to read macros into an existing worksheet, you'll need to recreate all the range names. To do so, move the cell pointer to the uppermost macro name, and select the usual Range Name Labels Right options from the menu. Use the ↓ key to highlight the entire range of macro names, as shown in Figure 3.6. Press Return after completing the highlighting.

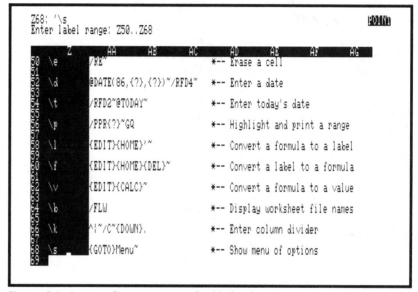

```
Z68: '\s                                                          POINT
Enter label range: Z50..Z68

      Z      AA       AB        AC      AD     AE      AF      AG
50  \e     /RE~                        *-- Erase a cell
51
52  \d     @DATE(86,{?},{?})~/RFD4~    *-- Enter a date
53
54  \t     /RFD2~@TODAY~               *-- Enter today's date
55
56  \p     /PPR{?}~GQ                  *-- Highlight and print a range
57
58  \l     {EDIT}{HOME}'~              *-- Convert a formula to a label
59
60  \f     {EDIT}{HOME}{DEL}~          *-- Convert a label to a formula
61
62  \v     {EDIT}{CALC}~               *-- Convert a formula to a value
63
64  \b     /FLW                        *-- Display worksheet file names
65
66  \k     ^!~/C~{DOWN}.               *-- Enter column divider
67
68  \s     {GOTO}Menu~                 *-- Show menu of options
69
```

Figure 3.6: Range of macro names highlighted

Range names that do not fit into the pattern of macro names (such as the cell named Menu in the UTILS worksheet) will need to be recreated independently. In this example, move the cell pointer to cell Z70 and use the Range Name Create options to name the cell Menu. (The Range Name Labels Right options work *only* in situations where the macro names are in a single column and where the associated macros are exactly one column to the right.)

Summary

In this chapter, we've developed ten simple, handy macros to help in your everyday work with 1-2-3. In addition, we've discussed the following methods.

- To copy the macros into an existing worksheet, use the 1-2-3 File Combine Copy Entire-File options.

- If you align range names in a single column and macro keystrokes in the column directly to the right, you can use the Range Name Labels Right options to name several macros at once.

In the next chapter, we'll discuss advanced macro *commands* that can add a great deal more power to your macros.

MACRO COMMANDS

4

IN THE LAST CHAPTER, we looked at several examples of fairly simple typing-alternative macros. In this chapter, we'll begin discussing more advanced macros that use the 1-2-3 *macro commands*. The macro commands represent a programming language that allows your macros to ask questions, make decisions, display menus, and perform other tasks that go beyond the basic typing-alternative capabilities we've seen.

Earlier versions of 1-2-3 included several simple macro commands (called /X commands). Version 2.0 offers the new macro commands listed below. Even though these commands may look strange and a little intimidating at first glance, you'll soon find that they are quite easy to use and very powerful.

{BEEP}	{GETNUMBER}	{QUIT}
{BLANK}	{GETPOS}	{READ}
{BRANCH}	{IF}	{READLN}
{BREAKOFF}	{INDICATE}	{RECALC}
{BREAKON}	{LET}	{RECALCCOL}
{CLOSE}	{LOOK}	{RESTART}
{CONTENTS}	{MENUBRANCH}	{RETURN}
{DEFINE}	{MENUCALL}	{SETPOS}
{DISPATCH}	{ONERROR}	{WAIT}
{FILESIZE}	{OPEN}	{WINDOWSOFF}
{FOR}	{PANELOFF}	{WINDOWSON}
{FORBREAK}	{PANELON}	{WRITE}
{GET}	{PUT}	{WRITELN}
{GETLABEL}		

We'll group these macro commands in categories and discuss each in this chapter. If you've never used these commands before, you should make an effort to try the sample macros presented throughout this chapter. Nothing explains a macro command better than seeing it in action.

Macro Command Grammar

The macro commands make up a macro *language*, and like all languages, there are certain rules of grammar, or *syntax*, which must be followed for the language to make sense. For example, even though the English sentences "John hit Mary" and "Mary hit John" contain exactly the same words, they have very different meanings because of the order (syntax) of the words. The sentence JohnhitMary has these same three words, but is incorrect because there are no spaces between the words.

The first rule of macro command syntax is that the commands are always enclosed in curly braces ({}). You can use either uppercase or lowercase letters, but the spelling of the command must be perfect.

The second rule of syntax concerns *arguments*. Some macro commands expect one or more arguments within the curly braces. An argument is some item of information that the command uses to perform its work. Any command that uses arguments must include a blank space after the command word and commas between arguments. For example, the LET command stores an item of information in a cell. It uses the syntax

> {**LET** *location,value*}

where *value* is an argument specifying data to be stored, and *location* is an argument describing where to store the data. For example, the command

> {**LET A1,"Over hill, over dale"**}

stores the words "Over hill, over dale" in cell A1. The macro command

> {**LET Target,123**}

stores the number 123 in a cell named "Target." The command below won't work at all, because there is no space after the LET command:

> {**LETTarget,123**}

The command below won't work, because there is no comma between the arguments:

{LET Target 123}

Different commands use different types of arguments. Like an @function, a single macro command might use numbers (like 123), character strings (like "Hello"), cell addresses (like J11), range specifications (like A1..Z10), or conditions (like K11>=22) as arguments. And, like @functions, using the wrong argument type will cause an error. The examples in this book will demonstrate the proper argument types for each macro command. The *Quick Reference* that comes with 1-2-3 is a useful resource for quickly looking up the syntax and argument types of macro commands.

User-Interface Commands

The user-interface commands allow a macro to pose a question and wait for an answer. We've already seen an example of the {?} macro keyword in the last chapter; it paused the macro to give us time to highlight a range. Other user-interface commands are discussed in this section.

{GETLABEL *prompt string,location*}   The GETLABEL command displays a *prompt string* in the control panel and waits for the user to type in some information, then press the Return key. Whatever the user types in is stored at *location,* which is a cell address or range name. If the *prompt string* contains a comma or colon, it must be enclosed in quotation marks. (For simplicity, it's just as easy to always enclose the prompt string in quotation marks.) For example, the command

{GETLABEL "What is your name? :",UserName} ˜

displays the message

What is your name? :

in the control panel and waits for the user to type in some information and press the Return key. Whatever the user enters is
stored in a cell named UserName. The Return symbol (˜) at the
end of the command makes sure the information goes into
the cell immediately.

{GETNUMBER *prompt string,location*}   The GETNUMBER
command is almost identical to GETLABEL, except that it stores
the entered data as a number rather than a label. For example, the
command

    {GETNUMBER "How old are you? :",UserAge} ˜

displays the message

    How old are you? :

in the control panel and waits for an answer followed by a press
on the Return key. The user's entry is stored as a number in the
cell named UserAge.

{GET *location*}   This command waits for a single key press and
stores that key press at *location* on the worksheet. GET does not
display a prompt string in the control panel. The keystroke is
stored as a label. If you press a "special key," such as Home,
GET stores the macro keyword for the key (e.g., {HOME}).

To get a better feel for these macro commands, take a
moment to enter the sample macro shown in Figure 4.1. After
entering the macro on your screen, use the Range Name Labels
Right options and highlight the range Z53..Z57 as range labels.

The exact contents of each cell are listed below. Use Worksheet Column-Width Set to make column Z ten spaces wide. All
other columns are the default nine spaces wide. Comments are
preceded with an asterisk and two hyphens to make them stand
out and to visually separate them from the macro commands. If
you want to save the macro, use the usual File Save options and
enter a file name, such as TestUser.

    Z50:   **'*-- TestUser macro tests the user-interface commands.**

    Z51:   **'*-- Range Names are listed in Z53..Z57.**

    Z53:   **'UserName**

Z54:	**'UserAge**
Z55:	**'KeyPress**
Z57:	**'\t**
AA57:	**'{GETLABEL "What is your name? :",UserName}** ˜
AF57:	**'*Get a label**
AA58:	**'{GETNUMBER "How old are you? :",UserAge}** ˜
AF58:	**'*Get a number**
AA59:	**'{GOTO}AA66** ˜
AF59:	**'*Move highlight**
AA60:	**'Press any key on the keyboard . . .** ˜
AF60:	**'*Print message**
AA61:	**'{DOWN}**
AF61:	**'*Move highlight**
AA62:	**'{GET KeyPress}** ˜
AF62:	**'*Get a keystroke**

After you've typed in the entire macro and named the ranges, type Alt-t to run the macro. First, the GETLABEL command will display its prompt on the screen. Type in your name and press Return. Notice that your answer is stored in the cell named UserName. Next, the macro will ask for your age. Type

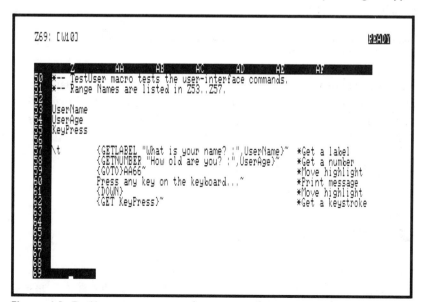

Figure 4.1: TestUser macro to test the user-interface commands

in your age and press Return. Notice that your answer is stored in the cell named UserAge.

Next, the macro prints the message "Press any key on the keyboard . . ." directly on the worksheet. (If you press the space bar, you won't be able to see the results, so press another key, such as Home.) You'll see the key press appear in the cell named KeyPress, as shown in Figure 4.2.

Figure 4.2: TestUser macro after answering prompts

{**LOOK** *location*}   This is a special user-interface command that checks to see if a key has been pressed but does not halt execution of the macro to do so. If a key has indeed been pressed, it stores that key press at *location,* as does the GET command. LOOK is most often used in conjunction with the other commands. We'll see an application of the LOOK command in Chapter 5.

Decision Making

One of the most powerful and important of the macro commands is the one that has the ability to make decisions based upon variable data (information that changes). The macro command for making decisions is IF.

{IF *condition*}   The IF command evaluates the *condition* argument. If the condition is true, the commands to the right of the IF command (on the same row, in the same cell) are processed. If the condition is false, the commands to the right of the IF command are ignored.

{BRANCH *location*}   The BRANCH command is often used in conjunction with the IF command to cause processing to continue in a different location of the macro. For example, look at the simple macro below, where \x is the name of the macro, and Endif is the name of the cell to the right (beneath the macro):

\x	**{IF UserName = "Bob"} Hi Bob! ˜ {BRANCH Endif}**
	Who are you? ˜
Endif	**{HOME}**

This macro checks to see if the cell named UserName contains the name Bob. If so, the macro types Hi Bob! into the currently highlighted cell, then continues processing at the HOME command. If the cell named UserName does not contain the name Bob, the macro types the message "Who are you?" into the currently highlighted cell, then continues processing at the HOME command.

Figure 4.3 shows a sample macro, named IfTest1, that uses the IF, BRANCH, and GETNUMBER commands. Type in the macro as shown in the figure, and use Range Name Labels Right to define the labels in cells Z53..Z59 as range names.

The exact contents of each cell are listed below:

Z50:	**'*--- IfTest1: First macro to test the IF command.**
Z51:	**'*--- Range Z53..Z59 contains range labels.**
Z53:	**'Answer**
Z55:	**'\a**
AA55:	**'{HOME}**
AA56:	**'{GETNUMBER "What is 1 + 1? :",Answer} ˜**

AA57:   '{IF Answer = 2}Nice work! ˜ {BRANCH Endif}
AA58:   'Back to kindergarten for you! ˜
Z59:   'Endif

To run the macro, type Alt-a. The GETNUMBER command will display the prompt

What is 1 + 1?

at the top of the screen. If you type 2 as your answer, the macro displays Nice work! in cell A1. If you type in a number other than 2, the macro displays the message "Back to kindergarten for you!" in cell A1.

The IF command can test for a certain key press. For example, the macro in Figure 4.4 displays the message "Press the Page Up key please . . ." in the home cell. The key press is stored in the cell named Answer. If the user does press PgUp, the macro displays the message "Nice work!" two rows below. Otherwise, the macro displays the message "Sorry, that's not right."

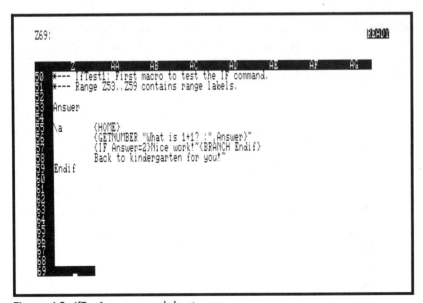

Figure 4.3: IfTest1 macro worksheet

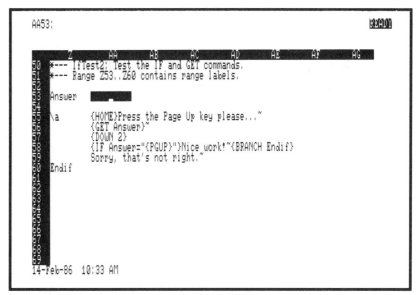

Figure 4.4: IfTest2 macro to test the IF and GET commands

Cells Z50..Z60 contain range names in this example. These are the exact contents of each cell:

Z50:	**'*--- IfTest2: Test the IF and GET commands.**
Z51:	**'*--- Range Z53..Z60 contains range labels.**
Z53:	**'Answer**
Z55:	**'\a**
AA55:	**'{HOME}Press the Page Up please... ~**
AA56:	**'{GET Answer} ~**
AA57:	**'{DOWN 2}**
AA58:	**'{IF Answer = "{PGUP}"}Nice work! ~ {BRANCH Endif}**
AA59:	**'Sorry, that's not right. ~**
Z60:	**'Endif**

It's quite possible that an IF command will have to decide between more than two alternatives. You can stack IF clauses on top of one another to make decisions from several alternatives, as shown in Figure 4.5. Use Range Name Labels Right to specify the labels in cells Z53..Z62 as range names.

Figure 4.5: IfTest3 macro with three IF commands

These are the exact contents of each cell:

Z50:	**'*-- IfTest3: Another test of the IF command.**
Z51:	**'*-- Range names are in cells Z53..Z62**
Z53:	**'Answer**
AA53:	**'a**
Z55:	**'\b**
AA55:	**'{HOME}**
AA56:	**'{GETLABEL "Enter a letter, A, B, or C : ",Answer} ~**
AA57:	**'{HOME}As in**
AA58:	**'{IF @UPPER(Answer) = "A"} Apple ~ {BRANCH Endif}**
AA59:	**'{IF @UPPER(Answer) = "B"} Banana ~ {BRANCH Endif}**
AA60:	**'{IF @UPPER(Answer) = "C"} Cherry ~ {BRANCH Endif}**
AA61:	**' Apple, Banana, or Cherry please! ~**
Z62:	**'Endif**

To run this macro, type Alt-b. The control panel will display the prompt:

Enter a letter, A, B, or C :

If you enter the letter A (or a), the home cell will display

As in Apple

If you enter the letter B (or b), the home cell will display

As in Banana

If you enter the letter C (or c), the home cell will display

As in Cherry

If you enter some other letter, the home cell will display

As in Apple, Banana, or Cherry please!

Notice that the macro uses the worksheet @UPPER function in the IF condition to convert the user's answer to uppercase before comparing it to the letter A, B, or C. One of the beauties of the IF command is that it allows you to use worksheet @functions in the condition portion. You'll see plenty of situations where this comes in handy throughout the book.

In cases where there are many alternatives from which to choose, you might be able to use the worksheet @CHOOSE function rather than a series of IF commands to make a decision in a worksheet. Or, you can have the macro type the @CHOOSE formula onto the screen.

For example, the macro in Figure 4.6 asks the user to enter a number between 1 and 10. If the user does so, the macro displays the words "That is" and the word for the number (e.g., "That is One" or "That is Nine"). If the number entered is not in the range from 1 to 10, the macro displays "That is not between 1 and 10!" Labels in the range Z53..Z61 are Range Name Labels Right range names.

These are the exact contents of each cell in the macro:

Z50:   '+--- IfTest4: Test the IF command and @CHOOSE
           function.

Z51:   '+--- Range Z53..Z61 contains range labels.

Z53:   'Answer

Z55:   '\a
AA55:   '{HOME}
AA56:   '{GETNUMBER "Enter a number from 1 to 10 :
      ",Answer} ~
AA57:   'That is ~ {RIGHT}
AA58:   '{IF Answer<1#OR#Answer>10}not between 1 and
      10! ~ {BRANCH Endif}
AA59:   '@CHOOSE(Answer-1,"One","Two","Three","Four",
      "Five","Six",
AA60:   ' "Seven","Eight","Nine","Ten") ~
Z61:   'Endif

Notice that rather than having a long series of IF commands to show the English words for each number, the macro simply types into the cell the formula

**@CHOOSE(Answer-1,"One","Two","Three","Four","Five",
"Six","Seven","Eight","Nine","Ten")**

(In the worksheet cell, the @CHOOSE formula must always be on a single line.) The @CHOOSE function makes a decision

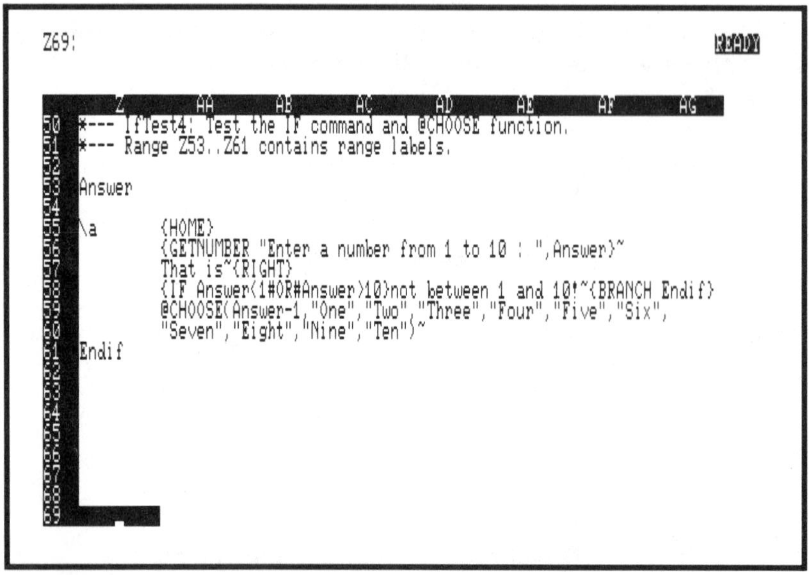

Figure 4.6: IfTest4 macro with IF command and @CHOOSE function

based on the first argument. If the first argument is zero, the first option is selected. If the first argument is one, the second option is selected, and so on. In this example, @CHOOSE operates on the value of Answer-1. Hence, if the Answer cell contains 8, then @CHOOSE(8-1 . . .) displays the word "Seven". If Answer-1 is zero, then @CHOOSE displays "One". The -1 offset is necessary because zero selects the first option.

As you might have figured out by now, @CHOOSE is handy for converting month numbers (1–12) to words (January–December), and day numbers (1–7) to words (Sunday–Saturday). We'll see examples of such macros in Chapter 6.

Looping

Another useful advanced macro technique is that of *looping,* or performing a group of macro commands or keywords repeatedly. 1-2-3 uses two macro commands for looping.

{**FOR** *start,stop,step,macro name*}   The first three arguments in the FOR command are numeric. They tell the macro where to start counting, how high to count, and how much to increment with each count. The last argument, *macro name,* is a range name that specifies a macro to execute.

Take a look at the simple macro below, which contains the named ranges Counter, \f, and DoThis.

```
Counter    0
\f         {FOR Counter,1,50,1,DoThis}
DoThis     /WCS3{RIGHT 2}
```

The macro subroutine named DoThis sets the column width of the currently highlighted cell to three spaces (/WCS3) then moves the cell pointer two columns to the right. However, this small routine is actually repeated 50 times when the \f macro is executed. That's because the FOR command starts counting at 1, and keeps counting until the value stored in the Counter cell is 50. Each time through the loop, the FOR command performs the commands in the DoThis subroutine, and increments the value of Counter by one.

You can watch a FOR command increment the Counter value by developing a macro like the one shown in Figure 4.7. These are the exact contents of each cell:

Z50:	**'*-- ForTest1. Test the looping command.**
Z51:	**'*-- Range names are in cells Z53..Z58**
Z53:	**'Counter**
AE53:	**'*-- Counter cell**
Z55:	**'\f**
AA55:	**'{HOME} + Counter ~**
AE55:	**'*-- Put formula in home cell**
AA56:	**'{FOR Counter,0,100,1,ShowNumb}**
AE56:	**'*-- Loop from 0 to 100**
Z58:	**'ShowNumb**
AA58:	**'{CALC}**
AE58:	**'*-- ShowNumb routine**

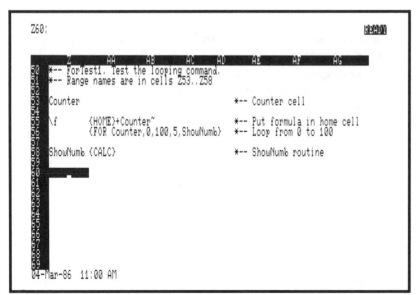

Figure 4.7: ForTest1 macro to test the FOR command

This simple macro places the formula +Counter in cell A1, which will show the contents of the Counter cell. Then, a FOR loop starts counting at zero, incrementing by one each time through the loop. For each pass through the loop, the ShowNumb routine recalculates ({CALC}) the value of Counter. Hence, when run, the macro appears to count from 0 to 100 in cell A1.

The *start, stop,* and *step* arguments can be variables. For example, the macro in Figure 4.8 uses the GETNUMBER command to ask for a starting, stopping, and stepping value for the loop.

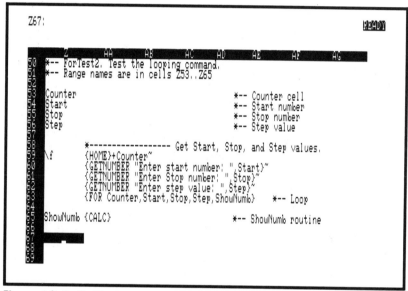

Figure 4.8: ForTest2 macro to test FOR command with GETNUMBER data

These are the exact contents of each cell:

Z50:	**'*-- ForTest2. Test the looping command.**
Z51:	**'*-- Range names are in cells Z53..Z65**
Z53:	**'Counter**
AE53:	**'*-- Counter cell**
Z54:	**'Start**
AE54:	**'*-- Start number**
Z55:	**'Stop**
AE55:	**'*-- Stop number**
Z56:	**'Step**
AE56:	**'*-- Step value**

```
AA58:    '*---------------- Get Start, Stop, and Step values.
Z59:     '\f
AA59:    '{HOME} + Counter ~
AA60:    '{GETNUMBER "Enter start number: ",Start} ~
AA61:    '{GETNUMBER "Enter stop number: ",Stop} ~
AA62:    '{GETNUMBER "Enter step value: ",Step} ~
AA63:    '{FOR Counter,Start,Stop,Step,ShowNumb}
AF63:    '*-- Loop
Z65:     'ShowNumb
AA65:    '{CALC}
AE65:    '*-- ShowNumb routine
```

Answers to the GETNUMBER questions are stored in the cells named Start, Stop, and Step in column Z. (Use Range Name Labels Right to highlight all the labels in column Z in this macro.) You might want to experiment with a few different numbers with this macro. Think before you act, though. For example, if you start the loop at 1, end the loop at 10, and make the step value zero, the loop will repeatedly display the number 1 and never stop, because the Counter value will never get closer to 10. The only way to stop the macro will be to press the BREAK key.

Similarly, if you enter a larger start number than stop number, the step value must be a negative number. For example, a loop that starts counting at 10 and stops counting at 1 needs to step -1 to eventually get to 1.

{FORBREAK} The FORBREAK command terminates a FOR loop whether or not the Stop value has been encountered. This command uses no arguments. For an example of the FORBREAK command, take a look at this macro:

```
Counter

\f              {FOR Counter,1,1000,1,RepMacro}
                Done! ~

RepMacro        {IF @CELLPOINTER("contents") = "Quit"}
                {FORBREAK}
                /RFC ~ ~
                {RIGHT 2}
```

This macro will select the Range Format Currency options in every other cell across a worksheet either until the counter reaches 1,000, or until the cell pointer lands in a cell that has the word Quit in it. In either case, the macro prints the word "Done!" when the FOR loop ends. (The @CELLPOINTER("contents") function returns the contents of the currently highlighted cell.) FORBREAK stops processing the FOR loop immediately and passes control to the first line beneath the FOR command. If the line beneath the FOR command is blank, the macro simply stops.

Manipulating Data

We've seen how the GETLABEL, GETNUMBER, and GET commands store information in named cells. Numerous other macro commands allow macros to store data in cells, pull data from cells, and recalculate current values. These commands are the topic of this section.

{LET *location,value:optional type*} The LET command allows you to place a *value* in a cell at *location*. Optionally, you can define that the stored data be a label (:string) or value (:value).

Figure 4.9 shows a simple macro that demonstrates several varieties of the LET command. The exact contents of each cell are listed below. Use the Range Name Labels Right options to specify the range Z53..Z60 as range names.

These are the exact contents of each cell:

Z50:	**'*-- TestLet macro tests various versions of the LET command.**
Z51:	**'*-- Range names are in cells Z53..Z60.**
Z53:	**'Cell1**
Z54:	**'Cell2**
Z55:	**'Cell3**
Z56:	**'Cell4**
Z57:	**'Cell5**
Z58:	**'Cell6**

Z60:   '\l

AA60:   '{LET Cell1,"Howdy"} ~

AA61:   '{LET Cell2,100} ~

AA62:   '{LET Cell3,300:value} ~

AA63:   '{LET Cell4,Cell2 + Cell3:value} ~

AA64:   '{LET Cell5,Cell2 + Cell3:string} ~

AA65:   '{LET Cell6,Cell1&" Podner"} ~

After typing Alt-l to run the macro, the named cells near the top of the screen will contain these values:

Cell1   'Howdy

Cell2   100

Cell3   300

Cell4   400

Cell5   'Cell2 + Cell3

Cell6   'Howdy Podner

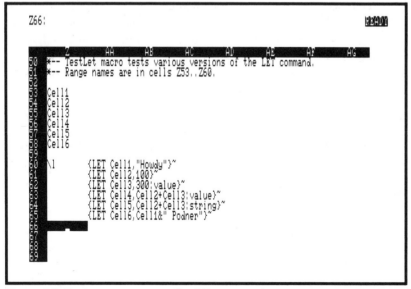

Figure 4.9: TestLet macro to test the LET command

The command {LET Cell1,"Howdy"} puts the label Howdy in Cell1. The commands {LET Cell2,100} and {LET Cell3,300} put the numbers 100 and 300 into Cell2 and Cell3. The command {LET Cell4,Cell2+Cell3:value} places the sum of Cell2 and Cell3 (400) in Cell4 as a value. The command {LET Cell5,Cell2+Cell3: string} places the string Cell2+Cell3 into Cell5 as a character string. Finally, the command {LET Cell6,Cell1&" Podner"} places the contents of Cell1 ("Howdy") plus the word Podner (preceded by a space) in Cell6, resulting in the label Howdy Podner.

If you do not specify a *:string* or a *:value* in the LET command, 1-2-3 will make a reasonable guess at the most likely result (like the summed cells in the example). Placing a Return (~) at the end of each LET command ensures that the cell will be updated immediately. Otherwise, you may need to press the CALC key to update a cell.

{CONTENTS *destination,source,optional* **width,*optional* *number*}** The CONTENTS command is similar to LET, except that it copies the contents of one cell to another and (optionally) formats the data in the process. The *optional width* parameter controls the width of the data entered into the destination cell, not the width of the column. *Optional width* uses the numeric formatting codes listed in Table 4.1 to format data in the destination cell.

Figure 4.10 shows a sample macro that takes data from cells Raw1, Raw2, and Raw3 and enters data into several cells using the CONTENTS command.

The exact contents of the cells are shown below. Note that cell AA56, which displays 8, actually contains the formula @SQRT(64).

Z50:	**'*-- ConTest Macro: Tests the CONTENTS command.**
Z51:	**'*-- Range names are in cells Z54..Z64.**
Z52:	**'*-- Cell Raw3 contains the formula @SQRT(64).**
Z54:	**'Raw1**
AA54:	**123**
Z55:	**'Raw2**
AA55:	**'ABC**
Z56:	**'Raw3**
AA56:	**@SQRT(64)**

Z58:   **'First**
Z59:   **'Second**
Z60:   **'Third**
Z61:   **'Fourth**
Z62:   **'Fifth**
Z64:   **'\c**
AA64: **'{CONTENTS First,Raw1}**
AA65: **'{CONTENTS Second,Raw2}**
AA66: **'{CONTENTS Third,Raw1,9,3}**
AA67: **'{CONTENTS Fourth,Raw2,2,4}**
AA68: **'{CONTENTS Fifth,Raw3,10,117}** ~

CODE	NUMERIC FORMAT
0 to 15	Fixed, 0 to 15 decimal places
16 to 32	Scientific, 0 to 15 decimal places
33 to 47	Currency, 0 to 15 decimal places
48 to 63	Percent, 0 to 15 decimal places
64 to 79	Comma, 0 to 15 decimal places
112	+/- horizontal bar graph
113	General
114	D1 (DD-MMM-YY)
115	D2 (DD-MMM)
116	D3 (MMM-YY)
121	D4 Full International Date
122	D5 Partial International Date
119	D6 (HH:MM:SS AM/PM)
120	D7 (HH:MM AM/PM)
123	D8 Full International Time
124	D9 Partial International Time
117	Text; formulas displayed as labels
118	Hidden
127	Default numeric display format

Table 4.1: Format options for the CONTENTS command

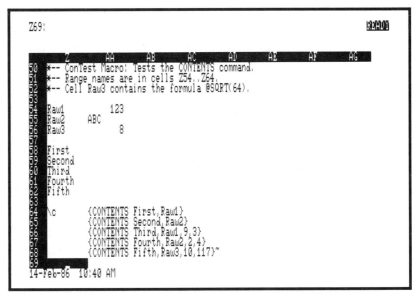

Figure 4.10: ConTest macro to test the CONTENTS command

After running the macro by typing Alt-c, the named cells will contain the following data. Note that *all* of the data are labels in the destination cells.

First	'	123
Second	'ABC	
Third	'	123.000
Fourth	'AB	
Fifth	'@SQRT(64)	

The command {CONTENTS First,Raw1} places the contents of cell Raw1 in the cell named First, converting the numeric 123 to a label. The formula {CONTENTS Second,Raw2} places the label ABC from the Raw2 cell into the cell named Second. The command {CONTENTS Third,Raw1,9,3} places 123.000 in the cell named Third, because the format argument (3) specifies three decimal places of accuracy.

The formula {CONTENTS Fourth,Raw2,2,4} places AB in the cell named Fourth. The result is narrowed to two spaces because of the 2 in the width argument. The format argument (4) has no effect, because the source datum was numeric. The cell named Fifth contains the label @SQRT(64) because the format argument (117) in the formula {CONTENTS Fifth,Raw3,10,117} specifies text as the display format.

{**BLANK** *location*}   The BLANK command erases the contents of cells specified in the *location* argument. The location can be a single cell address (e.g., {BLANK A1}), a range (e.g., {BLANK A1..A50}), or a named range (e.g., {BLANK WorkArea}). The simple macro below erases the contents of all cells in the range A1..G20 and types the heading "Dear Sir" into the Home cell.

> \h   {**BLANK A1..G20**}
>   {**HOME**}
>   **Dear Sir:** ~

{**PUT** *range location,column,row,data*}   The PUT command allows you to specify a range of cells and to enter data into the range by row and column position. Column 0, row 0 is always the upper-leftmost corner of the range, regardless of its location on the worksheet.

The opposite of the PUT command is the @INDEX function, which reads data by row and column position in a range. Take a look at this macro:

> \p   {**PUT C4..G12,0,0,123**}
>   {**PUT C4..G12,2,4,HoHoHo**}
>   {**PUT C4..G12,4,8,@INDEX(C4..G12,0,0)∗10**} ~

Now look at the worksheet in Figure 4.11. The highlighted area shows the range defined by the PUT commands (C4..G12). The number 123 appears in the upper-left corner of the range because of the command

> {**PUT C4..G12,0,0,123**}

The word HoHoHo appears near the middle of the range (column 2, row 4) because of the command

> {**PUT C4..G12,2,4,HoHoHo**}

The number 1230 appears in the lower-right corner of the range because of the command

{PUT C4..G12,4,8,@INDEX(C4..G12,0,0)∗10} ~

This command tells 1-2-3 to put into the fourth column, eighth row of the range, the contents of the upper-left corner or the range (@INDEX(C4..G12,0,0)) times 10.

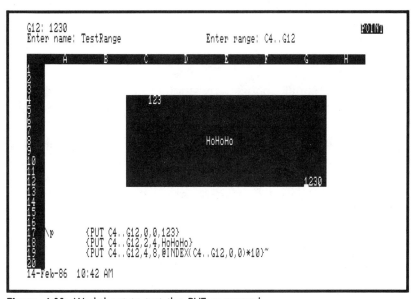

Figure 4.11: Worksheet to test the PUT command

Controlling the Display

Numerous macro commands allow you to control the appearance of the screen while a macro is running. These are, basically, BEEP, INDICATE, RECALC, RECALCCOL, PANELON, PANELOFF, WINDOWSON, WINDOWSOFF, and WAIT.

{BEEP *number*}   This command sounds the computer's beeper or bell. The optional *number* argument can be a number from 1

to 4. The simple macro below plays all four tones. BEEP with no argument elicits the same tone as {BEEP 1}.

       \b   {BEEP 1}
               {BEEP 2}
               {BEEP 3}
               {BEEP 4}

{INDICATE *message*}   This command lets you change the mode indicator in the upper-right corner of the screen. The *message* can be up to five characters long. INDICATE with no argument returns to the READY indicator. The command INDICATE " " removes the indicator. The indicator you assign will remain on the screen until changed by another INDICATE command. Normal indicator changes are overruled by INDICATE.

{PANELOFF}   The PANELOFF command uses no arguments. It suppresses redrawing of the control panel during macro execution. If a macro begins with a PANELOFF command, you will not see the macro selecting items from the menu.

{PANELON}   PANELON is the opposite of PANELOFF and is the normal state of 1-2-3. When PANELON is used in a macro, control panel messages and menus are visible during macro execution.

{WINDOWSOFF}   The WINDOWSOFF command suppresses redrawing of the worksheet during macro execution. For example, suppose you have a macro that moves the highlighter from cell to cell and makes changes to the cell contents. If the macro began with the WINDOWSOFF command, you would not see the cell pointer moving about or the changes being made. Instead, you'd see the end results only after the macro stopped executing.

{WINDOWSON}   The WINDOWSON command restores normal redrawing of the worksheet. Neither the WINDOWSOFF command nor the WINDOWSON command accepts arguments.

{WAIT *serial time specification*}   The WAIT command displays the message WAIT in the indicator at the top of the screen and pauses a macro for a specified length of time. The *serial time specification* argument is usually a calculation of the @NOW and @TIME functions. Once the WAIT indicator is flashing, the only way to interrupt the macro is with the BREAK key.

This sample macro beeps, displays the message "Ten seconds until next beep . . .", flashes the WAIT indicator for ten seconds, then beeps again:

\b   **{BLANK A1}{HOME}{BEEP 4}**
         Ten seconds until next beep . . . ˜
         {WAIT @NOW + @TIME(0,0,10)}
         {BEEP 2}

{RECALC *location,optional condition,optional iteration*} The RECALC command gives you complete control over worksheet recalculation during macro execution. It performs row-by-row re-calculations of a range on a worksheet specified by the *location* argument.

{RECALCCOL *location,optional condition,optional iteration*} RE-CALCCOL is similar to RECALC, but recalculates the worksheet in a columnwise manner.

The {CALC} keyword will recalculate an entire worksheet from within a macro. Both RECALC and RECALCCOL are partic-ularly useful on large worksheets because they allow you to recalculate only specified portions of the worksheet.

If you have set the recalculation method to manual, your macros will require the CALC, RECALC, or RECALCCOL com-mands to accurately reflect new values on the worksheet. Also, if you do not use a Return (˜) with updating commands like LET and CONTENTS, you may need to use one of the recalculation commands to update cells during macro execution.

When recalculating only a portion of a worksheet, you need to think about the relationships between interdependent cells. If a formula in a worksheet depends on a calculated value in another cell, be sure to calculate the dependent cell after the independent cell. If the dependent cell is below and to the left of the independent cell, use RECALC. If the dependent cell is above and to the right of the independent cell, use RECALCCOL.

The optional *condition* and *iteration* arguments allow you to be even more specific about recalculations. The *condition* argument can be used as an "until." Iterations are the number of times the range is recalculated. Hence, the command

{RECALC MyIrr,Converg<.0000002,55}

recalculates a range named MyIrr until the number in the cell named Converg falls below .0000002, or until 55 iterations have occurred.

Subroutines

We discussed the BRANCH command earlier; it passes control directly to another part of a macro. With the use of the *Routine Name* and RETURN commands, you can pass control to an external subroutine temporarily from within a macro.

{Routine Name, optional arguments}   The *Routine Name* command allows you to call a subroutine by any name inside the braces. The routine may not, however, have the same name as a macro command (such as BEEP). The *optional arguments* are discussed under DEFINE in the next section.

{RETURN}   When a subroutine is called with a *Routine Name* command, the RETURN command returns control to the first command beyond the *Routine Name* command. Control is also returned to the calling program when the subroutine finishes naturally by encountering a blank row.

Take a look at this macro, which uses two subroutines, named Numeric and Character:

*-- Macro to test subroutines.

\s	**{HOME}**
LoopTop	**{IF @CELLPOINTER("type")="v"}{Numeric}**
	{IF @CELLPOINTER("type")="l"}{Character}

                              {**RIGHT**}
                              {**IF @CELLPOINTER("type")<>"b"**}
                                   {**BRANCH LoopTop**}

Numeric   /**RFC**~~ **∗--Subroutine to format a number.**
                     {**RETURN**}
Character   /**RLC**~   **∗--Subroutine to format a string.**
                     {**RETURN**}

The name of the macro is \s. When executed, the macro homes the cursor. Then, if the type of data in the currently highlighted cell is a value (@CELLPOINTER("type")="v"), the macro passes control to a subroutine named Numeric. The subroutine formats the cell in Currency format, then the RETURN command returns control to the main body of the macro (the next IF command).

If the currently highlighted cell contains a label, the macro passes control to a subroutine named Character, which formats the cell with the Centered prefix and then returns control to the main body of the macro. Next, the macro moves the cell pointer one cell to the right. If the currently highlighted cell is not a blank (@CELLPOINTER("type")<>"b"), then the BRANCH command passes control to the cell named LoopTop, and the macro continues processing.

Breaking a program into subroutines like this can help keep individual routines in a macro down to a manageable size. Also, you can better structure macros that involve many IF commands. Recall that the IF command processes all commands to the right if the condition is true. Therefore, if several commands are necessary when the IF condition is true, as below:

             {**IF X1>10**}{**WINDOWSOFF**}/**WGRM**~{**LET X10,123**}
                  {**WINDOWSON**}{**CALC**}

you can simply place them in a subroutine and access them with a *Routine Name*, as below:

                    {**IF X1>10**}{**ManuCalc**}

ManuCalc   {**WINDOWSOFF**}
                    /**WGRM**~

```
{LET X10,123}
{WINDOWSON}
{CALC}
{RETURN}
```

Another advantage to subroutines is that they can be accessed from many different places in a macro. For example, suppose the ManuCalc subroutine above is one that your macro uses in several different places. Rather than repeating the six lines throughout your macros, you can simply use the command

```
{ManuCalc}
```

at any time in any macro to call the subroutine. The only requirement is, of course, that the subroutine be on the current worksheet.

Parameter Passing

To give your subroutines added flexibility, you can define any number of *parameters* to them. Parameters are much like arguments in @functions and macro commands. The DEFINE command determines parameters passed to a subroutine.

{DEFINE *argument 1:type,argument 2:type . . .argument n:type*} This command specifies cells for storing subroutine parameters and optionally their data *type*, either :value or :string.

An example of a subroutine with parameters is shown in Figure 4.12.

The named ranges Len and Width will hold data for the subroutine that calculates area (Len * Width). The named range Answer will store the results of the calculation. The macro itself, executed by typing Alt-a, first homes the cursor, then asks for a length and width using two GETNUMBER commands.

After the user enters the length and width, the macro calls the CalcArea subroutine, and passes the Len and Width data to the subroutine. The DEFINE command in the CalcArea subroutine intercepts the incoming data and defines them as numbers (values). Then the subroutine places the answer in the cell

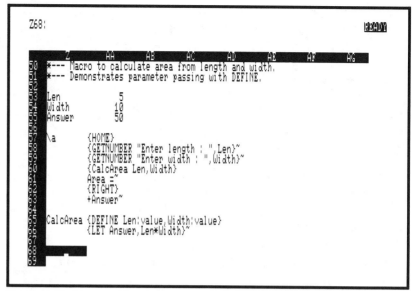

Figure 4.12: Macro with subroutine and parameters

named Answer using the LET command. The subroutine then returns control to the calling macro.

When the subroutine is done, the macro enters Area = into the currently highlighted cell, moves the cell pointer one cell to the right, and enters the formula +Answer into the currently highlighted cell. Since Answer is a named range, +Answer will show the contents of that cell anywhere on the worksheet.

We'll have a chance to see large macros with subroutines and parameter passing later in the book. For now, it is sufficient to be familiar with the basic concepts.

Miscellaneous Commands

There are still other macro commands in 1-2-3. However, we will discuss these commands as relevant throughout the book. We've covered a lot of ground already in this chapter, and have discussed enough commands and techniques to write plenty of powerful macros. Other macro commands are summarized below, and demonstrated in later chapters.

Error Handling

Error handling commands allow you to determine how a macro deals with an error. The primary error-handling commands are summarized next.

{ONERROR *branch location,message location***}**   This command sends control to the *branch location* cell when a macro execution error occurs and optionally records the 1-2-3 error message at *message location.*

{BREAKOFF}   The BREAKOFF command disables the BREAK key during macro execution. BREAKOFF should only be used in macros that have been thoroughly tested and debugged.

{BREAKON}   The BREAKON command restores the BREAK key to its normal interrupt status.

More Branching

{DISPATCH *variable location***}**   The DISPATCH command is another option for branching, like BRANCH and *Routine Name.* However, the *variable location* argument is the name of the cell that contains information telling where to branch to. For example, if the cell named BranchTo contained the label 'J22, the command {DISPATCH BranchTo} would send control to cell J22. If the cell named BranchTo contained the label 'SubRout1, the command {DISPATCH BranchTo} would send control to a range named SubRout1.

{RESTART}   The RESTART command acts like a RETURN command, but returns control all the way back to the original calling macro, bypassing any other subroutines in between. For example, look at the macro structure below, and notice how the

RETURN command in Subroutine 2 returns control to its calling subroutine (as indicated by the arrow).

\t   **Main body of macro**
           {Sub1}
           More commands . . .

Sub1   **Subroutine 1**
           {Sub2}
           More commands ◄─────┐
           {RETURN}   │

Sub2   **Subroutine 2**
           More commands   │
           {RETURN} ─────────────┘

In the macro below, Subroutine 2 ends with a RESTART command. Rather than returning control to the subroutine that called it (Subroutine 1), RESTART sends control back to the first subroutine call in the main body of the macro.

\t   **Main body of macro**
           {Sub1}
           More commands.. ◄─────┐

Sub1   **Subroutine 1**
           {Sub2}
           More commands   │
           {RETURN}   │

Sub2   **Subroutine2**
           More commands   │
           {RESTART} ────────────┘

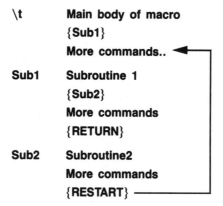

Cancelling a Macro

{QUIT} The QUIT command, placed anywhere inside a macro, terminates macro execution and returns control to the worksheet READY mode.

External File Operations

There are several macro commands that can access, read, and write data to external ASCII files. These macro commands are all discussed and demonstrated in Chapter 13. A summary of these file-handling commands follows.

{**OPEN** *file name,access mode*}   This command allows you to open an external ASCII text file in either (R)ead, (W)rite, or (M)odify mode.

{**CLOSE**}   This command closes an external file opened with the OPEN command.

{**FILESIZE** *location*}   This command determines the size of the currently open file (in bytes) and places that number at the cell specified in *location*.

{**GETPOS** *location*}   This command determines the position of the pointer in the currently open external file, and places the result at the cell specified in *location*.

{**SETPOS** *file position*}   This command moves the pointer to the position specified in *file position* in the currently open ASCII file.

{**READ** *byte count,location*}   This command reads the number of bytes specified in *byte count* from the currently open file and places them in *location*.

{**READLN** *location*}   This command reads a single line of text from the currently open ASCII text file and places it at the cell specified by *location*.

{**WRITE** *string*}   This command writes characters specified in *string* to the currently open ASCII file.

{**WRITELN** *string*}   This command writes characters specified in *string*, followed by a carriage return linefeed sequence, to the currently open ASCII file.

Menus

The MENUBRANCH and MENUCALL macro commands allow you to build custom menu systems with 1-2-3. These are discussed in detail in Chapters 11 and 12.

The /X Commands

Version 2.0 of 1-2-3 uses several /X commands that exactly duplicate the functions of other macro commands. The only purpose of these /X commands in version 2.0 is to make old macros compatible with the new version. The /X commands, and their version 2.0 equivalents, are listed below:

/X COMMAND	VERSION 2.0 MACRO COMMAND
/XI	{IF}
/XG	{BRANCH}
/XC	{*Routine Name*}
/XR	{RETURN}
/XQ	{QUIT}
/XL	{GETLABEL}
/XN	{GETNUMBER}
/XM	{MENUBRANCH}

Summary

We've covered many macro-building techniques in this chapter, all of which will come in handy with the macros we develop over the next few chapters. The macro commands we discussed in this chapter are summarized below.

- The user-interface commands

  {GETLABEL}   Displays a prompt and asks user to enter a label

{GETNUMBER}	Displays a prompt and asks user to enter a number
{GET}	Gets a single keystroke; does not display a prompt
{LOOK}	Checks for a recent keystroke without halting macro

- The decision-making commands

| {IF} | Executes commands to the right if condition is true |
| {BRANCH} | Often used with IF to pass control to another part of the macro depending on IF condition |

- The looping commands

| {FOR} | Repeats a macro while an incrementing number is within a specified range |
| {FORBREAK} | Terminates a FOR loop immediately |

- The data-manipulation commands

{LET}	Places a string or label value in a cell
{CONTENTS}	Places a formatted string in a cell
{BLANK}	Erases the contents of a cell or range
{PUT}	Places a number in a cell within a specified range

- The display-controlling commands

{BEEP}	Makes an audible tone
{INDICATE}	Changes the mode indicator at the top of the screen
{PANELOFF}	Suppresses display of control panel activity
{PANELON}	Displays control panel activity

{WINDOWSOFF}	Suppresses display of worksheet activity during macro execution
{WINDOWSON}	Displays worksheet activity during macro execution
{WAIT}	Displays WAIT indicator for a specified time
{RECALC}	Recalculates a portion of the worksheet, row by row
{RECALCCOL}	Recalculates a portion of the worksheet, column by column

■ The subroutine-controlling commands

{*Routine Name*}	Calls the subroutine whose name is inside the braces
{RETURN}	Returns control from a subroutine to a calling macro
{DEFINE}	Specifies locations and data types for parameters passed to a subroutine

■ Miscellaneous commands

{ONERROR}	Passes control to a new routine when a macro execution occurs
{BREAKOFF}	Disables the interrupting effect of the BREAK key during macro execution
{BREAKON}	Restores the interrupting effect of the BREAK key
{DISPATCH}	Passes control to a macro whose name is stored in another cell
{RESTART}	Bypasses all intermediate subroutines, returning control to the initial calling macro
{QUIT}	Terminates macro execution and returns control to the worksheet READY mode

- ASCII file-handling commands

{OPEN}	Opens an ASCII text file
{CLOSE}	Closes an open ASCII file
{FILESIZE}	Determines the size of an external ASCII file
{GETPOS}	Determines the pointer position in an ASCII file
{SETPOS}	Sets the pointer position in an ASCII file
{READ}	Reads data from an ASCII file into a worksheet
{READLN}	Reads a line of text from an ASCII file into a worksheet
{WRITE}	Writes a string of characters from a worksheet to an ASCII file
{WRITELN}	Writes a record to an ASCII file

- Menu commands

{MENUBRANCH}	Displays a custom menu
{MENUCALL}	Displays a custom menu, then returns control to the next cell

- /X commands. The /X macro commands from earlier versions of 1-2-3 can still be used in version 2 of 1-2-3, but all have new macro command equivalents.

5

WORKSHEET
MACROS

IN **THIS CHAPTER WE'LL** develop several macros using 1-2-3 macro commands. These macros will demonstrate numerous applications for the macro commands and give you some more handy tools for your worksheets.

Macros to Use the Numeric Keypad

If you own an IBM PC or similar computer where you can use either the numbers on the numeric keypad or the arrows, but not both simultaneously, you're sure to like these two simple macros. One allows you to enter numbers down a column; the other allows you to enter numbers across a row. Both macros also allow you to pause to format a cell.

The keypad macros are shown in Figure 5.1. Use Range Name Labels Right to name Z55..Z58 as the range of labels.

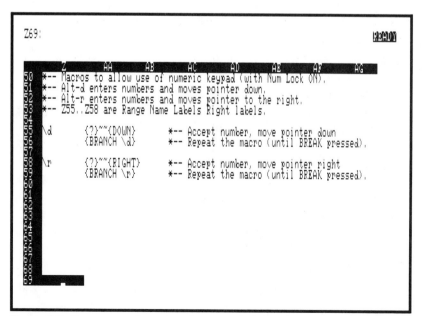

Figure 5.1: Two macros for using the numeric keypad

To use the macros, first position the cell pointer on the top-most row or leftmost column of a range of cells in which to enter numbers. If you want to enter numbers down a column, type Alt-d. If you want to enter numbers across a row, type Alt-r. Then, press the Num Lock key so that the numbers, rather than the arrows, work on your keypad. Enter numbers as usual, but press Return after entering each number. The macro will enter the number into the cell, then move the cell pointer down or to the right, depending on which macro you use.

To switch to cursor arrows, just press the Num Lock key. After repositioning the cell pointer, press the Num Lock key to continue entering numbers. To format a number, press Num Lock to turn the arrows back on, then highlight the cell to format, and select the Range Format options from the menu. Specify the format and press Return.

To terminate the macro altogether and return to normal worksheet keystrokes, press the BREAK (Ctrl-Scroll Lock) and Escape keys. The CMD indicator at the bottom of the screen will disappear when the macro is deactivated.

Let's take a moment to discuss how the macros work. First, the {?} keyword lets you type in anything until you press Return. If Num Lock is ON, the {?} simply accepts the numbers as an entry. The two Returns (~ ~) are used only when formatting numbers, so that the macro doesn't perform the {DOWN} or {RIGHT} command prematurely during formatting. The {RIGHT} command then moves the cell pointer to the right (in the Alt-r macro), or the {DOWN} command moves the cell pointer down a row (in the Alt-d macro). The BRANCH command then repeats the macro, which accepts the next number from the keypad. Since the BRANCH command always repeats the macro, the only way to stop this macro is with the BREAK key.

If you want your macro to put a number in every other row or every other column, just change the {DOWN} or {RIGHT} commands to {DOWN 2} or {RIGHT 2}:

\d   {?} ~ ~ {DOWN 2}
      {BRANCH \d}

\r   {?} ~ ~ {RIGHT 2}
      {BRANCH \r}

To put data in every third row or column, change {DOWN 2} to {DOWN 3}, or {RIGHT 2} to {RIGHT 3}, and so forth.

Changing Multiple Column Widths

Changing several column widths in 1-2-3 can be a time-consuming and tedious task. Here are a few macros that allow you to change several column widths with a few keystrokes. The first and simplest is shown in Figure 5.2.

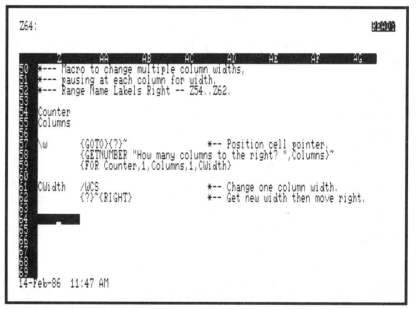

Figure 5.2: The ColWide1 macro

Use the Range Name Labels Right command to specify cells in the range Z54..Z61 as range labels. To use the macro, type Alt-w. The macro will give you an opportunity to move the cell pointer to the leftmost cell on which you want to change the width. Move the cell pointer, then press Return. The macro will display the message:

How many columns to the right?

Type in the number of columns on which you want to change the width and press Return.

The macro will highlight a column, then give you a chance to change its width by typing in a column number or by using the ← and → keys. Press Return after setting the width, and the macro will move to the next column and again allow you to specify a width. The macro will do this for as many columns as you specified when prompted earlier.

A slight variation of the basic column-width macro is shown in Figure 5.3. This macro is named ColWide2. When executed, the ColWide2 macro allows you to position the cell pointer on the leftmost column to be changed. Then the macro displays the prompt

How many columns to the right?

as with the previous macro. Next, the macro asks

How wide each column?

Enter a number from 1 to 240 and press Return. The macro will then change the column widths. For example, suppose you begin by placing the cell pointer in cell A1. Then you specify that you want to change the width of 10 columns to the right, and type in 5 as the column width for each column. The macro will set the column width for columns A through J to five spaces each.

Let's take a moment to discuss how the ColWide2 macro works. Beneath the top comment lines, two range names, Counter and Columns, are set to store data. The macro name, \w, appears in column Z, and the first step of the macro, which uses the keywords {GOTO}{?} ˜ to give the user a chance to position the cell pointer, appears in column AA.

Next, the GETNUMBER command asks for the number of columns on which to change the width. Your answer is stored in the cell named Columns. Then the GETLABEL command asks for the width of each column. In this macro, we use GETLABEL to get the width of the column because the answer is stored in the cell named Width, which is actually part of the macro.

Next, a FOR loop repeats the portion of the macro that changes column widths for as many times as you requested. The

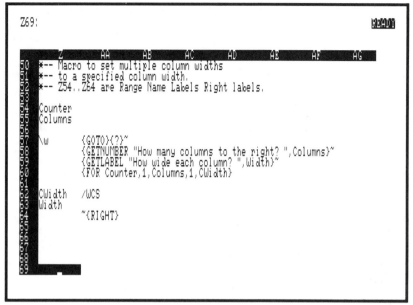

Figure 5.3: The ColWide2 macro

routine that changes the width of a single column is named CWidth. Notice that there is a gap in the macro at the cell named Width:

CWidth	**/WCS**
Width	
	~{**RIGHT**}

This gap is filled in when the user answers the prompt about the width of each column. Hence, if the user enters the number 5 in response to the prompt, this routine becomes

CWidth	**/WCS**
Width	**5**
	~{**RIGHT**}

which causes the column width to be set to five characters (/WCS5 ~). The closing {RIGHT} keyword simply moves the cell pointer to the right to adjust the next column width.

Another interesting variation of the column-width macro is the ColWide3 macro shown in Figure 5.4. It allows you to specify a "skip" factor between columns.

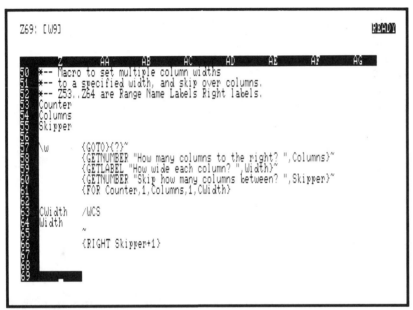

Figure 5.4: The ColWide3 macro

Like the other column-width macros, ColWide3 gives the user a chance to position the cell pointer, then presents the prompts

How many columns to the right?

and

How wide each column?

Then the macro asks:

Skip how many columns between?

You can then enter a "skip" factor. The macro will then change the column width for as many columns as you specify, skipping over the number of columns you specify. For example, if you start with the cell pointer in column A and tell the macro to change the width of each of 5 columns to 15 spaces wide, skipping one column, then columns A, C, E, G, and I will be set to 15 spaces wide. The remaining columns will be left unchanged.

The ColWide3 macro is similar to the ColWide2 macro, except that rather than simply moving {RIGHT} for each column, the command {RIGHT Skipper+1} skips over the appropriate number of cells to the right. It is necessary to add 1 to the original value in Skipper because pressing the Return key twice skips past one cell, and so on for all numbers.

Selective Arithmetic

Macros can help you to process information selectively on a worksheet. In this section we'll discuss some macros that can "decide" whether to include an item in a total. In Chapter 9 we'll look at macros that also work selectively on worksheet data, by processing only certain rows or columns, rather than only certain types of data.

Selecting Account Numbers

The worksheet in Figure 5.5 shows a fairly common problem with account numbers on a worksheet. The total shown in the last row is actually the sum of only the account numbers ending in the numbers 00. The other accounts are individual units subtotaled into the 00 accounts.

You could, of course, simply enter a formula that adds up only the appropriate cells to calculate the total. For example, the formula

+C3+C6+C8+C11+C14

will calculate an appropriate total for the worksheet in Figure 5.5. This can become quite inconvenient, however, if you often want to modify the worksheet by adding or deleting

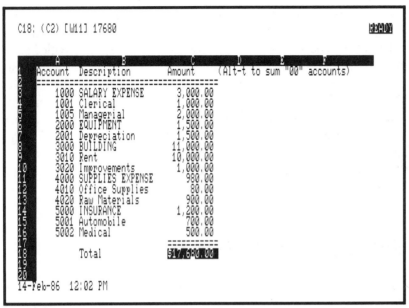

```
C18: (C2) [W11] 17680                                    READY

        A          B              C         D       E       F
1  Account  Description        Amount    (Alt-t to sum "00" accounts)
2  ------------------------------------------------
3     1000  SALARY EXPENSE     3,000.00
4     1001  Clerical           1,000.00
5     1005  Managerial         2,000.00
6     2000  EQUIPMENT          1,500.00
7     2001  Depreciation       1,500.00
8     3000  BUILDING          11,000.00
9     3010  Rent              10,000.00
10    3020  Improvements       1,000.00
11    4000  SUPPLIES EXPENSE     980.00
12    4010  Office Supplies       80.00
13    4020  Raw Materials        900.00
14    5000  INSURANCE          1,200.00
15    5001  Automobile           700.00
16    5002  Medical              500.00
17                            -----------
18          Total              $17,680.00
19
20
14-Feb-86  12:02 PM
```

Figure 5.5: Worksheet with account numbers and subtotals

columns. You'll need to re-enter the totaling formula each time you modify the worksheet.

A macro can handle this a little more elegantly by simply summing only those amounts for account numbers that are evenly divisible by 100. Figure 5.6 shows just such a macro.

Labels in the range Z54..Z65 are range names (assigned with the usual Range Name Labels Right options). You also need to name the cell where the total will be displayed (Total). In this example, cell C18 is named Total. Finally, the entire range of account numbers, names, and amounts needs to be named FulRange before the macro can be run for the first time. (If this range changes size in the future, the macro will adjust accordingly, so long as there is always a blank row beneath the last account number.) In this example, cells in the range A3..C16 are named FulRange.

Once the macro is entered and all the cells are named, pressing Alt-t will calculate and display the total of the selected accounts. Let's take a moment to discuss each line in the macro and describe how it works.

The first few comment lines describe what the macro does, and the label Counter acts as a range name for the cell to the

```
Z67:                                                                    READY

        Z       AA        AB       AC        AD       AE       AF       AG
50 *-- Macro to selectively sum accounts with numbers
51 *-- that are evenly divisible by 100.
52 *-- (Account numbers are numeric -- not labels)
53
54 Counter
55
56 \t           /RNCFulRange~{ESC}.            *-- Draw current FulRange
57               {END}{DOWN}{END}{RIGHT}~
58               {LET Total,0}
59               {FOR Counter,0,@ROWS(FulRange)-1,1,Accum}
60               {CALC}
61
62               *-- Routine below increments total if "00" account ---
63 Accum         {IF @MOD(@INDEX(FulRange,0,Counter),100)<>0}{BRANCH NoTotal}
64               {LET Total,Total+@INDEX(FulRange,2,Counter)}~
65 NoTotal       {LET Counter,Counter+1}
66
67
68
69

14-Feb-86  12:03 PM
```

Figure 5.6: Macro to selectively sum accounts

right. Next, \t acts as the macro name, and the first two lines of the macro redraw the FulRange range, which ensures that if any rows have been added or deleted, the macro will take them into consideration. Because this routine uses {END}{RIGHT} and {END}{DOWN} to highlight FulRange, it is important that there be a blank row under the last account number. Also, the first row of the range must have an account number, title, and amount. The routine that redraws the FulRange range is shown below:

\t   /RNCFulRange ~ {ESC}.
         {END}{DOWN}{END}{RIGHT} ~

In the next line, the macro simply sets the cell named Total to the initial value of zero:

{LET Total,0}

Next, a FOR loop is set up to repeat the subroutine named Accum for as many rows as there are in the range. The number of rows is calculated by using the @ROWS worksheet function and subtracting one to accommodate the fact that ranges begin at row zero and column zero:

{FOR Counter,0,@ROWS(FulRange)-1,1,Accum}

Next, the Accum subroutine determines whether the account number is evenly divisible by zero. It uses the @INDEX function to isolate the account number on the current row:

@INDEX(FulRange, *column zero, current row*)
@INDEX(FulRange,2,Counter)

It uses the @MOD function to see if the account number is evenly divisible by zero. If not, the IF clause passes control to the routine named NoTotal, which simply increments the FOR Counter. If the account number is evenly divisible by 100, the LET command increments the Total by the amount in the current row. These lines are shown below:

```
                 *— Routine below increments total if "00" account —
Accum        {IF @MOD(@INDEX(FulRange,0,Counter),100)<>0}
                 {BRANCH NoTotal}
                 {LET Total,Total+@INDEX(FulRange,2,Counter)} ~
NoTotal      {LET Counter,Counter+1}
```

Figure 5.7 shows a similar problem worksheet, but in this case the account numbers are stored as labels rather than numbers. The main account numbers (evenly divisible by 100) are left-aligned using the ' label prefix. The subaccount numbers are right-aligned using the " label prefix.

Figure 5.8 shows a macro that will sum only those accounts with 00 as the last two digits, even though the account numbers are labels.

You'll notice that the two macros for summing accounts (Figures 5.6 and 5.8) are almost identical, except that the macro that works with account numbers stored as labels uses the following IF clause to determine if the account number ends in the numbers 00:

{IF @MID(@INDEX(FulRange,0,Counter),2,2)<>"00"}
{BRANCH NoTotal}

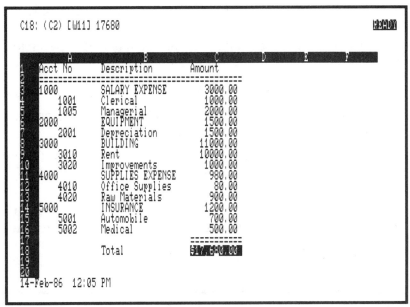

Figure 5.7: Worksheet with account numbers stored as labels

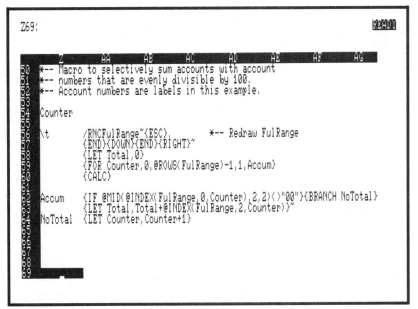

Figure 5.8: Macro to selectively sum label account numbers

This IF command uses the @MID function, which can isolate a portion of a character string (or label). Again, the @INDEX function isolates the account number on the current row. The entire

@MID(@INDEX(FulRange,0,Counter),2,2)<>"00"

expression isolates the two rightmost characters in the account number and compares them to the characters 00.

Odd-Even Analysis

Figure 5.9 shows the results of a macro that can independently sum the odd and even numbers in a range. It demonstrates another technique for selective arithmetic. Figure 5.10 shows the macro that provided the results.

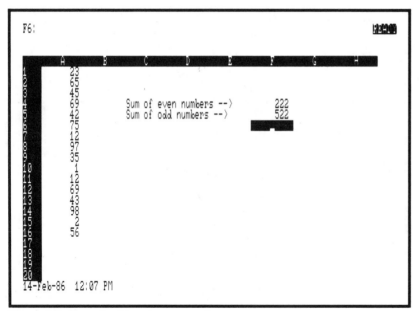

Figure 5.9: Sum of odd and even numbers

Use Range Name Labels Right to highlight the names in the range Z52..Z65. Answers are stored in cells named Answer1 and Answer2. In this example, name cell F4 Answer1, and cell

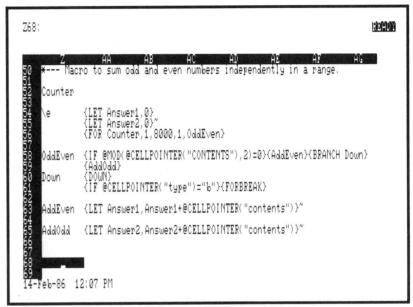

Figure 5.10: Macro to selectively sum odd and even numbers

F5 Answer2 using Range Name Create. To use the macro, place the cell pointer at the top of the column to be summed, and press Alt-e.

Like most macros, this one begins with an opening comment. A range label, Counter, appears above the macro, for use with the FOR command.

Next, the macro initializes the Answer1 and Answer2 cells with zero values, and a FOR loop, which will count as high as 8000, begins. The FOR command repeats the subroutine named OddEven:

{FOR Counter,1,8000,1,OddEven}

The OddEven subroutine checks to see if the currently highlighted cell is evenly divisible by two using the @MOD function with the currently highlighted cell:

@CELLPOINTER("CONTENTS")

If so, the macro performs the AddEven subroutine then branches to the Down subroutine. If the number is not evenly divisible by two, the macro performs the AddOdd subroutine, as shown below:

OddEven	**{IF @MOD(@CELLPOINTER("CONTENTS"),2) = 0}**
	{AddEven}{BRANCH Down}
	{AddOdd}
Down	**{DOWN}**

(Note: To make this macro work with a row, rather than a column of numbers, replace {DOWN} with {RIGHT}.) Before repeating the next FOR loop, the macro checks to see if the currently highlighted cell is blank:

@CELLPOINTER("type") = "b"

If so, the FORBREAK command stops the FOR loop and stops the macro:

{IF @CELLPOINTER("type") = "b"}{FORBREAK}

The AddEven and AddOdd subroutines simply increment either the Answer1 or the Answer2 cell by the contents of the currently highlighted cell, as shown below:

AddEven	**{LET Answer1,Answer1 + @CELLPOINTER**
	("contents")} ˜
AddOdd	**{LET Answer2,Answer2 + @CELLPOINTER**
	("contents")} ˜

Comparing Entries to a Standard

Occasionally, you might need to compare a series of numbers in a worksheet to a standard, perhaps to see at a glance how many numbers exceed, equal, or fall below some relevant parameter. Figure 5.11 shows a worksheet with a standard for comparison on the top row, and a series of numbers in a column below the standard. The +, − and = signs were entered automatically by a macro. Numbers marked with a + sign are greater than the standard, those marked with a − sign are less than the standard, and those marked with an = sign are equal to the standard.

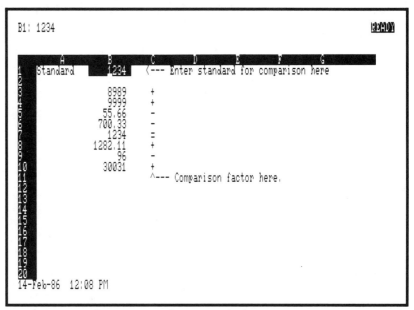

Figure 5.11: Numbers compared to a standard

Figure 5.12 shows the macro used to compare the column of numbers to the standard. Cells in the range Z54..Z62 are range labels. In addition, the cell containing the standard is named Standard (cell B1 in this example).

To use the macro, type Alt-c then position the cell pointer at the top of the column of numbers to be compared to the standard. Then just press Return and the macro will fill in the appropriate +, −, or = sign.

The macro begins by using {GOTO}{?} ˜ to allow the user to first position the cell pointer, as shown below:

\c   {GOTO}{?} ˜

Next, an IF command terminates the macro when the cell pointer lands on a blank cell below the column of numbers being analyzed:

{IF @CELLPOINTER("type") = "b"}{BRANCH Done}

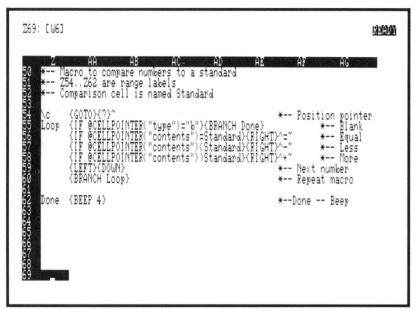

Figure 5.12: Macro to compare numbers to a standard

The next IF clause types an equal sign with the centered (^) label prefix in the cell to the right of the number if the cell contents equal the standard:

{IF @CELLPOINTER("contents")=Standard}{RIGHT} ^ = ~

The next IF command places a centered minus sign into the cell to the right, if the number is less than the standard:

{IF @CELLPOINTER("contents")<Standard}{RIGHT} ^ – ~

The next IF command places a centered + sign in the column to the right if the number equals the standard:

{IF @CELLPOINTER("contents")>Standard}{RIGHT} ^ + ~

The next line moves the cell pointer back to the column of numbers, then down a row:

{LEFT}{DOWN}

Then the BRANCH command repeats the comparison for the currently highlighted number:

{BRANCH Loop}

When the macro is done (indicated by the cell pointer landing on a blank cell), control is passed to the subroutine named Done, which simply beeps and stops the macro, as shown below:

{BEEP 4}

Macros to Print Worksheets

In this section we'll develop some macros to help you print worksheets. These include macros for using special printer attributes, printing multiple copies, double spacing, and printing row numbers and column letters.

Special Print Attributes

Version 2.0 of 1-2-3 allows you to place special printer codes directly into a worksheet to use compressed print, expanded print, underlining, boldface, and other special attributes your printer may have. The trick here, however, is knowing what the codes are for your printer. Since all printers use different codes, you need to refer to your printer manual to find the codes for your printer.

Once you know what the codes are, you need to translate them to three-digit ASCII code numbers, and place them into the worksheet preceded by two ¦ characters. The row containing the special code will not print at all, so you can use /WIR (Worksheet Insert Row) to make room for the special code if necessary. Be forewarned that, even though you enter two ¦ characters with the code, only one appears on the worksheet.

Figure 5.13 shows a portion of a worksheet with special codes for the Microline 83A embedded in it. Comments next to the special codes indicate what each code does. Figure 5.14 shows how this worksheet looks when printed. Notice that the heading fills the entire page width, and that the very wide worksheet fits across an ordinary 8½ × 11-inch sheet of paper. (The margin was set to 240 using the /PPOMR options to accommodate the smaller print.) The text beneath the worksheet is normal print.

```
H20: [W3]                                                              READY

       A        B        C     D        E        F        G      H     I
 1  |\031     *--Expanded Print On
 2
 3  Quarterly Sales of Three Products
 4  ---------------------------------
 5
 6  |\029     *--Compressed Print On
 7
 8           Quarter 1                        Quarter 2
 9           ---------                        ---------
10   Apples   Bananas Cherries     Apples  Bananas Cherries      Apples
11
12    345.43   473.76   654.87     232.65   195.83   345.43      395.58
13    624.77   453.00   866.14     116.86   275.85   234.76      296.10
14    634.88   654.00   497.89     991.45   347.98   634.88      361.06
15    376.09   443.76   326.55     343.76   645.09   147.87      354.76
16  ===========================  ===========================  =========
17   1981.16  2024.52  2345.45    1684.72  1464.75  1362.94     1407.50
18
19  |\030     *--Normal Print On
20  This is normal print for the Microline 83A printer.
14-Feb-86  12:12 PM
```

Figure 5.13: Worksheet with embedded printer codes

```
                   Quarterly Sales of Three Products
                   ---------------------------------------

        Quarter 1                 Quarter 2                 Quarter 3                 Quarter 4
        ---------                 ---------                 ---------                 ---------
 Apples  Bananas Cherries   Apples  Bananas Cherries   Apples  Bananas Cherries   Apples  Bananas Cherries

  345.43  473.76  654.87    232.65  195.83  345.43     395.58  409.77  195.83     354.67  486.88  333.65
  624.77  453.00  866.14    116.86  275.85  234.76     296.10  881.78  345.76     866.14  664.09  275.85
  634.88  654.00  497.89    991.45  347.98  634.88     361.06  296.98  347.98     497.89  397.89  465.33
  376.09  443.76  326.55    343.76  645.09  147.87     354.76  286.98  333.65     277.00  336.99  645.09
=========================  ========================  ========================  ========================
 1981.16 2024.52 2345.45   1684.72 1464.75 1362.94    1407.50 1875.51 1223.22    1995.70 1885.85 1719.92

   This is normal print for the Microline 83A printer.
```

Figure 5.14: Printed worksheet with special attributes

Figure 5.15 shows three macros that will embed some printer codes (and comments) for the Microline printer in a worksheet. Remember to put the apostrophe label prefix in front of the ¦¦ characters when creating the macros (e.g., '¦¦\029).

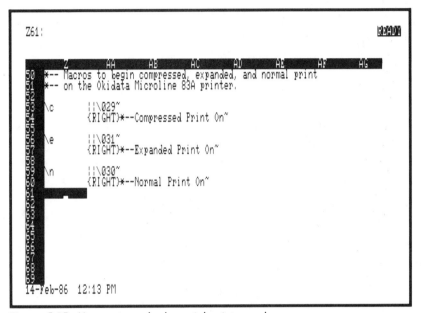

```
Z61:                                                              READY


       Z      AA       AB       AC       AD       AE       AF       AG
50  *-- Macros to begin compressed, expanded, and normal print
51  *-- on the Okidata Microline 83A printer.
52
53  \c        ¦¦\029~
54            {RIGHT}*--Compressed Print On~
55
56  \e        ¦¦\031~
57            {RIGHT}*--Expanded Print On~
58
59  \n        ¦¦\030~
60            {RIGHT}*--Normal Print On~
61



14-Feb-86  12:13 PM
```

Figure 5.15: Macros to embed special printer codes

Cells in the range Z53..Z59 contain range labels. The Alt-c macro enters code for compressed print; the Alt-e macro enters code for expanded print; the Alt-n macro enters code for normal print.

When you locate special attribute codes in your printer manual, they may not be expressed as three-digit numbers. Some printer codes may involve an *escape sequence,* which is the Escape key followed by another key. For example, Esc= means press the Escape key, then the equal sign key. The code for the Escape key is always 027. The code for the equal sign key is 61. Therefore, the numeric codes are \027 and \061. Enter these onto the worksheet as ¦¦\027\061.

You can always find the ASCII code for a keyboard character by going to any blank cell on the worksheet and typing in the

@CODE function and the character. For example, I found the code for the equal sign by entering the formula

@CODE(" = ")

on the worksheet.

The code for printing eight lines to the inch on a Microline printer is ESC-8 (Escape-8). The ASCII code for the character 8 is 56, which can be found by entering the formula

@CODE("8")

on the worksheet. Therefore, the code to place on the worksheet is ¦¦\027\056.

The IBM PC printer uses ASCII code 18 for normal printing, 15 for compressed print, and 14 for expanded print. Therefore, the macros for the IBM PC printer are as listed below:

\c	¦¦\015 ~
	{RIGHT} *--Compressed Print On ~
\e	¦¦\014 ~
	{RIGHT} *--Expanded Print On ~
\n	¦¦\018 ~
	{RIGHT} *--Normal Print On ~

Printing Multiple Copies

Here is a handy macro that allows you to print multiple copies of the same worksheet. The macro is shown in Figure 5.16. Labels in column Z are, as usual, labels used as range names.

To use the macro, first prepare to print a single copy of the worksheet. Select your basic margin and other settings as needed. Then type Alt-p to print the worksheet. The macro will give you an opportunity to highlight the range to print. Highlight the range then press Return. The macro will then ask how many copies. Enter a number and press Return. Then the macro will remind you to align the paper. Do so, then press Return to begin printing. The macro will print the number of copies you require, starting each on a new page.

Figure 5.16: Macro to print multiple copies of a worksheet

Let's briefly discuss how the macro works. The first lines name some cells (Copies, Counter, and Hold) used to store data while the macro is running.

The actual macro calls up the Print menu, selects the Printer and Range options, and waits for you to highlight the range. Then it quits the Print menu, as shown in the line below:

\p   /PPR{?} ˜ Q

The next line asks how many copies to print and waits for you to enter a number. Your answer is stored in the cell named Copies:

{GETNUMBER "How many copies : ",Copies} ˜

The next line displayed gives the user a chance to line up the paper in the printer, then press Return to begin printing. Since the GETLABEL command requires that data be stored some-where, the cell named Hold stores the keystroke from the GETLABEL command:

{GETLABEL "Align paper, then press <--'...",Hold} ˜

(Note: To compose the Return arrow in this prompt, type Alt-F1 m g for the arrow head, then two hyphens and an apostrophe for the rest of the arrow.)

The next line calls up the Print menu and selects the Printer Align Quit options to ensure that 1-2-3 is current with the alignment of paper in the printer:

/PPAQ

Next, a FOR loop repeats the subroutine named PrintOne for as many copies as are required. The PrintOne subroutine prints one copy of the worksheet using /Print Printer Go. After the worksheet is printed, the macro selects the Page option to move the paper in the printer to a new page, then the Quit option to leave the Print menu. These two lines of the macro are presented below:

	{FOR Counter,1,Copies,1,PrintOne}
PrintOne	**/PPGPQ**

Double- and Single-Spacing

Here are a pair of macros that can change a worksheet to double-spacing for printing, then back to single-spacing if you so desire. Since these macros insert and delete rows on the worksheet, they should be used with caution. The safest bet is to save the worksheet before changing the spacing. Then use the appropriate spacing macro and then print the worksheet. After printing, use /WEY to erase the modified worksheet.

Figure 5.17 shows the two macros: Alt-d to double-space a worksheet, and Alt-s to single-space a worksheet that has been double-spaced. Range labels are in column Z as usual.

To double-space a worksheet, place the cell pointer on the top row of the range to be double-spaced, and type Alt-d. The macro will continue inserting blank rows between lines until you press any key to stop it. After double-spacing, you can return to single-spacing by moving the cell pointer to the top of the double-spaced rows and typing Alt-s. Press any key to stop the single-spacing.

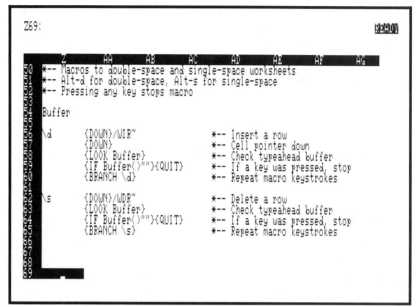

Figure 5.17: Macros to single- and double-space a worksheet

Let's take a look at how the macros work. First, a cell named Buffer is created to store the input from the LOOK command used later in the macro. Next, the Alt-d macro moves the cell pointer down a line and inserts a row (/WIR˜), then moves the cell pointer down another row:

    \d   **{DOWN}/WIR˜**
          {DOWN}

Next, the LOOK command checks to see if a key has been pressed since the macro started. The unique feature of the LOOK command is that it can check to see if a key has been pressed without interrupting the macro. It does so by checking the *typeahead buffer,* which is an area where keystrokes waiting to get into the computer are stored. If a key has indeed been pressed, the line below will store that keypress in the cell named Buffer:

    {LOOK Buffer}

Next, an IF command decides whether to stop processing the macro. If the cell named Buffer is not blank (<>""), the macro stops processing because of the QUIT command. Otherwise, the macro branches back to the first line and continues inserting blank rows, as shown below:

> **{IF Buffer<>" "}{QUIT}**
> **{BRANCH \d}**

The Alt-s macro works in basically the same fashion, except that it deletes rows instead of inserting them.

Printing Row Numbers and Column Letters

Normally, 1-2-3 does not display row numbers or column letters when you print a worksheet. Here is a macro that will put row numbers and column letters into a worksheet for printing. This is a useful technique for documenting worksheets on paper. The macro is fairly large; it is shown in Figure 5.18. (The figure itself was printed using this macro.)

```
                Z       AA      AB      AC      AD      AE      AF
    50 *-- Macro to fill in column letters and row numbers
    51 *-- prior to printing a worksheet.
    52
    53 Rows
    54 Cols
    55 ColNo
    56 Counter
    57 Lead
    58
    59 \b         {HOME}
    60            {GETNUMBER "How many rows? ",Rows}~
    61            {GETNUMBER "How many columns? ",Cols}~
    62            /WIR~/WIC{RIGHT}~
    63            /WCS5~{RIGHT}/WCS4~
    64            {HOME}{DOWN}
    65            /DF{BS}.{DOWN Rows}~1~1~~
    66            {GOTO}C1~
    67            {FOR Counter,1,Cols,1,PutLet}
    68            {GOTO}C1~/RLC{END}{RIGHT}~{HOME}
    69
    70 PutLet     {LET ColNo,@CELLPOINTER("col")-2}~
    71            {IF ColNo<=26}@CHAR(ColNo+64){CALC}~{BRANCH Next}
    72            {IF @MOD(ColNo,26)=0}+Lead&"Z"{CALC}~{BRANCH Next}
    73            {LET Lead,@CHAR(@INT(ColNo/26)+64)}~
    74            +Lead&@CHAR(@INT(@MOD(ColNo,26)+64)){CALC}~
    75 Next       {RIGHT}
```

Figure 5.18: Macro to print row numbers and column letters

Since this macro inserts rows and columns, you should use it only to print a worksheet. As soon as the macro is typed into a worksheet, save the worksheet using File Save. Then retrieve the worksheet containing this macro, move the cursor to cell A1, and use File Combine to read in the worksheet to be printed. Type Alt-b to run the macro. After all the row and column letters are inserted into the worksheet, use the usual Print Printer options to highlight the range to print and to select other options.

To ensure that column labels and row numbers appear on all printed pages, you can select the Other and Border options from the Print menu, and specify cell A1 as the border for both the Rows and Columns submenu options. After printing the worksheet, clear the screen with /WEY so that neither the macro nor the printed worksheet will be permanently affected by row and column insertions.

Since this is a large, complex macro, we'll discuss each line in some detail. The first lines, as usual, are comments and named cells used to store data.

To avoid wasting time filling in unnecessary labels, the macro asks the user for an estimate of the number of columns and rows to fill in. The user's answer is stored in the cells named Rows and Cols:

```
\b      {HOME}
        {GETNUMBER "How many rows? ",Rows} ~
        {GETNUMBER "How many columns? ",Cols} ~
```

To accommodate the additional row and column labels, the macro next inserts a blank row at the top of the worksheet and two blank columns at the left. The new columns are assigned widths of 5 spaces and 4 spaces respectively:

```
/WIR ~ /WIC{RIGHT} ~
/WCS5 ~ {RIGHT}/WCS4 ~
```

Next, the macro uses Data Fill to fill in row numbers down the left column, starting one row beneath the column letters. These lines handle this task:

```
{HOME}{DOWN}
/DF{BS}.{DOWN Rows} ~ 1 ~ 1 ~ ~
```

To enter column letters, the cursor moves the cell pointer to cell C1. (Cell C1 is always the position for starting column letters, hence the cell reference rather than a named range is used here.) Then a FOR loop repeats the PutLet subroutine for as many times as required to fill in all the columns. The lines below handle this task:

{GOTO}C1 ~
{FOR Counter,1,Cols,1,PutLet}

The PutLet subroutine is somewhat tricky, because it must determine column letters (such as AC) from column numbers (such as 59). It begins by storing the current column number in the cell named ColNo. The -2 offset is to accommodate for the two newly inserted columns at the left:

PutLet {LET ColNo,@CELLPOINTER("col")-2} ~

If the column number is in the range from 1 to 26, the column letter is simply the ASCII character of the column number plus 64. For example, the uppercase alphabet begins at ASCII character 65. Therefore, if the column number is 1, the column letter is @CHAR(64+1), which is A. The macro enters the appropriate formula into the cell, presses {CALC} to change the formula to a value, and continues with the next cell. The IF clause below takes care of all cell letters for columns A through Z:

{IF ColNo< =26}@CHAR(ColNo+64){CALC} ~ **{BRANCH Next}**

Two-letter column letters (e.g., AA) are a bit trickier. To handle these, the macro calculates the first character of the column letters by taking the integer value of the column number divided by 26 and adding 64 to it. This character is stored in the cell named Lead:

{LET Lead,@CHAR(@INT(ColNo/26)+64)} ~

The second character for the two-letter combination is calculated by taking the integer value of the modulus of the column number divided by 26, then incremented by 64. The Lead character and the second character are placed into the cell, then made into a value (with {CALC}) rather than a formula, as shown below:

+Lead&@CHAR(@INT(@MOD(ColNo,26)+64)){CALC}˜

There is one circumstance that requires special handling in creating cell labels. When the column number is evenly divisible by 26, the integer portion is too high and the modulus is too low. Therefore, the line below traps the potential error, and places the existing Lead character into the cell followed by the letter Z:

{IF @MOD(ColNo,26)=0}+Lead&"Z"{CALC}˜{BRANCH Next}

The subroutine named Next simply moves the cell pointer to the next column to calculate the column letters:

Next {RIGHT}

After the FOR loop processes all the columns, the line below centers all the column letters to make them line up properly above the columns. The usual Range Label Center options are used to perform this task:

{GOTO}C1˜/RLC{END}{RIGHT}˜{HOME}

The only disadvantage to this macro is that it takes a couple of minutes to fill in all the row and column labels even on a fairly small worksheet. You can speed up the macro considerably by turning off the windows, panel, and automatic recalculation from within the macro. You won't see anything happening on the screen while the macro is working; you'll need to wait for the beeps and for the WAIT indicator to disappear. The appropriate commands to add to the macro are shown below and indicated by arrows. Use /WIR (Worksheet Insert Row) to insert the new lines into the existing macro.

```
\b    {HOME}
      {GETNUMBER "How many rows? ",Rows} ~
      {GETNUMBER "How many columns? ",Cols} ~
      {INDICATE wait}                               <---
      {WINDOWSOFF}{PANELOFF}/WGRM                   <---
      /WIR ~ /WIC{RIGHT} ~
      /WCS5 ~ {RIGHT}/WCS4 ~
      {HOME}{DOWN}
      /DF{BS}.{DOWN Rows} ~ 1 ~ 1 ~ ~
      {GOTO}C1 ~
      {FOR Counter,1,Cols,1,PutLet}
      {GOTO}C1 ~ /RLC{END}{RIGHT} ~ {HOME}
      /WGRA{CALC}{INDICATE " "}                     <---
      {BEEP 4}{BEEP 2}                              <---
```

Summary

In this chapter we've developed some general-purpose macros for use on the worksheet, including the following:

- Macros to use the numeric keypad to enter numbers
- A macro to change the widths of multiple columns
- Macros to selectively sum numbers in a worksheet
- A macro to compare numbers to a standard
- Several macros for printing worksheets

6

DATE AND TIME
MACROS

IN THIS CHAPTER WE'LL discuss some general macros and formulas for managing dates in 1-2-3. If you are new to version 2.0 of 1-2-3, you might want to read up on all the new date functions and formats prior to reading this chapter. Doing so will help you to gain full control over dates and times in 1-2-3. These new functions are presented in Appendix A.

Full Time and Date Stamp

Here is a handy macro that "stamps" a worksheet with the current date and time. The macro displays the current date in plain English format (e.g., January 1, 1986). It displays the time in the Time-2 format in the cell below the date. The date-stamp macro is shown in Figure 6.1.

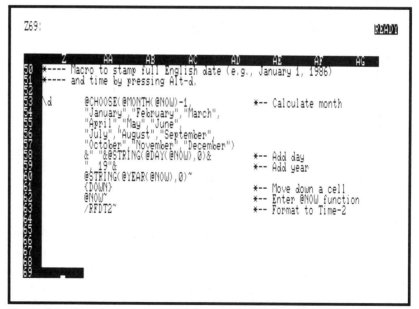

Figure 6.1: Macro to stamp a worksheet with the date and time

To use the macro, position the cell pointer in any blank cell that has another blank cell beneath it, then type Alt-d. The date and time will appear on the worksheet as below:

January 1, 1986
11:07 AM

The macro leaves the date and time as formulas, which means that they will change automatically as time passes and the worksheet is recalculated. To make the date and time remain stable as time passes, convert the formulas to values. Figure 6.2 shows a modification of the date-stamp macro that will do this for you.

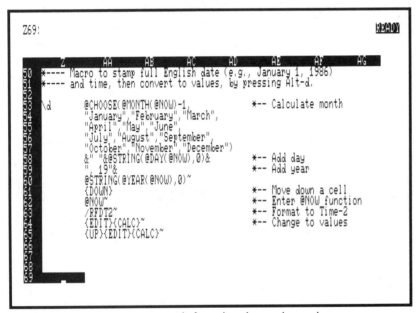

Figure 6.2: Date-stamp macro with formulas changed to values

The macro works in the following fashion. First, it enters into the currently highlighted cell the @CHOOSE formula below, which converts the month number to the appropriate month name:

    @CHOOSE(@MONTH(@NOW)-1,"January","February", "March",

      "April","May","June","July","August","September",

      "October","November","December")

Then the macro tacks onto the month a blank space and the character string equivalent to the day, using this line:

&"   "&@STRING(@DAY(@NOW),0)&   *-- Add day

The next two lines of the macro add a comma, the number 19, and the year of the current date to the month and day:

", 19"&   *-- Add year
@STRING(@YEAR(@NOW),0) ~

Next, the macro moves the cell pointer down a row to get ready to enter the time. Then it puts the @NOW function into the cell, and formats the cell to the Time-2 format, using these lines:

{DOWN}   *-- Move down a cell
@NOW ~   *-- Enter @NOW function
/RFDT2 ~   *-- Format to Time-2

If you use the version of the macro that changes the formulas to values, the next two lines in the macro convert the formulas to values by bringing each formula to the control panel for editing ({EDIT}) and pressing the CALC key ({CALC}):

{EDIT}{CALC} ~   *-- Change to values
{UP}{EDIT}{CALC} ~

This macro is especially useful for date stamping worksheets that need a plain English date format for printing, as in the case of worksheets that are used to print form letters. (Form letters are discussed in detail in Chapter 10.)

Same Day of the Month

Billing systems often require that a payment be made on the same day of each month. If the initial date is the 29th of the month or later, a formula is required to determine the last day of the month, because different months end on different days. This is the basic formula for calculating the same day of the month for every month in the year (for dates between 1900 and 1999) where SD is the name of the cell containing the original starting date:

@IF(@DAY(SD)>3,SD + 28-@DAY(SD + 28),SD + 31-@DAY(SD + 31)) +

@IF(@MONTH(SD) = 1,@MIN(@IF(@MOD(@YEAR(SD),4) =

0,29,28),@DAY($SD)),@IF(@MONTH(SD) = 3#OR#@MONTH

(SD) = 5#OR#@MONTH(SD) = 8#OR#@MONTH(SD) = 10,@MIN

(30,@DAY($SD)),@DAY($SD))) ~

(Note that the formula needs to be entered as a single line in a single cell.)

Since this is a rather long formula, it's to your advantage to put it in a macro. That way, you can enter the formula into a cell just by pressing a couple of keys. A simple macro to enter this formula into a cell is shown in Figure 6.3.

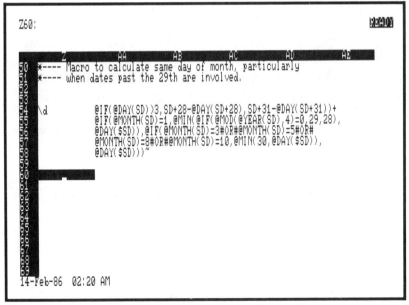

Figure 6.3: Macro to calculate the same day of the month

To use this macro, type it in as shown in the figure and use Range Name Labels Right to assign \d as the macro name. Then move the cell pointer to an out-of-the-way area and enter a serial-number date, such as @NOW or @DATE(86,1,31). Use the usual Range Name Create or Range Name Labels Right options to assign the name SD to the cell that holds the date.

Next, move the cell pointer to the cell below or to the right of the cell containing the date and type Alt-d. The same day for the next month (in serial-number format) will appear in this cell. Then you can use the Copy option to copy the formula as you wish. In Figure 6.4, I've copied the cell down eleven rows. Use Range Format Date to format these cells. (You may need to adjust the column width for date formats requiring lots of space.) In Figure 6.4, I've used the Date-1 format and adjusted the column width to 12 spaces.

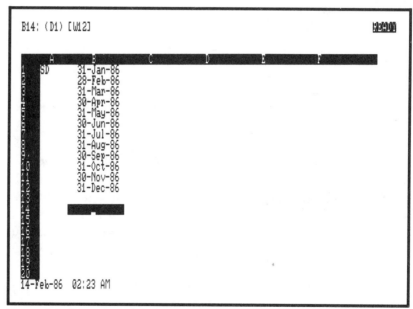

Figure 6.4: Same day of the month for a year

The one disadvantage to this formula is that it is large and uses a lot of memory. You can reclaim about 70 percent of this memory by converting the formulas to values. Figure 6.5 shows a macro that can automatically copy the same-day-of-the-month formula to a range of cells and convert them all to values.

```
        Z          AA          AB          AC          AD          AE          AF
50 *-- Macro to enter same-day-of-the-month formula
51 *-- and optionally convert formulas to values.
52
53 YN         n
54 RC         r
55 Err
56 Counter
57
58 \s         {ONERROR ErrMsg}~           *-- Prepare for range name error.
59            {GOTO}SD~
60 GetRc      {GETLABEL "(R)ows or (C)olumns? : ",RC}~
61            {IF @UPPER(RC)<>"C"#AND#@UPPER(RC)<>"R"}{BEEP}{BRANCH GetRc}
62            {MoveIt}{Formula}           *-- Move pointer, enter formula.
63            /C~.{?}~                    *-- Copy formula
64            {Convert}                   *-- Convert to values, if requested.
65
66 MoveIt     {IF RC="R"}{DOWN}           *-- Move cell pointer
67            {IF RC="C"}{RIGHT}
68
69 Formula    @IF(@DAY(SD)>3,SD+28-@DAY(SD+28),SD+31-@DAY(SD+31))+
70            @IF(@MONTH(SD)=1,@MIN(@IF(@MOD(@YEAR(SD),4)=0,29,28),
71            @DAY($SD)),@IF(@MONTH(SD)=3#OR#@MONTH(SD)=7#OR#
72            @MONTH(SD)=8#OR#@MONTH(SD)=10,@MIN(30,@DAY($SD)),
73            @DAY($SD)))~
74
75 Convert    {GETLABEL "Convert formulas to values? (Y/N) : ",YN}~
76            {IF @UPPER(YN)<>"Y"}{QUIT}
77            {GOTO}SD~
78            {MoveIt}
79 EdCalc     {EDIT}{CALC}~{MoveIt}
80            {IF @CELLPOINTER("type")<>"b"}{EdCalc}
81            {QUIT}
82
83 ErrMsg     {BEEP 2}{BEEP 4}
84            {GETLABEL "Whoops! Press <--' then name SD cell",Err}~
85            {QUIT}
86
87
```

Figure 6.5: Macro to copy the same-day-of-the-month formula

To use this macro, first type it in exactly as shown, then use Range Name Labels Right to highlight all the cell names in column Z. Then move to an out-of-the-way area and enter a serial date, such as @NOW or @DATE(86,1,31). Name this cell SD using Range Name Create or Range Name Labels Right. You may want to format this cell, and other cells that will contain dates, with one of the date formats.

Next, type Alt-s to run the macro. The control panel will ask if you want

(R)ows or (C)olumns

Type R to spread calculated dates down the same row, or C to spread calculated dates across the same column, then press Return. The macro will enter the same-day-of-the-month macro into the appropriate adjacent cell, then ask you to highlight the range to copy the cell to. Use → or ↓ to highlight the appropriate range of cells, then press Return.

The macro will fill in the highlighted range with the appropriate dates, then ask if you want to

Convert formulas to values? (Y/N) :

Enter Y to convert to values, or N to keep formulas, then press Return. The macro will perform accordingly then stop. If necessary, use the Range Format Date options to format the serial dates and the Worksheet Column Width options to set column widths.

This complex macro deserves some discussion because it demonstrates a number of powerful macro techniques. The macro begins with the usual comments, then names some cells for storing macro data, as shown below:

*-- Macro to enter same-day-of-the-month formula

*-- and optionally convert formulas to values.

YN

RC

Err

Counter

Next, the macro prepares for a potential error in the cell named SD by branching to the subroutine named ErrMsg should an error occur:

\s   {ONERROR ErrMsg} ˜   *-- Prepare for range
**   name error.**

Then the macro attempts to send the cell pointer to the cell named SD. If there is no such cell, an error occurs and the previous ONERROR command passes control to the routine named ErrMsg:

{GOTO}SD ˜

(If no error occurs, the macro proceeds normally.)

In the event of an error, the Err routine takes over, beeps, and displays the message "Whoops! Press <--' then name SD cell". Should this occur, you'll need to press Return to terminate the macro, assign the name SD to the cell containing the starting date, and then run the macro again.

Assuming that an error did not occur, the macro asks if formulas should be copied to (R)ows or (C)olumns, using the GETLABEL command:

GetRc   {GETLABEL "(R)ows or (C)olumns? : ",RC} ~

The next line traps a potential error by beeping and passing control back to the previous line (named GetRc) if the user enters something other than r, R, c, or C:

{IF @UPPER(RC)<>"C"#AND#@UPPER(RC)<>"R"}{BEEP}
{BRANCH GetRc}

Assuming that no errors have occurred yet, the macro positions the cell pointer on the appropriate cell and types in the same-day-of-the-month formula by calling the MoveIt and Formula subroutines:

{MoveIt}{Formula}   *-- Move pointer, enter formula.

Next the macro selects the Copy option from the menu and gives the user the opportunity to extend the highlight through the range of cells to copy the formula to:

/C ~.{?} ~   *-- Copy formula

Then the macro calls the Convert subroutine, which gives the user the option to convert formulas to values, and then converts if the user requests:

{Convert}   *-- Convert to values, if requested.

The MoveIt subroutine, which moves the cell pointer to the next row or column depending on the user's earlier response, is shown below:

MoveIt	{IF RC = "R"}{DOWN}	*-- **Move cell pointer**
	{IF RC = "C"}{RIGHT}	

The Formula subroutine, which enters the same-day-of-the-month formula into the currently highlighted cell, is shown below:

Formula @IF(@DAY(SD)>3,SD + 28-@DAY(SD + 28),SD + 31-
@DAY(SD + 31)) + @IF(@MONTH(SD) = 1,@MIN
(@IF(@MOD(@YEAR(SD),4) = 0,29,28),@DAY
($SD)),@IF(@MONTH(SD) = 3#OR#@MONTH(SD)
= 5#OR#@MONTH(SD) = 8#OR#@MONTH(SD)
= 10,@MIN(30,@DAY($SD)),@DAY($SD)))~

The Convert subroutine asks if you want to convert formulas to values then performs accordingly. This subroutine moves the cell pointer back to the original date (in the cell named SD), then converts formulas to values using the EdCalc subroutine. The Convert subroutine is shown here:

Convert {GETLABEL "Convert formulas to values?
(Y/N) : ",YN}~
{IF @UPPER(YN)< >"Y"}{QUIT}
{GOTO}SD~
{MoveIt}

The EdCalc subroutine converts a formula to a value until it encounters a blank cell, at which point it terminates the macro:

EdCalc {EDIT}{CALC}~{MoveIt}
{IF @CELLPOINTER("type")< >"b"}{EdCalc}
{QUIT}

Finally, this is the ErrMsg subroutine:

ErrMsg {BEEP 2}{BEEP 4}

```
{GETLABEL "Whoops! Press <--' then name SD
    cell",Err} ~
{QUIT}
```

The cell named Err simply holds the press on the Return key so
that the GETLABEL command works properly.

This is indeed a complex macro, but it is exceptionally easy
to use. It demonstrates useful techniques for responding to user-
input errors and is therefore worth studying if you plan to develop very complex macros and to fully master the macro
commands. But before we get too far off track, let's get back to
some basic date macros.

Day of the Week

Here is a fairly simple, though very handy, formula that can
determine the day of the week from a date. The formula is
shown below:

```
@CHOOSE(@MOD(Date,7),"Saturday","Sunday","Monday",
    "Tuesday","Wednesday","Thursday","Friday") ~
```

Of course, the formula must be entered as a single line in a
single cell. The Date argument is a cell named Date that contains
a 1-2-3 serial date. The formula works by taking the modulus of
the date divided by seven, and using that value to choose the
appropriate day from the seven days listed. (It just so happens
that serial dates follow such a pattern.)

Figure 6.6 shows a couple of macros that expediate entering
the day-of-the-week formula into a cell. The \l macro enters the
formula where the date is stored in the cell to the left of the currently highlighted cell. The \u macro enters the formula in a cell
where the date is above the currently highlighted cell.

For example, suppose you type in these macros and use
Range Name Labels Right to highlight the labels in column Z.
Then you enter a column of dates in the worksheet, as in
column B of Figure 6.7. You could then position the cell pointer

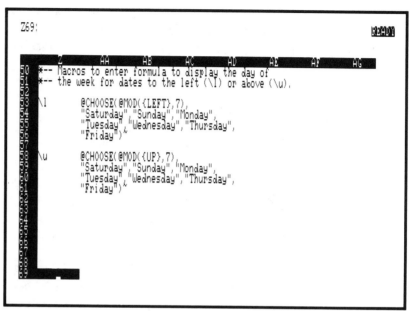

Figure 6.6: Macros to enter the day-of-the-week formula

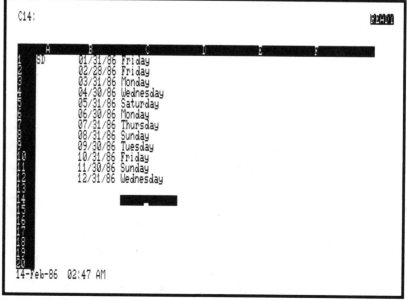

Figure 6.7: Calculated day-of-the-week in column C

on cell C1 and type Alt-l to see the weekday. Then you could use the Copy command to copy the formula down to other cells to see the days for the remaining dates, as shown in column C of Figure 6.7.

Of course, you can use {EDIT} {CALC} to convert these days to values if you wish. We will not go into detail on how to do that here, since we've discussed this topic in the previous macro and in previous chapters.

Converting Imported Dates

Chapter 13 discusses general techniques for importing ASCII text files from foreign software systems and mainframe computers. In this chapter, we'll focus on techniques for converting foreign dates to 1-2-3 serial dates. You really don't need macros to help with this, since formulas will suffice. Nonetheless, we'll discuss these formulas because such conversions are often necessary.

The chances are that your imported dates will be in one of these four formats:

FORMAT	EXAMPLE
Label	'010186
Reverse Label	'19860101
Number	10186
Reverse Number	19860101

All of the formulas that follow assume that the date to be converted is in cell A1. You'll need to change the A1 reference to the appropriate cell containing the foreign date format. Once entered, you can copy the formula to other cells as required. Note that these formulas need to be entered as a single line, with no spaces, on your worksheet.

To convert a date in label format, such as '010186, to a serial date, use the formula

@DATE(@VALUE(@RIGHT(A1,2)),@VALUE(@LEFT(A1,2)),
@VALUE(@MID(A1,2,2)))

To convert a date in reverse label format, such as '19860101, use the formula

**@DATE(@VALUE(@MID(A1,2,2)),@VALUE(@MID(A1,4,2)),
@VALUE(@MID(A1,6,2)))**

To convert a date in numeric format, such as 10186, use the formula

**@DATE(@MOD(A1,100),@INT(A1/10000),@INT(@MOD
(A1,10000)/100))**

To convert a date in reverse numeric format, such as 19860101, use the formula

**@DATE(@INT((A1-19000000)/10000),@INT(@MOD(A1,10000)/100),
@MOD(A1,100))**

Of course, you can develop macros to enter these formulas using techniques similar to those in the macros discussed previously in this chapter. However, the formulas are small enough that you might prefer just to copy them as necessary.

Changing the System Date and Time

You cannot use a macro to change the DOS system time and date, but since the capability to do so is a new feature in version 2.0 of 1-2-3, the technique deserves some discussion. All you need to do is select the System option from the Main menu. Doing so will temporarily leave 1-2-3 and bring you to the DOS A> or C> prompt. At the DOS prompt, type in the command

DATE

and press Return. DOS will show the current system date and

allow you to enter a new date. Use the MM-DD-YY format to enter the new date (e.g., 3-31-86) then press the Return key.

To change the system time, type in the command

TIME

at the DOS prompt and press Return. DOS will show you the current system time and allow you to enter a new time. Enter the time in HH:MM:SS (e.g., 12:01:00). For times past noon, use a 24-hour-clock format (e.g., 13:30:00 for 1:30 in the afternoon). Press Return after entering the new time to return to the DOS prompt.

To return to 1-2-3 after changing the date or the time, type

EXIT

at the DOS prompt, then press Return. When the worksheet reappears on the screen, press {CALC} (F9) to update date and time formulas in your worksheet to the new system date and time.

Summary

In this chapter we've developed a number of handy macros for managing 1-2-3 date and time data, including the following:

- A macro to stamp a worksheet with the current date and time
- A macro to calculate the same day of several months
- A macro to display the day of the week
- Several macros to convert dates imported from foreign files to 1-2-3 dates

ACCUMULATION AND CONSOLIDATION MACROS

M

ANY FINANCIAL APPLICATIONS require accumulated totals. There are several types of accumulation that worksheets might require. The simplest is the running total as shown in Figure 7.1. Notice that the simple formula @SUM(B4..$B4) is sufficient to maintain the running total. Once entered, you can simply copy this formula down as many rows as required for calculating the running totals. For running totals across columns, vary only the column letter in the second argument, as in the formula @SUM(B4..B$4).

```
E4: (T) [W18] @SUM($B$4..$B4)                              READY

         A            B            C            D         E         F
1                   Month      Cumulative
2      Month        Income       Income
3    ==============================================
4    January        3,225.55    $3,225.55   <-- @SUM($B$4..$B4)
5    February       4,354.22    $7,579.77
6    March          3,999.08   $11,578.85
7    April          5,121.55   $16,700.40
8    May            2,936.45   $19,636.85
9    June           2,299.22   $21,936.07
10   July           8,207.44   $30,143.51
11   August         4,492.11   $34,635.62
12   September      5,131.55   $39,767.17
13   October        6,201.77   $45,968.94
14   November       4,230.00   $50,198.94
15   December       7,121.55   $57,320.49
16
17
18
19
20
17-Feb-86   09:01 AM
```

Figure 7.1: Worksheet with simple running total

Not all accumulations are quite so simple. Let's look at an example of a year-to-date accumulation that requires a little more work.

Year-to-Date Accumulation

Figure 7.2 shows the skeleton of a worksheet that can calculate and display an income statement. The formulas are shown in text format, although, of course, they will display results on the actual worksheet.

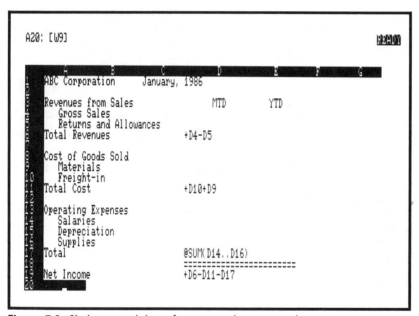

```
A20: [W9]                                                    READY

         A            B         C         D         E       F      G
  1 ABC Corporation      January, 1986
  2
  3 Revenues from Sales                MTD       YTD
  4     Gross Sales
  5     Returns and Allowances
  6 Total Revenues                 +D4-D5
  7
  8 Cost of Goods Sold
  9     Materials
 10     Freight-in
 11 Total Cost                     +D10+D9
 12
 13 Operating Expenses
 14     Salaries
 15     Depreciation
 16     Supplies
 17 Total                          @SUM(D14..D16)
 18                                ===========================
 19 Net Income                     +D6-D11-D17
 20
```

Figure 7.2: Skeleton worksheet for year-to-date accumulation

Figure 7.3 shows this same worksheet after entering data for the month of January. Notice that the year-to-date (YTD) column is still empty. That's because the accumulator macro has not been put to use yet.

After using the accumulator macro, the current month's data accumulates to the YTD column, as shown in Figure 7.4. Note that the message "*Posted" appears in cell E1 as a reminder that the current month's data have been accumulated into the YTD totals.

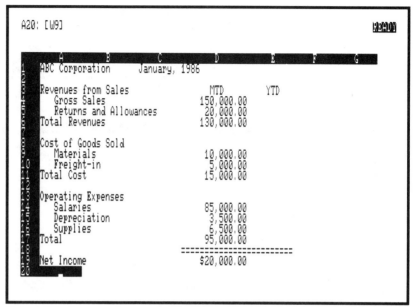

Figure 7.3: January data in the month-to-date column

Figure 7.4: January data posted to the year-to-date column

When February rolls around, you can erase the *Posted reminder, then enter February data into the month-to-date column, as shown in Figure 7.5.

```
A20: [W9]                                                    READY

          A         B          C          D          E          F
1  ABC Corporation     February, 1986
2
3  Revenues from Sales               MTD        YTD
4     Gross Sales               175,000.00  150,000.00
5     Returns and Allowances     55,000.00   20,000.00
6  Total Revenues               120,000.00  130,000.00
7
8  Cost of Goods Sold
9     Materials                  12,500.00   10,000.00
10    Freight-in                  7,500.00    5,000.00
11 Total Cost                    20,000.00   15,000.00
12
13 Operating Expenses
14    Salaries                   80,000.00   85,000.00
15    Depreciation                5,500.00    3,500.00
16    Supplies                    7,000.00    6,500.00
17 Total                         92,500.00   95,000.00
18                              ============================
19 Net Income                    $7,500.00  $20,000.00
20
```

Figure 7.5: February data in the month-to-date column

After entering the February data, you can use the accumulator macro to accumulate the new month's data, as shown in Figure 7.6. Once again, the *Posted reminder in cell E1 lets you know that the current month has been accumulated.

At first glance, it may appear as though you need only enter the formula +E4+D4 into cell E4 to accumulate YTD totals as each new month's data are entered into the worksheet. This will not work, however, because the formula is circular (that is, it refers to the cell it is stored in), and therefore will grow each time the worksheet recalculates. Instead, you need a macro that can control when the accumulation takes place.

The most elegant way to handle this accumulation is to extract the current month's data from the worksheet, then read these data back, additively, into the YTD column. A named range, the File Xtract options, and the File Combine options will provide all the tools you need.

Figure 7.6: February data accumulated to year-to-date totals

First, use the Range Name Create options to assign the name Month to the cells in the range D4..D19. Use the same options to assign the name Hold to cell E1. These named ranges will make building the rest of the macro easier. Then, enter the Alt-a macro shown in Figure 7.7. Use Range Names Labels Right to highlight the labels in column Z.

Let's discuss this macro now. The macro begins by moving the cursor to the home cell. Then it checks to see if the cell named Hold (cell E1) is blank. If not, the macro passes control to the subroutine named Caution, which displays the message

Are you sure? (see ∗Posted)

This is a safety device to help keep accidental accumulations from occurring. If the cell name Hold contains the word ∗Posted, then the current month may have already been posted, and therefore should not be posted again. You must first erase the ∗Posted message, then perform the update. The extra effort required helps ensure that an update is not performed accidentally.

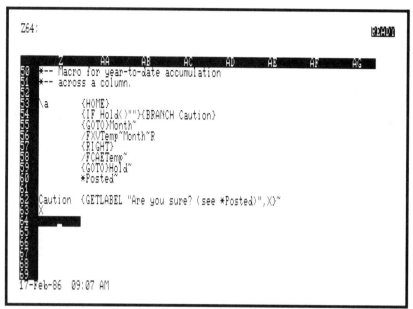

Figure 7.7: Year-to-date accumulator macro

Next, the macro uses the File Xtract Values options to store the Month range in a file named Temp, using these keystrokes:

/FXVTemp ˜ Month ˜ R

Then the macro moves the cell pointer over to the YTD column, and uses the File Combine Add Entire-File options to add (accumulate) the contents of the Temp file to the current YTD values, using these keystrokes:

{RIGHT}
/FCAETemp ˜

The macro finishes by simply placing the *Posted message in the cell named Hold:

{GOTO}Hold ˜
＊Posted ˜

One point to keep in mind when accumulating data with the File Combine Add options is that the YTD cell may not contain any formulas. However, as shown in this example, the File Xtract range may indeed contain formulas, which will in turn be properly accumulated into the YTD column.

Worksheet Consolidation

Along the same lines as accumulations are macros to consolidate data from separate worksheets. These are most often used in businesses where different departments manage their own worksheets and the corporate level combines these worksheets to see the overall picture.

Figure 7.8 shows a skeleton worksheet that can be used by several departments to record financial data. (The formulas are shown in text format in the figure, although they will, of course, show results of calculations in the actual worksheets.)

Figures 7.9, 7.10, and 7.11 show how three individual departments—Appliances, Housewares, and Sporting Goods—might fill in their worksheets. Each department uses a different file name for their worksheet (Applianc, Housewar, and Sports).

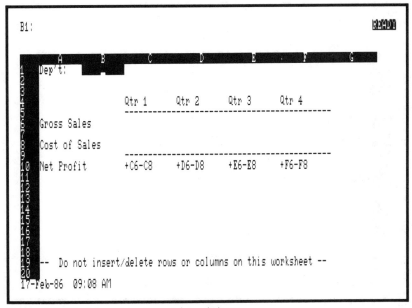

Figure 7.8: Skeleton departmental worksheet

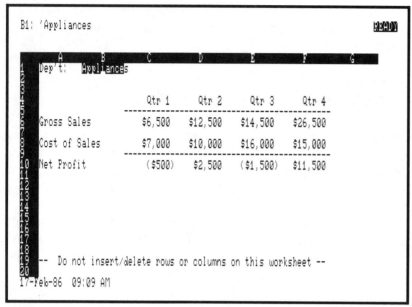

Figure 7.9: Financial statement on Applianc worksheet

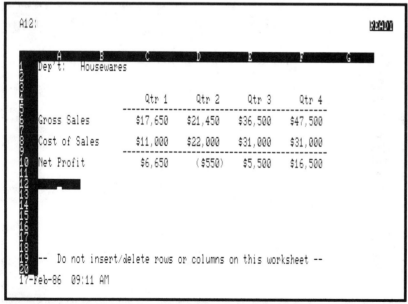

Figure 7.10: Financial statement on Housewar worksheet

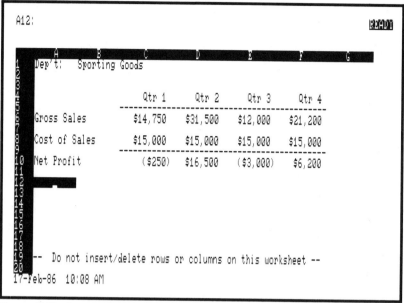

```
A12:                                                        READY

      A         B        C         D         E         F        G
 1  Dep't:   Sporting Goods
 2
 3
 4                      Qtr 1     Qtr 2     Qtr 3     Qtr 4
 5                    ---------------------------------------
 6  Gross Sales       $14,750   $31,500   $12,000   $21,200
 7
 8  Cost of Sales     $15,000   $15,000   $15,000   $15,000
 9                    ---------------------------------------
10  Net Profit          ($250)  $16,500   ($3,000)   $6,200
11
12        ____
13
14
15
16
17
18
19  -- Do not insert/delete rows or columns on this worksheet --
20
17-Feb-86  10:08 AM
```

Figure 7.11: Financial statement on Sports worksheet

Figure 7.12 shows a skeleton corporate worksheet that can be used to summarize the data from the three departmental worksheets. In this example, the corporate worksheet is named Corporat.

The macro to perform the consolidation, shown in Figure 7.13, is also stored on the Corporat worksheet.

This fairly simple macro uses a series of File Combine Add options to read in the three departmental worksheets. The command

   {HOME}

makes sure the cell pointer is properly placed for reading in the worksheets. Then the keystrokes

   /FCAEHousewar~

read in the Housewares (Housewar) department's data. The keystrokes

   /FCAESports~

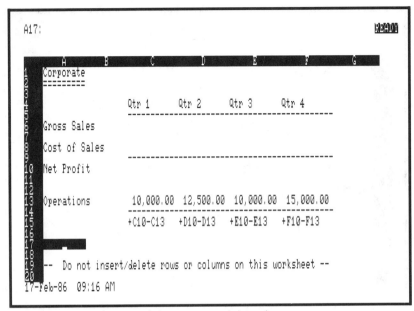

Figure 7.12: Corporate worksheet to consolidate departments

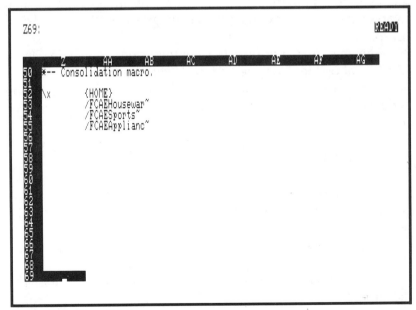

Figure 7.13: Consolidation macro

read in the Sporting Goods (Sports) department's data, and the keystrokes

/FCAEApplianc ‾

read in the Appliances (Applianc) department's data. Figure 7.14 shows the corporate worksheet after all the other worksheets have been consolidated.

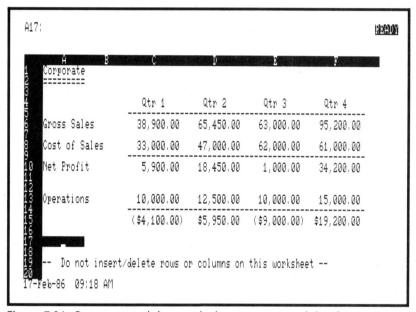

Figure 7.14: Corporate worksheet with departments consolidated

Consolidation with Pause for Disk Change

One variation on the consolidation macro is the addition of a pause to allow you to change data disks. This variation is practically essential on computers with two floppy disks, particularly if the departmental worksheets are large. Figure 7.15 shows a variation of the

consolidation macro with a subroutine added to allow for a pause
for changing disks between File Combine commands.

```
Z51: [W12]

50 *-- Consolidation macro with pause for data disk change.
51
52 Parameter
53 KeyPress
54
55 \x          {HOME}{BLANK C1}~
56             {ChangeDisk "Housewares"}
57             /FCAEHousewar~
58             {ChangeDisk "Sporting Goods"}
59             /FCAESports~
60             {ChangeDisk "Appliances"}
61             /FCAEApplianc~
62             {ChangeDisk "Corporate"}
63
64 ChangeDisk  {DEFINE Parameter:String}
65             {LET C1,+"Enter "&Parameter&" disk, then press any key..."}~
66             {BEEP 2}
67             {GET KeyPress}
68             {BLANK C1}~
69             {RETURN}
```

Figure 7.15: Consolidation macro with disk-change subroutine

The two cells named Parameter and KeyPress store data as
the macro runs. The macro begins by blanking cell C1, which is
used for displaying instructions:

\x {HOME}{BLANK C1} ~

Next the macro calls the ChangeDisk subroutine, and passes
the department name "Housewares" along the way:

{ChangeDisk "Housewares"}

The ChangeDisk subroutine defines the passed parameter
(Housewares in this example) as a character string, then uses that
word in the instructions displayed in cell C1:

Enter Housewares disk, then press any key . . ."

The first two lines of the ChangeDisk subroutine define the parameter and display the instructions:

```
ChangeDisk {DEFINE Parameter:String}
             {LET C1, + "Enter "&Parameter&" disk, then press
             any key . . . "} ~
```

Next, the macro beeps so the user hears when it is time to change disks. The macro assumes the user will change disks, then press a key, so it waits for a key press:

```
{BEEP 2}
{GET KeyPress}
```

When the user presses a key to continue, the subroutine erases the instructions from cell C1 and returns control to the main body of the macro where the File Combine takes place:

```
{BLANK C1} ~
{RETURN}
```

The main body of the macro includes the lines:

```
{ChangeDisk "Housewares"}
{ChangeDisk "Sporting Goods"}
{ChangeDisk "Appliances"}
{ChangeDisk "Corporate"}
```

so that the macro pauses for each required disk change and displays the appropriate department name with each pause. The last call to the ChangeDisk subroutine reminds the user to place the corporate disk back in drive B to proceed.

Partial Consolidation

Another way to consolidate worksheets is to pull only certain ranges of data from individual departments onto the corporate worksheet. For example, Figure 7.16 shows a version of the corporate worksheet where only the calculated net profits are consolidated from the individual departments. The corporate worksheet shown here simply totals the net profits using @SUM commands at the bottom of each Qtr column.

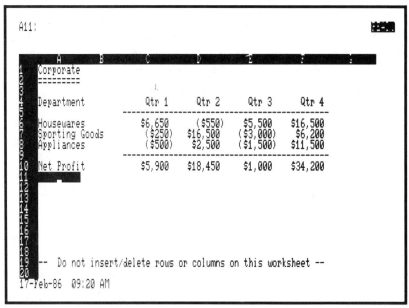

Figure 7.16: Consolidation of only parts of worksheets

To accomplish this, each departmental worksheet must have a named range that will be read into the corporate worksheet. Figure 7.17 shows the Sports worksheet with the net profits highlighted and named Total using the Range Name Create options from the menu. All departmental worksheets (Sports, Housewar, and Applianc) must have the range name Total assigned to the Net Profit row.

The corporate worksheet must include range names for incoming data. These are the named ranges for incoming data on the corporate worksheet shown in Figure 7.16:

RANGE NAME	CELLS
HTotal	C6..F6
STotal	C7..F7
ATotal	C8..F8

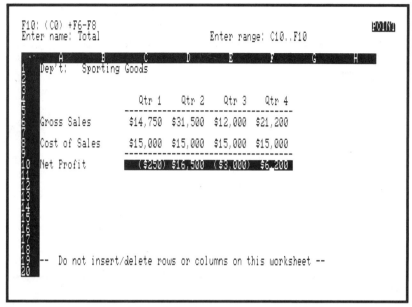

Figure 7.17: Departmental worksheet with range named Total

Next, the consolidation macro needs to position the cell pointer on the appropriate row for the incoming data, then use the File Combine Add Named-Range options to read in only the named range at the current cell pointer location. The macro for this is shown in Figure 7.18. (This macro also includes the ChangeDisk subroutine, which we discussed earlier.)

This is the routine that reads in the totals for the Housewares worksheet:

56   {GOTO}HTotal ~

57   {ChangeDisk "Housewares"}

58   /FCANTotal ~ Housewar ~

The line that reads {GOTO}HTotal ~ positions the cell pointer on the range named HTotal on the corporate worksheet, since this is where the incoming net profits will be stored. The next line, which reads

   {ChangeDisk "Housewares"}

```
            Z               AA                  AB
     50  *-- Consolidation macro with pause for data disk change.
     51  `
     52  Parameter
     53  KeyPress
     54
     55  \x              {HOME}{BLANK C1}~
     56                  {GOTO}HTotal~
     57                  {ChangeDisk "Housewares"}
     58                  /FCANTotal~Housewar~
     59                  {GOTO}STotal~
     60                  {ChangeDisk "Sporting Goods"}
     61                  /FCANTotal~Sports~
     62                  {GOTO}ATotal~
     63                  {ChangeDisk "Appliances"}
     64                  /FCANTotal~Applianc~
     65                  {ChangeDisk "Corporate"}
     66
     67  ChangeDisk      {DEFINE Parameter:String}
     68                  {LET C1,+"Enter "&Parameter&" disk, then press any key..."}~
     69                  {BEEP 2}
     70                  {GET KeyPress}
     71                  {BLANK C1}~
     72                  {RETURN}
```

Figure 7.18: Consolidation macro for partial worksheets

calls the ChangeDisk subroutine, which waits for the user to put
the Housewares department data disk in drive B. The line that
reads

/FCANTotal ˜ Housewar ˜

selects the File Combine Add Named-Range options from the
menu, specifies the range named Total in the incoming worksheet,
and specifies the worksheet named Housewar. The same procedure
is repeated for the Sporting Goods and Appliances worksheets,
using the STotal and ATotal ranges on the corporate worksheet.

Trapping Wrong-Disk Errors

If your consolidation macro requires that data disks be changed
several times, you may want to build in a routine to trap potential errors. For example, previous macros will bomb (go back to
the READY mode) should you accidentally insert the Appliances

disk when the macro asks for the Sporting Goods disk. The macro in Figure 7.19 will not bomb when such an error occurs. Instead, it will emit a low beep, present the message

Wrong Disk! Press a key to try again . . .

then allow you to try again.

```
               Z        AA       AB       AC       AD
49
50   *-- Consolidation macro with pause and error trapping.
51
52   Parameter
53   KeyPress
54
55   \x          {HOME}{BLANK C1}~
56   Housewares  {ChangeDisk "Housewares"}
57               /FCAEHousewar~
58   Sports      {ChangeDisk "Sports"}
59               /FCAESports~
60   Appliances  {ChangeDisk "Appliances"}
61               /FCAEApplianc~
62               {ChangeDisk "Corporate"}
63
64   ChangeDisk  {ONERROR ErrTrap}
65               {DEFINE Parameter:String}
66               {LET C1,+"Enter "&Parameter&" disk, then press any key . . ."}~
67               {BEEP 2}
68               {GET KeyPress}
69               {BLANK C1}~
70               {RETURN}
71
72   ErrTrap     {BLANK C1}
73               {BEEP 4}
74               {LET C1,"Wrong Disk! Press a key to try again..."}~
75               {GET KeyPress}
76               {DISPATCH Parameter}~
77
78
```

Figure 7.19: Consolidation macro with wrong-disk error trap

We need not discuss all of the macro in detail, since most of its contents should be familiar by now. However, the new error handling is a bit tricky and therefore deserves some discussion. The first modification is the use of the ONERROR command in the ChangeDisk subroutine:

{ONERROR ErrTrap}

This means that should an error occur in the macro, control will be passed to the routine named ErrTrap. The ErrTrap routine looks like this:

```
ErrTrap    {BLANK C1}
           {BEEP 4}
           {LET C1,"Wrong Disk! Press a key to try
              again . . ."} ~
           {GET KeyPress}
           {DISPATCH Parameter} ~
```

It clears the message area (C1), emits a low beep {BEEP 4}, then displays the "Wrong Disk! . . ." message. Then it waits for a key press and returns control to the main body of the program, using the DISPATCH command.

Recall that the DISPATCH command returns control to the destination named by the argument cell, not to the destination cell itself. Therefore, if the cell named Parameter contains the label Housewares, the command {DISPATCH Parameter} sends control to the cell named Housewares. In this macro, the cell named Parameter always contains a department name (Appliances, Sports, or Housewares). Furthermore, each routine in the main body of the macro has a department name assigned to it, as in the Housewares routine below:

```
Housewares    {ChangeDisk "Housewares"}
              /FCAEHousewar ~
```

So the cell named Parameter now serves two functions instead of one: it becomes part of the instructions shown on the screen in cell C1, and it contains the name of the cell to branch to after an error is handled by the ErrTrap routine.

A few notes about the ONERROR command are in order at this point. First of all, the ONERROR command branches control as soon as an error occurs in a macro, whether or not it is the error you are "expecting." Therefore, you should not place ONERROR commands in your macro until all the bugs are out, and until you can reasonably predict what error may occur (such as a "File Does Not Exist" error in this example).

Also note that once an error occurs in a macro, the ON-ERROR command is deactivated. Therefore, unless another

ONERROR command is issued, a second error will cause the macro to bomb. In the macro in Figure 7.19, the ONERROR command is issued in the ChangeDisk subroutine so that it is reinstated every time the macro pauses for a disk swap.

You can use a second parameter in the ONERROR command to record the error message that 1-2-3 normally displays at the lower-left corner of the screen. For example, the command

{ONERROR ErrTrap, ErrMsg}

passes control to the cell named ErrTrap and stores the error message in the cell named ErrMsg. If your ONERROR commands cause problems in a macro, use this two-argument version of the command, and check the contents of the ErrMsg cell to see what error triggered the ONERROR command.

Summary

The worksheets used in the examples in this chapter are all quite small. Perhaps macros do not seem justified for managing such small worksheets. However, keep in mind that these same techniques for accumulating and consolidating worksheets will work with worksheets of any size. Therefore, any time spent studying the File Xtract and File Combine options is time well spent. Virtually all worksheet accumulations and consolidations will depend on proper use of these 1-2-3 menu options. In addition, the use of the ONERROR command will give you some freedom to make mistakes while juggling lots of data disks.

The macros we discussed in this chapter include the following:

- A macro for year-to-date accumulations
- Macros for consolidating several worksheets
- Consolidations with pauses for changing disks
- Partial consolidations
- Consolidations with built-in error traps

8

MACRO-BUILDING AIDS

IN THIS CHAPTER WE'LL create some macros that can help you develop and manage other macros. The first is a macro that allows you to record keystrokes in macro form as you type them. The other macros are tools to help you manage range names on the worksheet.

A Macro-Building Macro

The macro-building macro is quite easy to use. When you type Alt-m, the cell pointer moves to the home cell and creates a range named Macro. Then it simply waits for you to type some keystrokes. Suppose you type in these keystrokes and menu options:

@SUM (End ↑ . End ↓) Return / C Return . Tab Tab Return
Home / Worksheet Global Format Currency 2 Return

The macro-building macro will translate each keystroke to its appropriate macro name and place those macro names on the worksheet. Just press the BREAK key when you are done recording keystrokes. Then use File Xtract Values to give the macro a file name, and highlight the recorded keystrokes, as shown in Figure 8.1. Later, you can call up the macro using File Retrieve or File Combine, and assign a macro name to it.

This macro is not quite as powerful as the Symphony Learn mode, nor as the external keyboard enhancers that allow you to see 1-2-3 perform while you record keystrokes. But it is valuable for quickly putting together a simple typing-alternative macro or a subroutine for a larger macro. Figure 8.2 shows the macro-building macro. Labels in column Z are, as usual, range names for cells to the right.

The macro-building macro begins with the usual descriptive comment, followed by a cell named Entry that stores keystrokes. The first line of the macro homes the cursor and uses the Range Erase options to clear any previously recorded macro from the worksheet. Then the macro puts the label Macro into cell A1

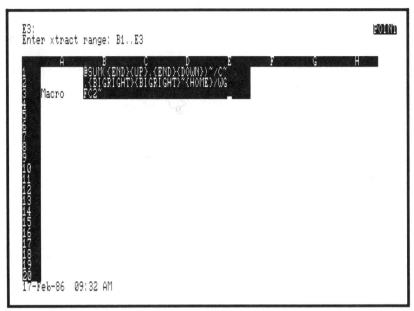

Figure 8.1: Recorded macro on the worksheet

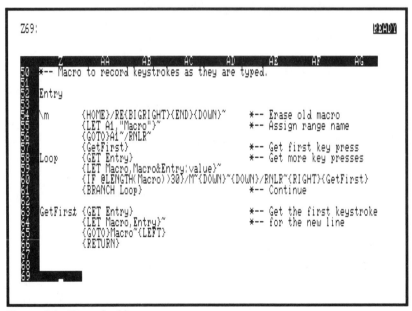

Figure 8.2: Macro-building macro

and uses the Range Name Labels Right options to assign this as the name of the cell to the right. The first three lines of the macro, shown below, perform these tasks:

```
\m   {HOME}/RE{BIGRIGHT}{END}{DOWN} ~     *-- Erase old
                                                  macro
     {LET A1,"Macro"} ~       *-- Assign range name
     {GOTO}A1 ~ /RNLR ~
```

Next, the macro calls the GetFirst subroutine, which records the first keystroke for a given row in the macro:

```
{GetFirst}                      *-- Get first key press
```

The next line uses the GET command to get the next keystroke and stores it in the cell named Entry:

```
Loop    {GET Entry}             *-- Get more key presses
```

The next LET command joins the current keystroke to the existing keystrokes stored in the cell named Entry:

```
{LET Macro,Macro&Entry:value} ~
```

The next line keeps the macro from becoming too long across a row:

```
{IF @LENGTH(Macro)>30}/M ~ {DOWN} ~ {DOWN}/RNLR ~
     {RIGHT}{GetFirst}
```

In English, this line means "If the current row of keystrokes is more than 30 characters long, then move the label Macro down to the next row, assign the range name to the new row, and get the first keystroke for this new row."

The BRANCH command repeats the macro, starting at the routine named Loop, so that the user can record more keystrokes:

```
{BRANCH Loop}                   *-- Continue
```

Only pressing the BREAK key will terminate this loop (and the macro).

The GetFirst subroutine, shown below, records the first keystroke for a new row. A separate routine is required for this because the LET command, which adds new keystrokes to existing keystrokes, will not work if the cell receiving the keystrokes is blank.

GetFirst   **{GET Entry}**   ***-- Get the first keystroke**

{LET Macro,Entry} ~   ***-- for the new line**

{GOTO}Macro ~ {LEFT}

{RETURN}

Deleting Range Names

When building macros, you need to create and manage a lot of range names. The Range Name Delete options allow you to delete a single range name, and the Range Name Reset options allow you to delete all range names on a worksheet. There are no options to selectively delete a group of range names. A couple of macros can give you the ability to selectively delete a group of range names. Both macros are shown in Figure 8.3.

The Alt-d macro simply displays a menu of range names and lets you delete a name by moving the highlighter to the name and pressing Return. You can continue to delete names for as long as you wish. To stop deleting range names, press the BREAK key. You'll find this method a considerable improvement over selecting the Range Name Delete options for each range name you want to delete.

The Alt-c macro allows you to delete a column of range names and labels by highlighting the labels on the worksheet. This is particularly useful with macro names, since these are usually stored in a single column next to the macro commands and keystrokes. (Don't use the Alt-c macro to delete a single range label.)

When you first run the Alt-c macro, it allows you to highlight the range of names to delete, as shown in Figure 8.4. After you

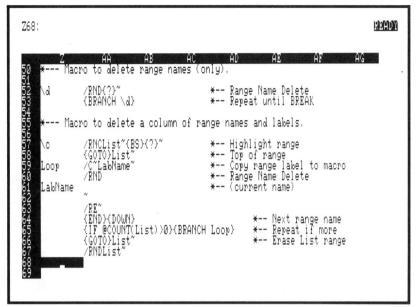

Figure 8.3: Macros to delete range names

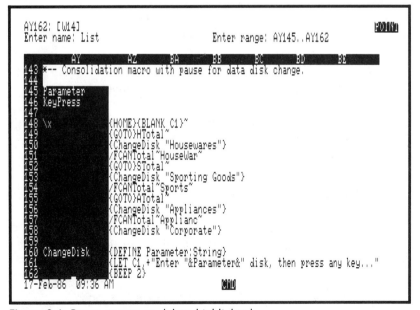

Figure 8.4: Range names to delete highlighted

press Return, the macro deletes the range names, as well as the range labels, within the highlighted range.

The Alt-c macro is a bit more complex than the Alt-d macro, and it deserves some discussion. The macro begins by creating a range named List, which you define by positioning and expanding the cell pointer:

\c   /RNCList˜{BS}{?}˜   •-- Highlight range

Next, the macro positions the cell pointer at the top of the range named List, and copies the first range label to the cell named LabName. The label, in turn, becomes part of the Range Name Delete options, which the macro performs next:

	{GOTO}List˜	**•-- Top of range**
Loop	**/C˜LabName˜**	**•-- Copy range label to macro**
	/RND	**•-- Range Name Delete**
LabName		**•-- (current name)**
	˜	

Next, the macro erases the label on the worksheet, using Range Erase, and then moves the cell pointer down to the next range name in the column:

/RE˜
{END}{DOWN}   •-- Next range name

As long as there are still labels in the range of range names (@COUNT(List)>0), the macro repeats the process of deleting range names:

{IF @COUNT(List)>0}{BRANCH Loop}   •-- Repeat if more

When there are no more range names to delete, the macro sends the cell pointer back to the starting position (the first cell in the range named List), and deletes the range:

{GOTO}List˜   •-- Erase List range
/RNDList˜

At this point, all of the range labels and range names in the previously highlighted range have been deleted from the worksheet, and the macro returns control to the READY mode.

Showing Range Names

Version 2.0 of 1-2-3 includes an option to display a list of all range names and their locations on a worksheet. The option is quite simple to use. Call up the menu, select the Range Name Tables options, then move the cell pointer to a good location for displaying range names. You should pick a location that has a blank column to the right and as many blank rows beneath as there are range names. You need only move the cell pointer to the upper-left corner of the range. Press Return, and 1-2-3 will show you all of the range names, along with their locations, as shown in Figure 8.5.

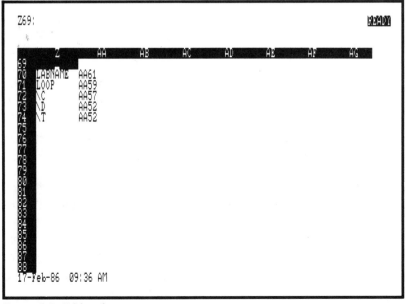

Figure 8.5: Table of range names

Of course, you can create a simple macro to show range names, like this:

\t   /RNT{BS}{?} ˜

Using External Keyboard Enhancers

Another way to build 1-2-3 "typing alternative" macros is to use an external macro processor or *keyboard enhancer*. Two examples of such programs are Borland's *SuperKey*, and Rose-Soft's *ProKey*. Both programs run in the "background" while you are using 1-2-3, and are invisible until you want them. To record a macro, you call up the background program, begin recording, then perform the keystrokes that you want to record. 1-2-3 will behave normally, and the background program will record the keystrokes.

When you have finished recording keystrokes, you inform the background program of this, and it disappears into the background once again. You can then replay the recorded keystrokes at any time by simply pressing a couple of keys (just like you do when using 1-2-3 macros).

Besides the ability to record keystrokes as they happen, the background programs are independent of any 1-2-3 worksheet. That means your macro can leave 1-2-3 to print graphs or run a program from DOS, then come back into 1-2-3 again. The background macro can also work with several separate worksheets, since no one worksheet needs to contain the macro.

The one disadvantage to background programs is that they require a good deal of memory. On a small computer with big worksheets, this might be a very large disadvantage. You can use an external keyboard enhancer to record a macro, then call that recorded macro into the worksheet and convert it to a 1-2-3 macro if you like. Of course, this will work only if the external macro performs a task that 1-2-3 macros are capable of performing.

Here's an example of techniques for recording a macro and pulling it into 1-2-3 using Borland's SuperKey. First, with SuperKey already in the background and 1-2-3 running normally, you type Alt / to call up the SuperKey menu, then select the Macro and Begin options to record keystrokes. SuperKey will ask that you enter a keystroke name for the macro (any letter preceded by the Alt or Ctrl key).

Next, you just type your keystrokes. 1-2-3 will perform the keystrokes normally, and SuperKey will record them. When you are done recording, you type Alt - . Then select the Macro and Save options to store the recorded keystrokes on a file. You can also play back the keystrokes by pressing the macro name, just as you can with 1-2-3 macros.

If you wish to change the SuperKey macro into a 1-2-3 macro, you can do so with a bit of translation. First, select the 1-2-3 File Import Text options from the menu. Enter the name of the SuperKey file, adding .MAC as the extension (e.g., SuperMac.MAC). The SuperKey macro will appear as shown in Figure 8.6.

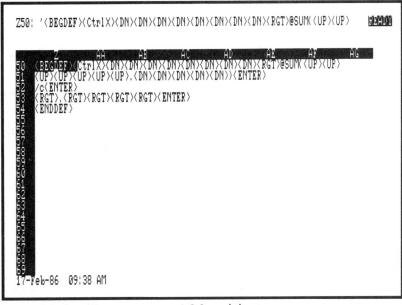

Figure 8.6: SuperKey macro on a 1-2-3 worksheet

It isn't too difficult to figure out what the various SuperKey key names mean, so these are easy to translate. The <BEGDEF> and <ENDEF> commands are strictly for SuperKey, so these can be eliminated. The <Ctrlx> is the SuperKey name, which can also be eliminated. Figure 8.7 shows the sample SuperKey macro converted to 1-2-3 syntax.

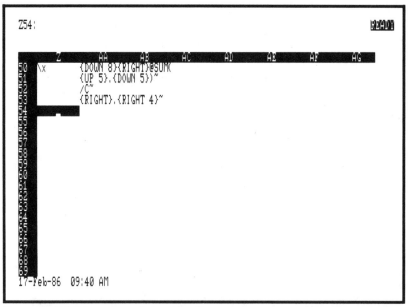

Figure 8.7: 1-2-3 version of the SuperKey macro

Of course, since even the external keyboard enhancers only record keystrokes, they cannot help you to develop complex macros that use macro commands. Nonetheless, they can come in handy for the simpler typing-alternative macros, and save some of the time and tedium involved in writing long macros with many keywords.

Summary

In this chapter we've developed some macros to help create and manage other macros. We've also discussed some external *keyboard enhancers* that you can use in conjunction with 1-2-3. The macros we've created include the following:

- A macro to record keystrokes
- Macros to delete range names and labels
- A macro to display a table of range names and locations

9

GRAPHICS
MACROS

IN THIS CHAPTER WE'LL discuss some macros along with some general techniques for creating 1-2-3 graphics. We'll include in this chapter a discussion of the 1-2-3 ASCII/LICS (American Standard Code for Information Interchange/Lotus International Character Set) characters that you can use as graphics aids on the worksheet.

Viewing ASCII/LICS Codes

In addition to the letters and numbers that you see on your keyboard, 1-2-3 has many foreign-language and small graphics characters. These are displayed in Appendix 2 of the *1-2-3 Reference Manual* that came with your 1-2-3 package. You can also develop a macro to place these characters on your screen, as shown in Figure 9.1. (Figure 9.1 shows only a portion of the full character set. Use PgUp and PgDn to view all the characters.)

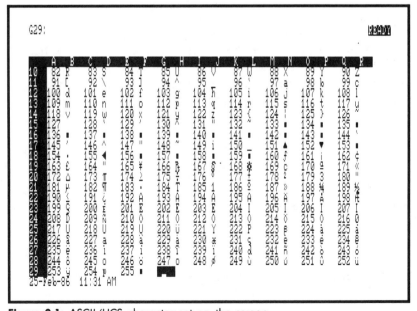

Figure 9.1: ASCII/LICS character set on the screen

The macro to display the character set is shown in Figure 9.2. Use Range Name Labels Right to make labels in column Z into range names for all the macros in this chapter.

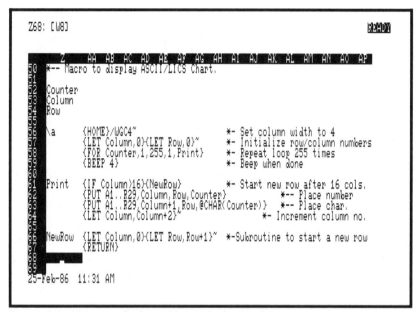

```
Z68: [W8]                                                    READY

       Z    AA  AB  AC  AD  AE  AF  AG  AH  AI  AJ  AK  AL  AM  AN  AO  AP
50   *-- Macro to display ASCII/LICS Chart.
51
52   Counter
53   Column
54   Row
55
56   \a        {HOME}/WGC4~                  *- Set column width to 4
57             {LET Column,0}{LET Row,0}~    *- Initialize row/column numbers
58             {FOR Counter,1,255,1,Print}   *- Repeat loop 255 times
59             {BEEP 4}                      *- Beep when done
60
61   Print     {IF Column>16}{NewRow}        *- Start new row after 16 cols.
62             {PUT A1..R29,Column,Row,Counter}        *-- Place number
63             {PUT A1..R29,Column+1,Row,@CHAR(Counter)}  *-- Place char.
64             {LET Column,Column+2}~               *- Increment column no.
65
66   NewRow    {LET Column,0}{LET Row,Row+1}~  *-Subroutine to start a new row
67             {RETURN}
68
69
25-Feb-86  11:31 AM
```

Figure 9.2: Macro to display ASCII/LICS characters

Let's discuss how the macro works. Notice the cells named Counter, Column, and Row. These are used to store data as the macro is working. The macro first homes the cursor and globally sets the worksheet column width to four characters:

\a   {HOME}/WGC4 ~

Then it sets the Column and Row cells to zero and begins a loop that counts from 1 to 255 (because there are 255 possible ASCII/LICS characters). This loop accesses the subroutine named Print:

{LET Column,0}{LET Row,0} ~
{FOR Counter,1,255,1,Print}

The Print subroutine makes sure the chart of characters fits reasonably well on the screen. It first checks to see if more than

16 columns across have been printed. If so, it branches to the subroutine named NewRow:

Print   **{IF Column>16}{NewRow}**

If not, the macro places the current value of the Counter cell in the next Row and Column in the range A1..R29. Next to this cell, the macro places the ASCII/LICS code using the @CHAR function. Then the macro increments the column number by two and proceeds through the FOR loop:

{PUT A1..R29,Column,Row,Counter}
{PUT A1..R29,Column+1,Row,@CHAR(Counter)}
{LET Column,Column+2} ˜

The NewRow subroutine resets the column number to zero and increments the row number by one, so the next row of characters begins in the first column of a new row:

NewRow   **{LET Column,0}{LET Row,Row+1} ˜**
            {RETURN}

You can use the usual Print Printer options to print the codes after the macro completes its task. It is unlikely that your printer will show exactly the same character set as you see on your screen because screens and printers rarely use identical graphics characters.

Once you know what ASCII/LICS characters are available to you, you need to learn to use them. We'll discuss that in the next section.

Using ASCII/LICS Characters

There are two ways to access ASCII/LICS characters. One is to use the @CHAR function with the appropriate number. The other is to use the Compose (Alt-F1) key with appropriate letter codes. Compose key codes are listed in Appendix 2 of the *1-2-3*

Reference Manual. Of course, you can also create macros for the special characters. Let's look at some examples.

Figure 9.3 shows some sample character strings and the formulas that are used to display them. All of the examples use the @CHAR function within a formula to display the text in the cell.

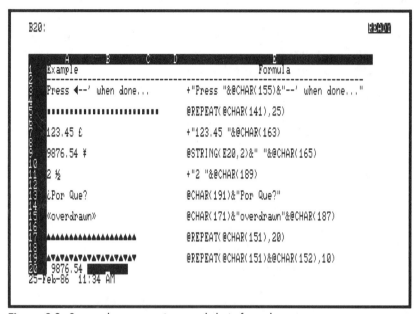

Figure 9.3: Some character strings and their formulas

These codes work fine except when you need to embed a special character in a string that cannot be calculated with a formula. For example, a GETLABEL command requires that the prompt string be whole, not built out of a formula.

When @CHAR will not work, you can use a *compose sequence.* Compose sequences are easy to use, but they require either memorizing or referring to Appendix 2 of the *1-2-3 Reference Manual.* To type a compose sequence, you press Compose (Alt-F1) then a one- or two-letter code. For example, the sequence for the left-pointing triangle is Compose-mg. Hence, to type a left-pointing triangle at any time, hold down the Alt key and press F1. Then type the letters mg. The appropriate character will appear at the current cursor position. Figure 9.4 shows some special characters, the compose sequences used to type them, and some examples of their usage. (Note the {COMPOSE} symbol is used to represent pressing the Compose key; {COMPOSE} is not a valid macro keyword.)

```
E20:                                                              READY

        A        B           C              D        E       F       G      H
    Symbol   Compose sequence        Example
    --------------------------------------------------------------------
    ◄        {COMPOSE}mg     {GETLABEL "Press ◄-' to continue...",X}~

    ¢        {COMPOSE}c/     21¢

    π        {COMPOSE}pi     π = 3.141592653589794

    ²        {COMPOSE}2^     πr²

    ▲        {COMPOSE}ba     ▲ Results in column above

    ▼        {COMPOSE}ea     ▼ Data in column below

    •        {COMPOSE}^.     • This item is bulleted.

    °        {COMPOSE}^0     97° Fahrenheit

    ±        {COMPOSE}+-     ±123.45

25-Feb-86  11:35 AM
```

Figure 9.4: Some compose sequences

If you use a particular set of special characters often, you may want to create macros to type them. The macros can type only a single character into a single cell, but you can, of course, move and copy these characters on the worksheet. Figure 9.5 shows some graphics-character macros. As usual, macro names are in column Z.

A Graphics Slide Show

The graphics slide show macro allows you to view a series of graphs in a slide show fashion. Let's look at an example. Figure 9.6 shows a simple worksheet. Figures 9.7 through 9.10 show four different named graphs that show these data in different ways. Once you have entered the slide show macro on the worksheet, pressing Alt-s displays these graphs on the screen,

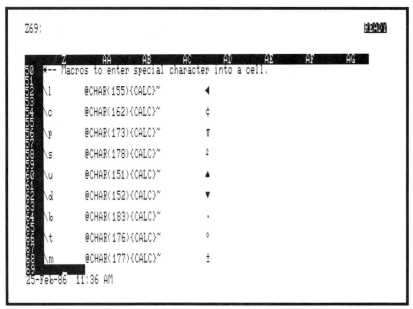

Figure 9.5: Macros to print graphics characters

```
A17:                                                    READY

         A         B         C         D         E
1
2                        ABC COMPANY
3
4                       Quarterly Sales
5
6  Product    Quarter 1   Quarter 2   Quarter 3   Quarter 4
7  -------    ---------   ---------   ---------   ---------
8  Apples     3,234.56    4,321.56    3,765.99    4,109.43
9  Bananas    3,999.02    4,401.12    3,765.09    4,001.33
10 Cherries   4,678.23    5,889.04    3,996.55    4,444.04
11 Zebras     3,567.76    4,825.76    3,593.67    4,910.40
12            ================================================
13 Total     $15,479.57  $19,437.48  $15,121.30  $17,465.20
14
15
16 Type Alt-s for graphics slide show.
17
18
19
20
25-Feb-86  11:37 AM
```

Figure 9.6: Worksheet data for which graphs are presented

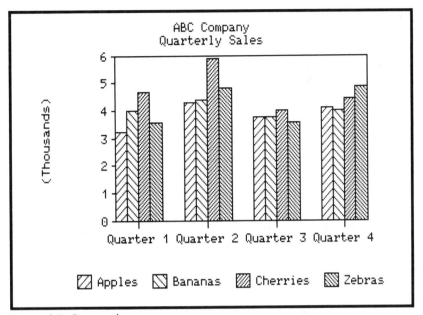

Figure 9.7: Bar graph

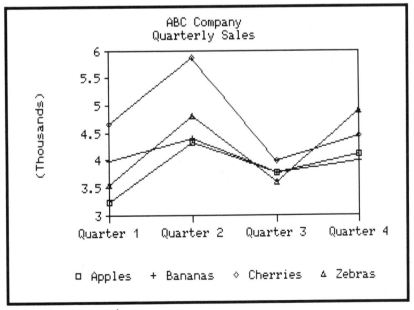

Figure 9.8: Line graph

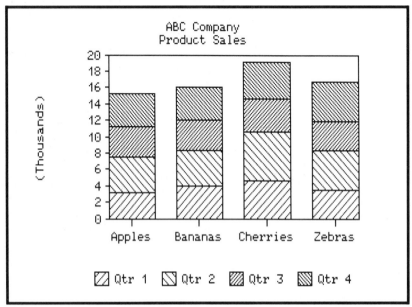

Figure 9.9: Stacked-bar graph

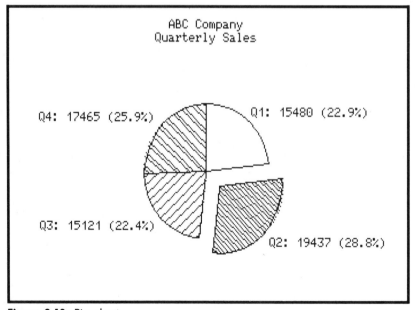

Figure 9.10: Pie chart

one at a time. While any graph is displayed, you can press any key to display the next graph.

To use the macro, you must first create a series of graphs and assign a name to each graph with the usual Graph Name Create options from the menu. You can assign any name you like to each of the graphs.

Figure 9.11 shows the macro capable of displaying the graphics slide show. The macro will work with any worksheet that contains named graphs, so long as the quantity in the cell named Figs is less than or equal to the number of named graphs in the worksheet. In this example, the cell named Figs contains the number 4, because there are four named graphs to display with this worksheet.

Figure 9.11: Macro to display a graphics slide show

Let's discuss the macro line by line. The cell named Figs must contain the number of cells to display before the macro is used—4 in this example. The Counter cell is used for the FOR loop.

The macro begins by turning the windows and panel off, so that the worksheet and menu do not reappear on the screen between graph displays:

\s   {WINDOWSOFF}{PANELOFF}

Next the macro calls up the Graph menu

/G

and then repeatedly accesses the subroutine named PikGraf, using the number stored in Figs to determine the number of repetitions:

{FOR Counter,0,Figs-1,1,PikGraf}

After displaying all of the graphs, the macro quits the Graph menu and returns to the worksheet READY mode:

Q

The PikGraf subroutine displays the graph by selecting the Name Use options from the Graph menu and moving the graph name highlighter to the right as many times as is specified by the number in the Counter cell:

PikGraf   NU{RIGHT Counter} ˜

The macro will work fine with any worksheet that contains named graphs. Just remember to place the appropriate number in the cell named Figs first. If you would like the macro to ask how many graphs to display each time it is run, insert the command

{GETNUMBER "How many graphs?",Figs} ˜

near the top of the macro, as below:

Figs
Counter

\s   {GETNUMBER "How many graphs?",Figs} ˜
**   {WINDOWSOFF}{PANELOFF}**
**   /G**

```
          {FOR Counter,0,Figs-1,1,PikGraf}
          Q

PikGraf   NU{RIGHT Counter} ~
```

Creating Pie Charts

Figure 9.10 shows a pie chart that uses some techniques that are new to version 2.0 of 1-2-3. Therefore, we'll take a moment to discuss how this pie chart was created. The techniques discussed here do not represent the only way to present these data on a pie chart, of course, but they do demonstrate some features that are new to version 2.0 of 1-2-3.

To create the sample pie chart, position the cell pointer in cell B13 and make its references absolute by pressing EDIT (F2) and ABS (F4), followed by a press on the Return key. The formula will then contain absolute references, as below:

@SUM(B8..B11)

Repeat this process to make all four formulas in row 13 refer to absolute ranges.

Next, transpose the formulas into an out-of-the-way area on the worksheet, such as column K. To do so, select the Range Transpose commands, specify B13..E13 as the range to copy from, and specify K1 as the range to copy to. Figure 9.12 shows the transposed totals in column K.

Next, place the special codes (0–7) for specifying types of crosshatching used in the pie chart into column L. To explode one slice of the pie, add 100 to the hatch code, as in cell L2. To display both the quarter and the total with each pie slice, you can calculate X-Range values as in column M in Figure 9.12. The text of the formulas stored in column M is listed in column P.

Finally, assign K1..K4 as the A-Range for the pie chart, assign the range L1..L4 as the B-Range, and assign the range M1..M4 as the X-Range. The resulting pie chart is shown in Figure 9.10.

The hatch marks (0–7) that you can use in a pie chart are shown in Figure 9.13. Notice the exploded seventh slice. This was achieved by entering 107, rather than 7, as the value to plot.

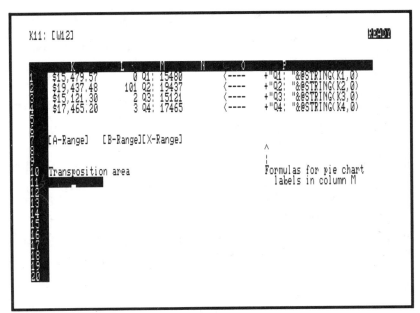

Figure 9.12: Specifications for the pie chart

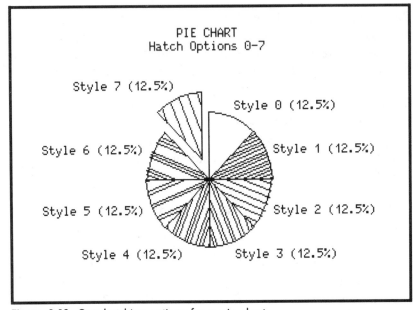

Figure 9.13: Crosshatching options for a pie chart

Automatic Graph Generation

Suppose that you have a series of identical departmental worksheets, such as the Appliances, Sporting Goods, and Housewares worksheets we developed in Chapter 7. Later, you decide to include a graph in each of these worksheets. To call up each individual worksheet and define ranges and graph names can be a tedious task. (Even more tedious if you have 10 or 15 such similar worksheets!) You can avoid the tedium by creating a macro that automatically creates and names a graph for each of the departmental worksheets.

To create such a macro, you call up one of the departmental worksheets and create the graph you want. Jot down every keystroke that you type to create the graph. Then, place these keystrokes in a new worksheet as a macro subroutine and have the macro repeat these keystrokes for each departmental worksheet. Figure 9.14 shows a macro that can automatically create graphs for the Appliances, Sporting Goods, and Housewares worksheets.

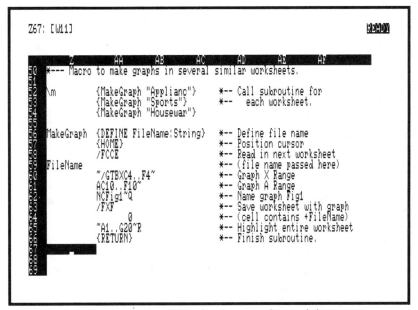

Figure 9.14: Macro to create graphs for three similar worksheets

This macro demonstrates the value of using subroutines with parameters, because the process of creating a graph can be accessed repeatedly for any number of worksheets. Let's discuss how the macro works.

The main body of the macro simply calls the MakeGraph subroutine once for each worksheet that needs a graph. In this example, the departmental worksheet file names are Applianc, Sports, and Housewar, as shown below:

*--- Macro to make graphs in several similar worksheets.

\m   {MakeGraph "Applianc"}
        {MakeGraph "Sports"}
        {MakeGraph "Housewar"}

The MakeGraph subroutine defines the passed parameter as a string, and stores the parameter in the cell named FileName, which is actually a part of the macro. The departmental file name is stored beneath the /FCCE (File Combine Copy Entire-File) options, so that the macro reads the appropriate departmental worksheet into the macro worksheet, as shown below:

MakeGraph   {DEFINE FileName:String}
                {HOME}
                /FCCE
FileName

Once the departmental worksheet is read into the macro worksheet, the macro names the range C4..F4 as the X-Range:

~/GTBXC4..F4~

Then the macro assigns the range C10..F10 as the A-Range:

AC10..F10~

Next, the macro uses the Name Create options to name the graph Fig1, then quits the Graph menu:

NCFig1~Q

Now the macro needs to extract the departmental worksheet and graph from the macro worksheet and put it back under its original departmental file name. Since the file name is already stored in the cell named FileName, the formula + FileName in cell AA64 supplies the appropriate file name to the File Xtract options. On the worksheet, the results of the + FileName formula appear only as a zero, but when the macro is executing, the appropriate file name is filled in. The lines below show the + FileName formula in text format in the cell:

/FXF

+ FileName   **∗-- (cell contains + FileName)**

Next the macro highlights the Xtract range, A1..G20, which is the original departmental worksheet, and replaces the original departmental worksheet file with the new departmental worksheet and graph:

˜ A1..G20 ˜ R

Then control is returned to the main body of the macro, and the macro repeats the graph-creation for the next departmental worksheet:

{RETURN}

This macro is particularly tricky because it uses the passed parameter to store the worksheet file name in two places within the macro. First, the file name is stored in the cell named File-Name, because of the DEFINE command and the cell named FileName. Then the file name appears a second time within the macro by using the formula + FileName in the body of the macro. The file name could actually be used any number of times within the macro using the + FileName formula, but this macro only required that the file name be used twice.

The MakeGraph subroutine could be used to create graphs in any number of similar worksheets. For example, if you had a series of similar worksheets stored under the file names January, February, March, April, May, June, and July, the main body of the macro would contain the commands

     \m   {MakeGraph "January"}
             {MakeGraph "February"}
             {MakeGraph "March"}
             {MakeGraph "April"}
             {MakeGraph "May"}
             {MakeGraph "June"}
             {MakeGraph "July"}

to create graphs in all six worksheets.

   If you wanted the macro to pause to allow you to type in a title for each graph, you could include the Options Titles First options in the MakeGraph subroutine as shown below:

     NCFig1 ~
     OTF{?} ~ QQ
     /FXF

   You can, of course, have the macro pause for any of the Graph menu options. Just be sure to put the appropriate letters (such as OTS for Other Title Second) in front of the Quit (Q) and File Xtract (/FX) keystrokes.

Plotting Every Other Column on a Graph

In most cases, the various graphics ranges (X, A, B, and so forth) will be in contiguous rows or columns in a worksheet. This makes them easy to highlight as ranges. However, many worksheets will require that noncontiguous rows or columns be displayed in a graph. Figure 9.15 shows a simple example.

   If you want to plot quarterly totals for apples in the A-Range, and quarterly totals for bananas in the B-Range, you cannot assign the ranges using the usual Graph Range options. The range of apple totals is split up by the banana totals, and vice

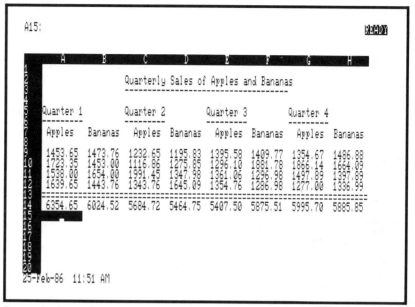

Figure 9.15: Worksheet with noncontiguous totals to plot

versa. The desired A-Range actually consists of the noncontiguous cells A14, C14, E14, and G14. The desired B-Range consists of the noncontiguous cells B14, D14, F14, and H14.

There are, of course, several ways to deal with this problem. The simplest way is to place formulas for the totals in rows or columns in an out-of-the-way area on the worksheet.

Plotting Noncontiguous Data with Formulas

Figure 9.16 shows an out-of-the-way area (starting at column M) that contains formulas for plotting a graph from the sample worksheet shown in Figure 9.15.

Column M contains the formulas shown below. Each references one of the cells containing a quarterly total for apples.

    +A14
    +C14
    +E14
    +G14

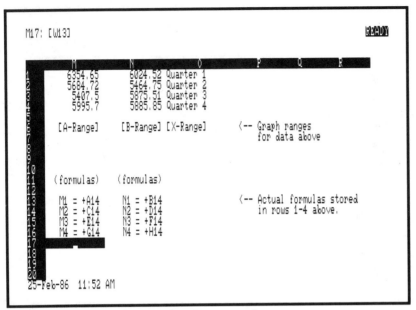

Figure 9.16: Calculated ranges for plotting graphs

This range of cells in column M (M1..M4) is then defined as the A-Range using the Graph A menu options.

Column N contains these formulas:

+B14

+D14

+F14

+H14

The formulas reference the cells containing the quarterly totals for bananas. These formulas (N1..N4) can be defined as the B-Range using the Graph B menu options.

Column O contains labels used in the graph. There are no formulas involved, only simple labels. These cells (O1..O4) are defined as the X-Range. The resulting graph is shown in Figure 9.17.

This method is simple and practical. Since the totals in columns M and N are actually references to other cells, the technique stands up to row insertions and deletions in the worksheet.

You can, of course, develop macros to help plot these non-contiguous columns on worksheets. However, unless you do this

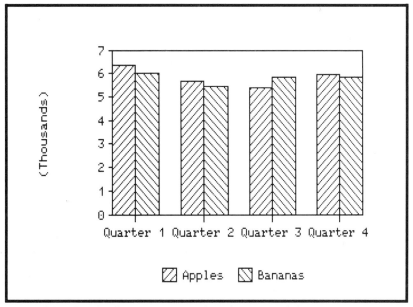

Figure 9.17: Graph of noncontiguous data from a worksheet

sort of thing often, it might be simpler to create the graph ranges without the macros.

Figure 9.18 shows a macro that can display a graph from a worksheet identical to the one shown in Figure 9.16. The macro requires that the data being plotted be in a range named Totals. (In the sample worksheet, cells in the range A14..H14 are named Totals, using the usual Range Name Create options.)

The macro also uses out-of-the-way ranges for placing data to be plotted, similar to the techniques we have already discussed. The only difference is that the macro automatically places the latest values to be displayed in the graph ranges, then displays the graph. In this example, you'll need to specify M1..M4 as the graph A-Range, and N1..N4 as the graph B-Range. Also, you might want to name O1..O4 as the X-Range and put some X-Range titles in the cells. Name the graph Hopper1 with the usual Graph Name Create options.

Let's discuss how this macro works. First, you need to put a number into the cell named Number, indicating the number of columns to be plotted in the graph. In this example, the number 8 is used (for columns A–H). The other named cells store data as

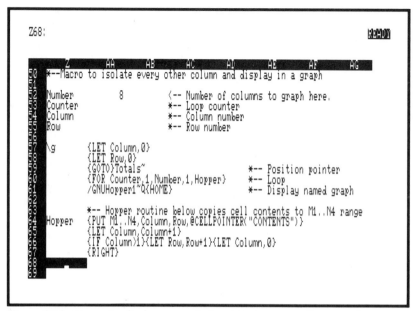

Figure 9.18: Macro to display a graph for data in noncontiguous columns

the macro is executing:

*--Macro to isolate every other column and display in a graph

Number	**8**	**<-- Number of columns to graph here.**
Counter		
Column		
Row		

Next, the macro initializes values for the Row and Column cells and moves the cell pointer to the start of the range named Totals. A FOR loop then repeats the subroutine named Hopper for each column of data being plotted:

```
\g      {LET Column,0}
        {LET Row,0}
        {GOTO}Totals ~
        {FOR Counter,1,Number,1,Hopper}
```

The Hopper subroutine takes the contents of the currently highlighted cell and places them into the appropriate cell in the

A- or B-Range. In this example, the A-Range and B-Range are in the range M1..N4. Other graphs might use other ranges. Larger graphs would require larger ranges. For example, a graph with 16 columns would need a range such as M1..N8 for two columns of data, each with eight rows.

The subroutine is a little easier to understand if you view the M1..N4 range as having these column and row coordinates:

	A-RANGE	B-RANGE
	M	**N**
1	(0,0)	(0,1)
2	(1,0)	(1,1)
3	(2,0)	(2,1)
4	(3,0)	(3,1)

The range M1..N4, of course, consists of the A- and B-Ranges plotted on the graph.

When the macro starts, the cell pointer is on the first value to be plotted, and the row and column numbers are zero. Therefore, the PUT command puts the first data item into the upper-left corner of the M1..N4 range:

Hopper {PUT M1..N4,Column,Row,
       @CELLPOINTER("CONTENTS")}

The next line adds one to the column number. At this point, the column number equals one, and the row number still equals zero. In this case, since the column number is not greater than one, the {IF Column>1} command has no effect. Then the RIGHT command moves the cell pointer to the next item of data in the Total range:

    {LET Column,Column + 1}
    {IF Column>1}{LET Row,Row + 1}{LET Column,0}
    {RIGHT}

This will be the total sales of bananas for the second quarter. The PUT command then places this value in column 1, row 0 of the M1..N4 range, which is actually the top of the graph's B-Range.

The macro then adds one to the column number again. The IF clause catches the fact that column 1 now equals 2, so it changes the column number back to zero and adds one to the row. The RIGHT command moves the cell pointer over one row, so that it is resting on the second quarter totals for apples. The PUT command copies its value to column 0, row 2 of the M1..N4 range, which is the appropriate place in the graph's A-Range. This process continues until both the A-Range and B-Range have been filled in.

In other words, while the cell pointer moves steadily across the values to be plotted on the graph, the macro calculates the Column and Row position of each value to be plotted, following the pattern

```
0,0
1,0
1,0
1,1
2,0
2,1
3,0
3,1
4,0
4,1
```

After the A-Range and B-Range have had the appropriate values filled in, the FOR loop finishes and the line below displays the graph:

/GNUHopper1 ~ Q{HOME}

Macro to Skip Blanks and Other Columns

It is conceivable that your worksheets are a bit more complex than the ones discussed so far. For example, Figure 9.19 shows a portion of a worksheet that displays quarterly sales totals for three different products—apples, bananas, and cherries. As an added problem (from a graphics point of view), there is a blank column between each quarter. Figure 9.20 shows a graph of these data.

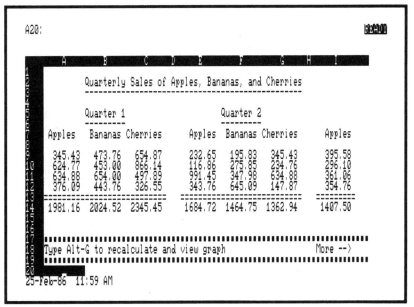

Figure 9.19: Worksheet with quarterly sales totals for three products

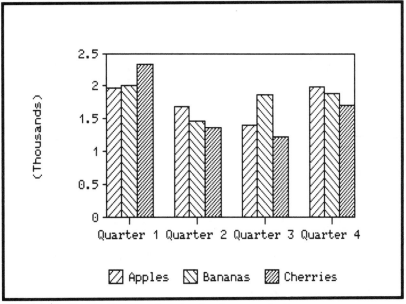

Figure 9.20: Graph of quarterly sales for three products

Figure 9.21 shows an out-of-the-way area on the worksheet with graph ranges defined for plotting these data. Column S is the graph's A-Range, column T is the graph's B-Range, column U is the graph's C-Range, and column V is the graph's X-Range.

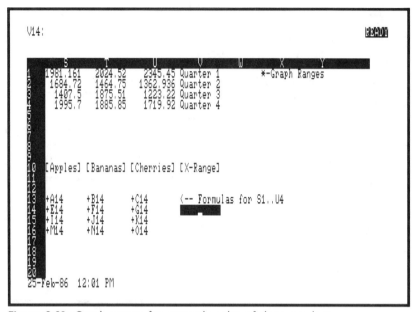

Figure 9.21: Graph ranges for quarterly sales of three products

You can either use the macro to place values in these graph ranges, or you can simply enter the appropriate formulas yourself. These are the formulas for the range S1..U4:

	A-RANGE	**B-RANGE**	**C-RANGE**
	S	**T**	**U**
1	+A14	+B14	+C14
2	+E14	+F14	+G14
3	+I14	+J14	+K14
4	+M14	+N14	+O14

Be sure to use options from the Graph menu to assign the A-, B-, C-, and X-Ranges after entering the formulas and before using the macro. Name the graph Hopper2.

Figure 9.22 shows a macro that can read the totals from row 14 into the appropriate graph ranges. Make sure to use the Range Name Create options to assign the range name Total to the row of totals (A14..P14) before using the macro.

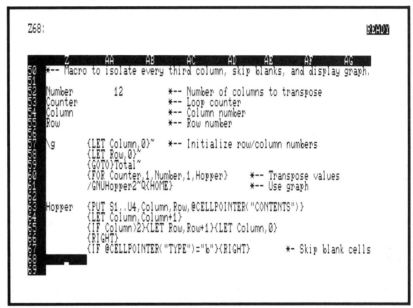

Figure 9.22: Macro to plot every third column and skip blank columns

This macro works on the same basic principle as the previous macro in this chapter. However, the Column counter for the PUT range resets the column number and increments the row number only after the column number exceeds two:

{**LET Column,Column + 1**}
{**IF Column>2**}{**LET Row,Row + 1**}{**LET Column,0**}

The macro also skips to the right through each value to be plotted. However, when the macro encounters a blank cell, it skips to the right once again:

{**RIGHT**}
{**IF @CELLPOINTER("TYPE") = "b"**}{**RIGHT**}

The named graph used by this macro is Hopper2, but you can change this to any graph name you like:

/GNUHopper2 ˜ Q{HOME}

Again, you may not even need these macros to plot graphs of noncontiguous columns, because you can manually build the range of values to plot fairly easily. Nevertheless, if you need to set up such ranges often, the macros might be worth the effort. And, of course, the macros illustrate numerous techniques for managing data in noncontiguous cells that can be used in many applications.

Summary

In this chapter we've discussed graphics macros that actually extend beyond the graphs of 1-2-3. These macros include the following:

- Macros to display and use ASCII/LICS characters
- A macro to display a graphics slide show
- A macro to automatically create graphs for similar worksheets
- Macros to graph data in noncontiguous rows and columns

DATABASE MANAGEMENT MACROS

IN THIS CHAPTER WE'LL create some useful 1-2-3 database management macros. We'll begin with a macro that can create a database from a list of field names. We'll generate a database with this macro, then we'll use the generated database in examples of some other database management macros.

Macro to Create a Database

Whenever you create a database, you need to arrange field names so that there is room for the 1-2-3 Input, Criterion, and Output ranges. If you assign names to these ranges, you can move the cell pointer easily from one range to the next by pressing the GoTo key.

Figures 10.1 and 10.2 show a macro that can easily set up the database ranges and names for you. These are the named ranges in the macro:

NAME	CELL
Instruct	AN1
\c	AA6
\d	AA3

Unlike most other examples in this book, this macro is stored at the top of the worksheet in cell Z1. The database itself needs the lower rows for the database ranges.

When you type Alt-d, the screen displays the instructions shown in Figure 10.2. You can enter field names in column A, as shown in Figure 10.3. Press Alt-c after entering all the database field names, and the macro will create the database Input, Criterion, and Output ranges. It will name these ranges Input, Criterion, and Output.

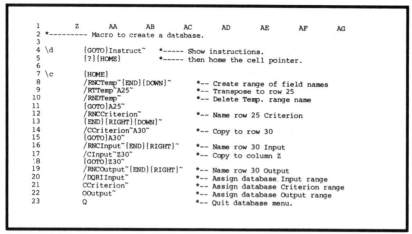

Figure 10.1: Macro to create a database

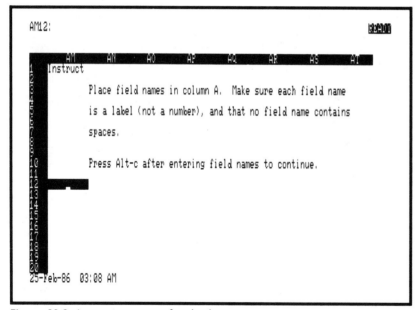

Figure 10.2: Instruction screen for database macro

To enter data into the database, press the GoTo key, and enter the range name Input. Then type in records as you normally would. Or, if you prefer, create a *data entry form* (which we'll do in the next section of this chapter).

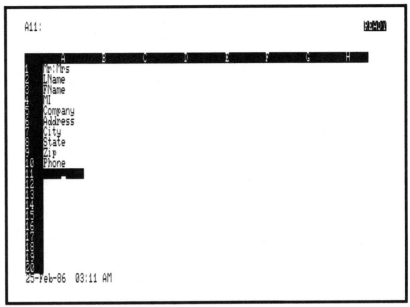

Figure 10.3: Database field names in column A

Let's take a moment to discuss how the database creation macro works. The small Alt-d macro simply displays the instruction screen and waits for the user to press Return. Then, the macro homes the cell pointer:

*--------- Macro to create a database.

\d   {GOTO}Instruct ~
      {?}{HOME}

The second portion of the macro, Alt-c, homes the cell pointer and assigns the range name Temp to the column of field names:

\c   {HOME}
      /RNCTemp ~ {END}{DOWN} ~

Next, the macro transposes the column of field names into a row of field names starting at cell A25:

/RTTemp ~ A25 ~

Then the macro deletes the range name Temp, since it is no longer needed:

/RNDTemp ˜

The macro moves the cell pointer to cell A25 and assigns the range name Criterion to the row of field names and a single row beneath:

{GOTO}A25 ˜
/RNCCriterion ˜
{END}{RIGHT}{DOWN} ˜

(Note: If you use #OR# database queries, you'll have to change the range specifications while using the database.)

Next the macro copies the row of field names to row 30 and assigns the range name Input to this row of field names. This is the range where database records will be stored:

/CCriterion ˜ A30 ˜
{GOTO}A30 ˜
/RNCInput ˜ {END}{RIGHT} ˜

Next the macro copies the row of field names to cell Z30 and assigns the name Output to the range. This range can be used with various Data Query options that require an Output range:

/CInput ˜ Z30 ˜
{GOTO}Z30 ˜
/RNCOutput ˜ {END}{RIGHT} ˜

Then the macro uses options under the Data Query menu to make the three named ranges into the Input, Criterion, and Output ranges for database management:

/DQRIInput ˜
CCriterion ˜
OOutput ˜
Q

The best way to use this macro is to bring the macro to the screen with the usual File Retrieve options. Use the macro to create the database, then use Range Erase to erase the macro and instructions. Next, use File Save to save the new database under a unique file name.

Data Entry Forms

1-2-3 allows you to enter data into a database in the same way that you enter data into worksheet cells. If you prefer, you can make a *database entry form*. The form offers a few advantages. For one, it can display *prompts* (such as "Last Name" and "First Name") rather than abbreviated field names (such as LName and FName). Also, the form can include instructions, if you wish. Another advantage is that the form can automatically place a label prefix in front of fields that mix numbers and characters. For example, the entry 123 Oak St. is illegal if you forget the label prefix.

Figure 10.4 shows a database entry form with some data typed in. Some of the field names originally placed into column A have been expanded into prompts that are more user-friendly. The column width has been expanded to 12 characters.

Figure 10.5 shows a macro that allows the user to enter data through a form. The Input range, in row 30, contains the same database field names as those in column A in Figure 10.3. The macro is activated by typing Alt-a. To quit the macro, enter only the capital letter Q in the Mr:Mrs field, then press Return.

Before using this macro, you should enter one record into row 31 using the usual method of positioning the cell pointer and typing in field data. (The macro uses the {END} and {DOWN} keys to find the first blank record at the bottom of the database and therefore needs to find at least one record at the top.)

Named ranges on the worksheet are listed below. The database ranges named Input, Output, and Criterion were created by the database creation macro.

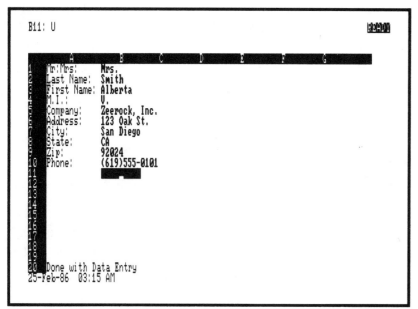

Figure 10.4: Data on a database entry form

```
49        Z       AA      AB      AC      AD      AE      AF      AG
50 *--------- Macro for data entry form on sample database.
51
52 \a        {HOME}
53          {LET A20,"In Data Entry Mode"}~
54          /RUA30..J1030~                  *-- Create Unprotect ranges
55          /RUB1..B11~
56          /WGPE                           *-- Global Protection on
57          {HOME}{RIGHT}
58 GetEntry  {IF @CELLPOINTER("ROW")=6#OR#@CELLPOINTER("ROW")>8#AND#@CELLPOINTER("TYPE")="b"}'
59          {?}{DOWN}
60          {IF B1="Q"}{BRANCH Done}
61          {IF @CELLPOINTER("ROW")>10}{TransRec}
62          {BRANCH GetEntry}                *-- GetEntry gets 1 record
63
64 TransRec  {GOTO}Input~                    *-- Transpose form data
65          {END}{DOWN}{DOWN}                *-- onto a database record
66          /RTB1..B10~~
67          /REB1..B10~                      *--Blank the form
68          {HOME}{RIGHT}
69          {RETURN}
70
71 Done      /WGPD                           *-- Turn off protection
72          {BLANK B1}~{BEEP 2}
73          {LET A20,"Done with Data Entry"}~
74          {HOME}
```

Figure 10.5: Macro to enter mailing list data on a form

RANGE NAME	CELL(S)
Criterion	A25..J26
Done	AA71
GetEntry	AA58
Input	A30..J30
Output	Z30..AI30
TransRec	AA64
\a	AA52

The macro begins by homing the cursor and placing the prompt "In Data Entry Mode" at the bottom of the screen:

*---------- Macro for data entry form on sample database.

\a   {HOME}
       {LET A20,"In Data Entry Mode"} ~

Next the macro unprotects 1,000 rows in the database Input range:

/RUA30..J1030 ~

(If your database is likely to have more than 1,000 records, you'll need to extend this range accordingly.)

The macro also unprotects the portion of the data entry form in which data are typed. In this example, data are typed into column B:

/RUB1..B11 ~

The macro then turns global protection on. This ensures that the user can enter data only in the form and cannot accidentally type over the prompts:

/WGPE

The keystrokes below move the cell pointer to column B:

{HOME}{RIGHT}

The long IF command that follows (which does not even fit on the screen) makes sure that the Address, Zip, and Phone fields are automatically preceded with an asterisk. Although it is broken in text below, be sure to enter this IF clause in a single cell on the worksheet:

{IF @CELLPOINTER("ROW") = 6#OR# @CELLPOINTER("ROW")
>8#AND# @CELLPOINTER("TYPE") = "b"}'

In English, the IF clause says "If the cell pointer is in row 6, or if the cell pointer is in row 8 or 9, and if the cell is currently blank, then type an apostrophe into the field." Row 6 accepts address data, rows 8 and 9 accept zip code and phone number data. Obviously, this IF clause works only for this database; it would need to be modified for a database with different fields.

The line below waits for the user to enter some data into the field, then it moves the cursor down to the next field:

{?}{DOWN}

The macro checks to see if the user entered the letter Q into the Mr:Mrs field. If so, it passes control to a subroutine named Done:

{IF B1 = "Q"}{BRANCH Done}

The IF clause below passes control to a subroutine named TransRec after the user fills in the form (that is, when the cell pointer reaches the eleventh row on the worksheet):

{IF @CELLPOINTER("ROW")>10}{TransRec}

The BRANCH command repeats the loop for entering data into a field:

{BRANCH GetEntry}

The TransRec subroutine positions the cell pointer on the first empty slot in the database Input range and transposes the data from the form into a record. Then the subroutine erases the current data in the form and repositions the cell pointer in column B to accept the next record:

TransRec   {GOTO}Input ˜
              {END}{DOWN}{DOWN}
              /RTB1..B10 ˜ ˜
              /REB1..B10 ˜
              {HOME}{RIGHT}
              {RETURN}

When the user is done, the macro disables the global protection, blanks cell B1, beeps, and displays the message "Done with Data Entry":

Done   /WGPD
          {BLANK B1} ˜ {BEEP 2}
          {LET A20,"Done with Data Entry"} ˜
          {HOME}

The entire worksheet returns to the READY mode.

Query Forms

The same form that is used for entering data can be used for performing a query (search). 1-2-3 allows you to perform database queries by setting up a Criterion range, entering data into the range, and selecting one of the Data Query options. A macro can significantly reduce the number of steps required to perform a query. For example, filling in the query form like this

Mr:Mrs:

Last Name: **Miller**

First Name:

Address:

City:

State:

Zip Code:

Phone Number:

will make the highlighter move directly to a record with Miller in the LName field. Pressing ↑ or ↓ moves the highlighter up and down to other Millers.

Filling in the query form like this

Mr:Mrs:

Last Name: Smith

First Name:

Address:

City:

State: CA

Zip Code:

Phone Number:

will cause the highlighter to highlight only people with the last name Smith who live in California. Notice that the use of multiple criteria implies an *and* relation. For example, the search

Mr:Mrs: Dr.

Last Name:

First Name:

Address:

City: Paris

State: TX

Zip Code:

Phone Number:

highlights only records that have Dr. in the Mr:Mrs field, *and* Paris in the City field, *and* TX in the State field.

Figure 10.6 shows the macro that presents the query form and performs the query. The Input, Criterion, and Output ranges contain field names in the database. In this example, these are the rows created and named automatically by the database creation macro in Figure 10.1. These are the ranges named in the worksheet:

RANGE NAME	CELL(S)
Criterion	A25..J26
Input	A30..J30
Output	Z30..AI30
\c	AA58
\f	AA53

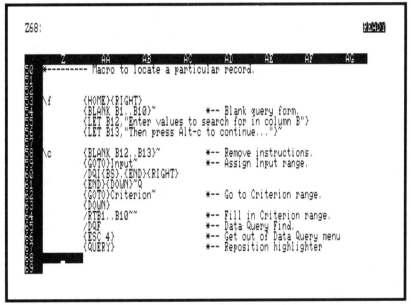

Figure 10.6: Macro to present a form and perform a query

The macro begins by placing the cell pointer at the top of column B and erasing the current contents in the query form. (If you prefer to have the query form retain data from one use to the next, just leave out the

{BLANK B1..B10} ~

command.)

The next two lines of the query present instructions and allow the user to fill in the query form:

> **{LET B12,"Enter values to search for in column B"}**
> **{LET B13,"Then press Alt-c to continue . . ."}** ˜

When the query form is filled in, the user presses Alt-c to continue. The macro erases the instructions from the screen

> **\c   {BLANK B12..B13}** ˜

then moves the cell pointer to the range named Input:

> **{GOTO}Input** ˜

Next, the macro assigns all the records in the database to the Data Query Input range:

> **/DQI{BS}.{END}{RIGHT}**
> **{END}{DOWN}** ˜ **Q**

(Note: The {END}{DOWN} used to highlight the range assumes that all records have data in the Phone field. If any records have a blank in the Phone field, the macro will not work properly.)

Next the macro moves the cell pointer to the Criterion range and transposes the data from the query form into the Criterion range:

> **{GOTO}Criterion** ˜
> **{DOWN}**
> **/RTB1..B10** ˜ ˜

Then the macro performs the query by selecting Data Query Find

> **/DQF**

and presses the Escape key four times to back out of the Data Query menu:

> **{ESC 4}**

This causes the cell pointer to leave the highlighted record. Therefore, the macro repositions the highlighter by pressing the Query key:

{**QUERY**}

The user will not have to back out of several menus after the search is complete because the {ESC 4} already took care of that.

Once the highlighter lands on the appropriate record, the user can use the ↑ and ↓ keys to move the highlighter to other records that match the query criteria or press Escape to leave the FIND mode and return to the READY mode. These are built-in features of Date Query Find, so the macro need not do anything more.

Mailing Labels

Databases are great for storing lists of data, and often those lists contain names and addresses. With the aid of a couple of macros, you can get 1-2-3 to print mailing labels and form letters from your database. Of course, you can use the Data Sort options to presort the records into zip code order for bulk mailing.

To make the labels look just right, the macro squeezes out blank company lines, so that a mailing label without a company is printed like this

Ms. Jane Doe
123 Oak St.
San Diego, CA 92122

rather than like this:

Ms. Jane Doe

123 Oak St.
San Diego, CA 92122

The label-printing macro is shown in Figure 10.7. You can use
Range Name Labels Right with the highlighter in column Z to assign
all the range names in column AA. The database-creation macro
discussed at the start of this chapter created and named the Input,
Output, and Criterion ranges. These are the named ranges for
this macro:

RANGE NAME	CELL(S)
Counter	AA53
Input	A50
Labels	A50..J53
LabLoop	AA69
Line1	AA55
Line2	AA56
Line3	AA57
Line4	AA58
Line5	AA59
Line6	AA60
NoCo	AA83
OneLab	AA55..AF59
PrintIt	AA74
Record	AA54
YesCo	AA78
\I	AA62

As you can see, the macro uses numerous named cells for
storing data. Counter is a loop counter, Record is the current
record (row) number in the database, and Line1 through Line6 is
a range of cells that stores a mailing label. The macro prints six
lines to make each label exactly one inch tall:

Counter
Record
Line1

Line2

Line3

Line4

Line5

Line6

The macro begins by setting the Record number to 1 and moving the cell pointer to the Input range. Then the macro assigns the range name Labels to the entire database:

\l   **{LET Record,1}** ~

     {GOTO}Input ~

     /RNCLabels ~ **{BS}.**

     {END}{RIGHT}{END}{DOWN} ~

As with the previous macro, this one will work only if all the Phone fields contain data. Otherwise, you'll need to create the Labels range name yourself prior to running the macro. Then

```
49    Z     AA     AB      AC      AD      AE      AF      AG
50  *————— Macro to print mailing labels from a database.
51  *————— Printed label is stored in range named OneLab (AA55..AF60).
52
53 Counter
54 Record
55 Line1
56 Line2
57 Line3
58 Line4
59 Line5
60 Line6
61
62 \l        {LET Record,1}~            *— Initialize record number
63           {GOTO}Input~              *— Move to Input range
64           /RNCLabels~{BS}.          *— Create range named Labels
65           {END}{RIGHT}{END}{DOWN}~
66           /PPOOUQQ                  *— Printer Unformatted output
67           {FOR Counter,1,@ROWS(Labels)-1,1,LabLoop}
68
69 LabLoop   {LET Line1,@INDEX(Labels,0,Record)&" "&@INDEX(Labels,2,Record)}~
70           {IF @ISSTRING(@INDEX(Labels,3,Record))}{LET Line1,Line1&" "&@INDEX(Labels,3,Record)}~
71           {LET Line1,Line1&" "&@INDEX(Labels,1,Record)}~
72           {IF @ISSTRING(@INDEX(Labels,4,Record))}{YesCo}{BRANCH PrintIt}
73           {NoCo}
74 PrintIt   /PPROneLab~GQ~            *— Print label
75           {LET Record,Record+1}     *— Increment record number.
76
77           *— YesCo routine makes a label with Company name.
78 YesCo     {LET Line2,@INDEX(Labels,4,Record)}~
79           {LET Line3,@INDEX(Labels,5,Record)}~
80           {LET Line4,@INDEX(Labels,6,Record)&", "&@INDEX(Labels,7,Record)&" "&@INDEX(Labels,8,Record)}~
81
82           *— NoCo routine makes a label without Company name.
83 NoCo      {LET Line2,@INDEX(Labels,5,Record)}~
84           {LET Line3,@INDEX(Labels,6,Record)&", "&@INDEX(Labels,7,Record)&" "&@INDEX(Labels,8,Record)}~
85           {BLANK Line4}~
86
```

Figure 10.7: Macro to print mailing labels

you'll also need to delete from the macro those lines that create the range named Labels.

Next the macro sets up the printer for unformatted display so that page breaks do not disrupt the alignment of the labels in the printer:

/PPOOUQQ

For each record in the database, the macro accesses the subroutine named LabLoop:

{FOR Counter,1,@ROWS(Labels)-1,1,LabLoop}

The LabLoop subroutine builds each line of the mailing label. First, the macro puts the individual's title and first name into the first line of the mailing label (Line1):

{LET Line1,@INDEX(Labels,0,Record)&" "&@INDEX
(Labels,2,Record)} ˜

(Note: This formula, like many in this chapter, must be entered into the macro as a single line. It is only broken into two lines to fit into text.)

Next, the macro checks to see if there is a middle name for this individual (using the @ISSTRING function). If so, the macro adds the middle initial to the first line of the mailing label:

{IF @ISSTRING(@INDEX(Labels,3,Record))} {LET Line1,Line1
&" "&@INDEX(Labels,3,Record)} ˜

(Note: This formula must be typed into a single cell.)

Next the macro adds the individual's last name to the first line of the mailing label:

{LET Line1,Line1&" "&@INDEX(Labels,1,Record)} ˜

If there is a Company associated with the mailing label, the macro branches to a subroutine named YesCo, then skips to the subroutine named PrintIt. Otherwise, the macro branches to the subroutine named NoCo, then falls into the subroutine named PrintIt:

```
{IF @ISSTRING(@INDEX(Labels,4,Record))}
    {YesCo}{BRANCH PrintIt}
{NoCo}
```

The PrintIt subroutine prints the mailing label (by printing the range named OneLab). It then increments the Record counter by one so that the next mailing label will be printed:

```
PrintIt    /PPROneLab ˜ GQ ˜
           {LET Record,Record + 1}
```

The YesCo subroutine places the Company on the second line of the mailing label, the Address on the third line, and the City, followed by a comma, the State, and the Zip on the fourth line:

```
*-- YesCo routine makes a label with Company name.
{LET Line2,@INDEX(Labels,4,Record)} ˜
{LET Line3,@INDEX(Labels,5,Record)} ˜
{LET Line4,@INDEX(Labels,6,Record)&", "&@INDEX
    (Labels,7,Record)&" "&@INDEX(Labels,8,Record)} ˜
```

(Note: The last line in this subroutine must be entered as a single line in a single cell.)

The NoCo subroutine is similar to the YesCo subroutine, except that it leaves out the Company, and that it blanks the fourth line of the label:

```
*-- NoCo routine makes a label without Company name.
{LET Line2,@INDEX(Labels,5,Record)} ˜
{LET Line3,@INDEX(Labels,6,Record)&", "&@INDEX
    (Labels,7,Record)&" "&@INDEX(Labels,8,Record)} ˜
{BLANK Line4} ˜
```

(The line beginning with LET Line3 should be entered as a single cell entry.)

To print labels, you'll probably first want to use Data Sort to put the data into zip code order, then load mailing labels into your printer and type Alt-l. If the labels are out of alignment, press BREAK, realign the labels in the printer, then type Alt-l to try again.

Envelopes

You can modify the label-printing routine slightly to print names and addresses directly onto envelopes. First, select the Worksheet Global Default Printer Wait Yes options to make sure the printer pauses between envelopes (or add the line /WGDPWYQQ to the macro, somewhere above the FOR loop). Then, change the line that reads

PrintIt   /PPROneLab ˜ GQ ˜

to

PrintIt   /PPROneLab ˜ GPQ ˜

so the macro starts each address on a new "page."

Form Letters

The form letter macro is a slight variation of the mailing label macro. In this section we'll develop a macro that can print form letters from the sample database. You'll need a form letter to print, of course, with the named ranges Line1, Line2, Line3, Line4, and Line5. The letter itself must be a range named Letter. Figure 10.8 shows a sample form letter on the worksheet.

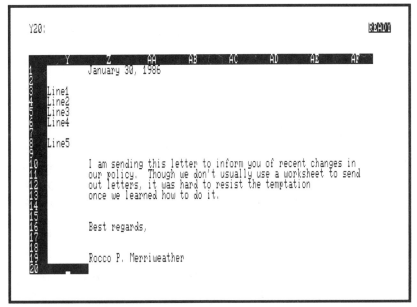

Figure 10.8: Form letter

These are the named ranges in the letter:

RANGE NAME	CELL(S)
Letter	Z1..AF20
Line1	Z3
Line2	Z4
Line3	Z5
Line4	Z6
Line5	Z8

The macro to print the form letters is shown in Figure 10.9. The Input range accessed by the macro is that created by the database-creation macro in Figure 10.1.

Like the mailing label macro, the form letter macro uses the Counter and Record cells to store data, then creates a range named Labels that includes all the records in the database:

Counter

Record

\I   **{LET Record,1} ˜**

            {GOTO}Input ˜

            /RNCLabels ˜ {BS}.

            {END}{RIGHT}{END}{DOWN} ˜

(Again, if one of the Phone fields is left blank, the macro won't work properly. Therefore, you might want to manually name and highlight the Labels range, rather than have the macro do it.)

    The macro then clears all previous printer settings and aligns the paper in the printer:

/PPCAQ

If you want your macro to pause for paper change between letters, you can add the line

/WGDPWYQQ

```
49    Z      AA     AB     AC     AD     AE     AF     AG     AH
50 *——————— Macro to print form letters from a database.
51 *——————— Form letter is stored at Letter (Z1..AF20).
52
53 Counter
54 Record
55
56 \l      {LET Record,1}~          *— Initialize record number.
57         {GOTO}Input~             *— Name range of records.
58         /RNCLabels~{BS}.
59         {END}{RIGHT}{END}{DOWN}~
60         /PPCAQ
61         {FOR Counter,1,@ROWS(Labels)-1,1,LabLoop}
62
63 LabLoop {LET Line1,@INDEX(Labels,0,Record)&" "&@INDEX(Labels,2,Record)}~
64         {IF @ISSTRING(@INDEX(Labels,3,Record))}{LET Line1,Line1&" "&@INDEX(Labels,3,Record)}~
65         {LET Line1,Line1&" "&@INDEX(Labels,1,Record)}~
66         {IF @ISSTRING(@INDEX(Labels,4,Record))}{YesCo}{BRANCH Dear}
67 Dear    {NoCo}
68 Dear    {LET Line5,+"Dear "&@INDEX(Labels,0,Record)&" "&@INDEX(Labels,1,Record)&":"}~
69         /PPRLetter~GPQ~          *— Print the letter.
70         {LET Record,Record+1}    *— Increment record number
71
72         *— YesCo routine prints heading with Company name.
73 YesCo   {LET Line2,@INDEX(Labels,4,Record)}~
74         {LET Line3,@INDEX(Labels,5,Record)}~
75         {LET Line4,@INDEX(Labels,6,Record)&", "&@INDEX(Labels,7,Record)&" "&@INDEX(Labels,8,Record)}~
76
77         *— NoCo routine prints heading without Company name.
78 NoCo    {LET Line2,@INDEX(Labels,5,Record)}~
79         {LET Line3,@INDEX(Labels,6,Record)&", "&@INDEX(Labels,7,Record)&" "&@INDEX(Labels,8,Record)}~
80         {BLANK Line4}~
81
```

Figure 10.9: Macro to print a form letter

to the macro as well. Next, a FOR loop repeats the LabLoop subroutine, which prints a letter:

{FOR Counter,1,@ROWS(Labels)-1,1,LabLoop}

The LabLoop subroutine is basically the same as the one in the mailing labels macro, except that it creates a salutation line (e.g., Dear Mr. Smith:). The subroutine named Dear handles this task:

{LET Line5, + "Dear "&@INDEX(Labels,0,Record)&" "&@INDEX (Labels,1,Record)&":"} ~

(This LET command is broken into two lines to fit into the book. Make sure to enter it as a single long command in your macro.)

The macro prints the letter for each record, starting each letter at the top of a new page using the Page option from the Print menu:

/PPRLetter ~ GPQ ~

Figure 10.10 shows a sample letter printed by the macro.

```
January 30, 1986

Mrs. Alberta V. Smith
Zeerock, Inc.
123 Oak St.
San Diego, CA 92024

Dear Mrs. Smith:

I am sending this letter to inform you of recent changes in
our policy.  Though we don't usually use a worksheet to send
out letters, it was hard to resist the temptation
once we learned how to do it.


Best regards,


Rocco P. Merriweather
```

Figure 10.10: Form letter printed by a macro

Frequency Distribution

The Data Distribution options can perform frequency distributions upon ranges of numbers. For example, if you had a database field named Amount, and it contained these numbers

Amount

100

150

200

250

300

325

350

400

you could use data distribution to display how many numbers fell within certain ranges, as below:

100	1
200	2
300	2
400	3

This tells you that one value falls within the range 0–100, two values fall within the range 101–200, and so on.

One weakness of data distribution is that it works only with numbers. A second weakness is that it does not generate values for comparison. You have to create your own "Bin range," often guessing at the range of possible values. These two weaknesses are overcome by the frequency distribution macro shown in Figure 10.11.

When run, the macro asks on which field you want to perform a frequency distribution. You type in any field name (such as LName or Zip), and press Return. The macro then displays all the unique items in the field and the number of occurrences of each. For example, a frequency distribution on a zip code field might yield these results:

12345	**120**
12346	**81**
42001	**36**
42002	**101**
54434	**200**

Note that this frequency distribution deals in exact numbers. For example, there are exactly 120 records with zip codes of 12345, and exactly 36 records with zip codes of 40021.

```
49      Z        AA       AB       AC       AD       AE       AF
50 *--- Macro to print frequency distribution from a selected field.
51
52 Counter
53 FldName
54 FldNum
55
56 \f        {HOME}{GOTO}Input~                      *- Get field name.
57           {GETLABEL "Enter field name : ",FldName}~
58           {IF @ISERR(FldNum)}{BRANCH \f}          *- Trap error.
59           {LET Crit,FldName}~                     *- Make Bin range.
60           {LET Bin,FldName}~                      *- Criterion range.
61           {GOTO}Input~
62           /RNCRecords~{BS}.                       *- Name Records range.
63           {END}{RIGHT}{END}{DOWN}~
64           /DQRI{BS}.                              *-- Query Input range.
65           {END}{RIGHT}{END}{DOWN}~
66           CCrit~OBin~UQ                           *-- Extract unique records.
67           /DSDBin~D{DOWN}.{END}{DOWN}~PBin~A~G        *-- Sort them.
68           {GOTO}Bin~
69           /RNCNumber~{BS}.{END}{DOWN}~            *-- Create Numbers range.
70           {GOTO}Bin~/C.{END}{DOWN}~List~          *-- Copy to List range.
71           {RIGHT 2}{DOWN}
72           {FOR Counter,1,@ROWS(Number)-1,1,Dformula}    *-- Loop...
73
74 Dformula @DCOUNT(Records,FldNum,{LEFT 2}{UP}.{DOWN})~ *-- Enter formula.
75           {EDIT}{CALC}~                           *- Change to value.
76           {LEFT 2}{UP}/C~{DOWN}~{DOWN 2}{RIGHT 2}
```

Figure 10.11: Frequency distribution macro

The macro in Figure 10.11 uses the Input range from the sample database we generated at the start of this chapter. These are the named ranges:

RANGE NAME	CELL(S)
Bin	BA51
Counter	AA52
Crit	AZ51..AZ52

RANGE NAME	CELL(S)
Dformula	AA74
FldName	AA53
FldNum	AA54
Input	A30..J30
List	BB51
Output	Z30..AI30
\f	AA56

The macro uses several named cells for storing data, including a formula for determining the column number of the database field being analyzed. The formula, in the cell named FldNum, is shown in text format below. The formula looks up the field name in the row of field names and returns the number for that row. You should type this formula into the cell as displayed, but you'll see only the results of the calculation on the screen:

```
Counter
FldName
FldNum      @HLOOKUP(FldName,Input,0)
```

The macro begins by moving the cell pointer to the range named Input so that some of the field names will appear on the screen. Then the macro asks for the name of the field to analyze and stores the answer in the cell named FldName:

```
\f    {HOME}{GOTO}Input ~
      {GETLABEL "Enter field name : ",FldName} ~
```

If the user enters a field name that does not exist, the formula in the cell named FldNum will generate an error. The next line in the macro detects this problem and repeats the question about the field to analyze:

```
{IF @ISERR(FldNum)}{BRANCH \f}
```

(Note: The @HLOOKUP function is case-sensitive, so entering "zip" as the field to analyze might cause the macro to ask the question again if the field name is "Zip.")

Next, the name of the field being analyzed is stored in the cells named Crit and Bin, which are used later to perform the frequency distribution:

> **{LET Crit,FldName}** ~
> **{LET Bin,FldName}** ~

The macro repositions the cell pointer on the Input range and assigns the name Records to the total range of database records:

> **{GOTO}Input** ~
> **/RNCRecords** ~ **{BS}.**
> **{END}{RIGHT}{END}{DOWN}** ~

The macro also assigns the database records to the Data Query Input range:

> **/DQRI{BS}.**
> **{END}{RIGHT}{END}{DOWN}** ~

The macro then assigns Crit as the database Criterion range, and Bin as the database Output range. Then the macro selects Data Unique to pull a list of all unique items from the field being analyzed into the output (Bin) range:

> **CCrit** ~ **OBin** ~ **UQ**

The macro sorts the data in the Bin range into ascending order:

> **/DSDBin** ~ **D{DOWN}.{END}{DOWN}** ~ **PBin** ~ **A** ~ **G**

The range name Number is assigned to the Bin range. The Bin range is then copied to a range named List:

> **{GOTO}Bin** ~
> **/RNCNumber** ~ **{BS}.{END}{DOWN}** ~

```
{GOTO}Bin ~ /C.{END}{DOWN} ~ List ~
{RIGHT 2}{DOWN}
```

Then a FOR loop repeats the routine named Dformula once for as many rows of records as there are in the Number range:

{FOR Counter,1,@ROWS(Number)-1,1,Dformula}

The Dformula routine enters an @DCOUNT formula into the cell to the right of the Bin range. This formula counts how many of the unique item are in the database and displays that value. To keep the formula from recalculating as the macro proceeds, {EDIT} {CALC} turns the formula to a value. The last line copies the field name being analyzed down a row in the Crit range, because the Crit range is used to calculate the @DCOUNT formula:

```
Dformula    @DCOUNT(Records,FldNum,{LEFT 2}{UP}.
                {DOWN}) ~
            {EDIT}{CALC} ~
            {LEFT 2}{UP}/C ~ {DOWN} ~ {DOWN 2}{RIGHT 2}
```

Needless to say, the frequency distribution macro is both complex and a bit abstract. It may take some study to understand all of its techniques. Watching the macro run will fill you in on some of its techniques, so you might want to give it a whirl on a database.

Totals and Subtotals in Reports

It's easy to put formulas into a worksheet to calculate subtotals and totals. But suppose you have a database like the one shown in Figure 10.12, and you want to print a report subtotaled by part number, as shown in Figure 10.13. You'll either have to do some manual reorganization, or you'll have to use a macro.

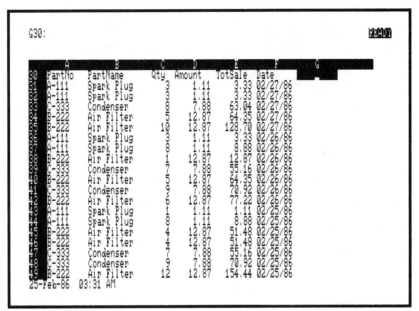

Figure 10.12: Database with part numbers

```
                         Current Sales              Page 1

         A-111    Spark Plug      1      1.11        1.11 02/25/86
         A-111    Spark Plug      3      1.11        3.33 02/27/86
         A-111    Spark Plug      3      1.11        3.33 02/27/86
         A-111    Spark Plug      3      1.11        3.33 02/26/86
         A-111    Spark Plug      8      1.11        8.88 02/26/86
         A-111    Spark Plug      8      1.11        8.88 02/25/86
         SubTotal:                                  28.86

         B-222    Air Filter      1     12.87       12.87 02/26/86
         B-222    Air Filter      4     12.87       51.48 02/25/86
         B-222    Air Filter      4     12.87       51.48 02/25/86
         B-222    Air Filter      5     12.87       64.35 02/26/86
         B-222    Air Filter      5     12.87       64.35 02/27/86
         B-222    Air Filter      6     12.87       77.22 02/26/86
         B-222    Air Filter     10     12.87      128.70 02/27/86
         B-222    Air Filter     12     12.87      154.44 02/25/86
         SubTotal:                                 604.89

         C-333    Condenser       7      7.88       55.16 02/26/86
         C-333    Condenser       7      7.88       55.16 02/25/86
         C-333    Condenser       8      7.88       63.04 02/27/86
         C-333    Condenser       9      7.88       70.92 02/25/86
         C-333    Condenser       9      7.88       70.92 02/26/86
         SubTotal:                                 315.20

         Total:                                    948.95
```

Figure 10.13: Subtotaled report printed by a macro

Figure 10.14 shows the macro that subtotaled the records in the sample database. These are the named ranges in the worksheet:

RANGE NAME	CELL(S)
BlankLine	AA52
BotLine	AA55..AF55
Counter	AA60
Done	AA97
Input	A30
LastPart	AA61
Loop	AA73
NewPage	AA90
Offset	AA63
PageNo	AA62
RepLine	AA76
Row	AA57
SubTot	AA58
SubTotal	AA84
Title	AA53..AG53
Total	AA59
TotLine	AA54..AF54
\r	AA65

The named cells at the top of the macro are actually parts of the printed report. The cell named BlankLine contains nothing; it is used to print blank lines on the report. The cell named Title contains the formula:

+"   Current Sales   Page "&@STRING(PageNo,0)

This formula prints the report title and calculated page number at the top of each page of the printed report. The page number is

```
49        Z        AA       AB       AC       AD       AE       AF
50 *------- Macro to print totaled and subtotaled report.
51
52 BlankLine
53 Title                    Current Sales                      Page 0
54 TotLine  SubTotal:                                 0.00
55 BotLine  Total:                                    0.00
56
57 Row
58 SubTot
59 Total
60 Counter
61 LastPart
62 PageNo
63 Offset
64
65 \r       {GOTO}Input~
66          {DOWN}
67          /DSD{BS}.{END}{RIGHT}{END}{DOWN}~
68          P{BS}~A~S{BS}{RIGHT 4}~A~G
69          /RNCRecords~{BS}.{END}{RIGHT}{END}{DOWN}~
70          {LET Row,0}{LET Offset,0}
71          {LET LastPart,@INDEX(Records,0,Row)}~
72          {LET PageNo,1}~
73 Loop     {FOR Counter,0,@ROWS(Records)-1,1,RepLine}
74          {BRANCH Done}
75
76 RepLine  {IF Counter+Offset/55=@INT(Counter+Offset/55)}{NewPage}
77          {IF @INDEX(Records,0,Row)<>LastPart}{SubTotal}
78          /PPR{BS}.{END}{RIGHT}~GQ
79          {LET LastPart,@INDEX(Records,0,Row)}~
80          {LET SubTot,SubTot+@INDEX(Records,4,Row)}~
81          {LET Total,Total+@INDEX(Records,4,Row)}~
82          {LET Row,Row+1}{DOWN}
83
84 SubTotal /PPRTotLine~GQ
85          {LET SubTot,0}~
86          /PPR{BS}BlankLine~GQ
87          {LET Offset,Offset+3}
88          {RETURN}
89
90 NewPage  /PPP
91          RTitle~G
92          RBlankLine~GQ
93          {LET PageNo,PageNo+1}~
94          {LET Offset,0}
95          {RETURN}
96
97 Done     /PPRTotLine~G
98          R{BS}BlankLine~G
99          R{BS}BotLine~G
100         PQ
```

Figure 10.14: Macro to print a subtotaled report

converted to a string (using @STRING) so that it can be linked to the character string "Current Sales."

The cell named TotLine prints a subtotal for each group of part numbers. TotLine contains the formula:

+"SubTotal:"&@REPEAT(" ",36-@LENGTH(@STRING(SubTot,2)))
&@STRING(SubTot,2)

(Note: Even though the formula is split into two lines to fit into the book, it must be entered into the cell as a single line.)

This formula prints SubTotal: followed by a calculated number of blank spaces (@REPEAT), followed by the subtotal converted to a string. The @REPEAT formula prints some blank spaces, calculated as "36 minus the length of the subtotal." This ensures that the subtotal is always properly aligned in its column, regardless of its size.

The cell named BotLine contains the formula:

+"Total:"&@REPEAT(" ",39-@LENGTH(@STRING(Total,2)))
&@STRING(Total,2)

(Again, the formula must be entered as a single line, and is only split to fit into the book.) Like the subtotal formula, this formula displays the title Total: followed by a calculated number of spaces, followed by the grand total. This line is printed once at the bottom of the report.

These named cells store data as the macro is printing the report:

Row

SubTot

Total

Counter

LastPart

PageNo

Offset

Row is the current row position in the report, SubTot is the current subtotal, Total is the current grand total, and Counter is a looping variable. LastPart stores the part number from the last record printed so that the macro can detect a part number change, and therefore, the need to print a subtotal. PageNo is the calculated page number.

The macro begins by sorting the sample database into part number order, and by the amount sold within common part numbers. The database need only be sorted by the subtotaling field for the macro to work, but sorting by the amount sold within the part numbers adds a little organization to the printed report:

```
\r    {GOTO}Input ~
      {DOWN}
      /DSD{BS}.{END}{RIGHT}{END}{DOWN} ~
      P{BS} ~ A ~ S{BS}{RIGHT 4} ~ A ~ G
```

Next the database assigns the name Records to the entire range of database records:

```
/RNCRecords ~ {BS}.{END}{RIGHT}{END}{DOWN} ~
```

The macro then initializes several variables. The LastPart variable is assigned the part number from the first record in the database:

```
{LET Row,0}
{LET LastPart,@INDEX(Records,0,Row)} ~
{LET PageNo,1} ~
```

Next, a loop repeats the subroutine named RepLine once for each record in the database:

```
Loop    {FOR Counter,0,@ROWS(Records)-1,1,RepLine}
        {BRANCH Done}
```

First, RepLine determines whether the next page of the report should be printed on a new page. It makes this decision by checking to see if 55 (or some multiple of 55) lines have been printed (plus an Offset value). If so, the macro passes control to the subroutine named NewPage to start printing on a new page:

```
RepLine    {IF Counter + Offset/55 = @INT(Counter + Offset/55)}
           {NewPage}
```

The next line determines whether a subtotal needs to be displayed. It decides by comparing the part number from the record about to be printed to the last part number printed. If the two are not the same, the macro passes control to a subroutine named SubTotal, which will display the subtotal on the report:

{IF @INDEX(Records,0,Row)< >LastPart}{SubTotal}

Then the macro prints the current record from the database:

/PPR{BS}.{END}{RIGHT} ˜ GQ

The LastPart variable is then assigned the part number of the record just printed:

{LET LastPart,@INDEX(Records,0,Row)} ˜

The SubTot variable is incremented by the amount in the record that was just printed:

{LET SubTot,SubTot + @INDEX(Records,4,Row)} ˜

The grand total is also incremented by the amount in the record just printed:

{LET Total,Total + @INDEX(Records,4,Row)} ˜

Next, the row counter and highlighter are moved down to the next record, and the process is repeated:

{LET Row,Row + 1}{DOWN}

The SubTotal subroutine displays the subtotal in the report. It prints the range named TotLine, which includes the Subtotal heading and current subtotal value. The subroutine then resets the SubTot value to zero for calculating the next part number subtotal. Finally, the subroutine prints a blank line, then increments the Offset counter by three. (Offset counts the number of blank lines printed on the page.) Then the subroutine returns control to the main body of the macro:

SubTotal   /PPRTotLine ˜ GQ
**   {LET SubTot,0} ˜**

```
          /PPR{BS}BlankLine ˜ GQ
          {LET Offset,Offset + 3}
          {RETURN}
```

The NewPage subroutine ejects the paper in the printer to the top of the next page, prints the range named Title, prints a blank line, increments the page number, resets the Offset, and returns control to the main body of the macro:

```
NewPage    /PPP
           RTitle ˜ G
           RBlankLine ˜ GQ
           {LET PageNo,PageNo + 1} ˜
           {LET Offset,0}
           {RETURN}
```

The subroutine named Done prints the last subtotal on the report, followed by a blank line and the grand total:

```
Done     /PPRTotLine ˜ G
         R{BS}BlankLine ˜ G
         R{BS}BotLine ˜ G
         PQ
```

Like the frequency distribution macro, the subtotaling macro is fairly complex. Unless you are a programmer, you may need to study it for a while to understand all of the techniques it uses.

It is possible to create a macro that asks the user for the field to subtotal (group) on and for the field to total. Then the macro could be used easily in a variety of databases. However, the macro would become quite complex because of the need to calculate column positions for subtotals and totals. Furthermore, the subtotaling macro already runs quite slowly, and it would be slowed down even more by the added flexibility.

The subtotaling macro presented here could easily be modified for any database. Most of the modification would simply involve changing column numbers in the @INDEX functions to reflect the columns being used for grouping and subtotals. The

@REPEAT(" ",36-@LENGTH(SubTotal),2)

calculations would need to be adjusted for the new database, and perhaps some other alignments would need to be changed. But once you become familiar with the macro, you'll find the changes relatively easy to make.

Summary

In this chapter we've developed numerous database management macros, including the following:

- A macro to create a database
- A macro to present a data entry form
- A macro to display and execute a data entry form
- Macros for mailing labels, envelopes, and form letters
- A macro to display a frequency distribution
- A macro to put totals and subtotals in a report

11

CUSTOM MENUS

IN THIS CHAPTER WE'LL discuss the 1-2-3 menu commands, which allow you to temporarily replace the built-in menu system with your own custom menus. This capability is great for developing worksheets for users with little or no 1-2-3 experience.

All 1-2-3 custom menus use a similar structure. The first row contains the menu name and the menu options that will appear on the screen. For example, this menu is named MainMenu (assuming you highlight the cell containing the label Main-Menu and select Range Name Labels Right):

MainMenu   Print   Graph   Save   Return

When activated, this menu displays the options

Print   Graph   Save   Return

in the control panel.

Each menu item must be in a separate cell on the same row, and there cannot be any blank columns between items. There can be up to eight options in a single menu.

Each item on the menu should begin with a different letter. This is because the user can select menu items either by highlighting an option and pressing Return, or by typing the first letter of the menu option (just like regular 1-2-3 menus). Therefore, if your menu had the options

GoTo-Cell   Graph   Print   Save

typing the letter G would always select GoTo-Cell, and never Graph.

You've undoubtedly noticed that whenever you highlight an option on the 1-2-3 Main menu, it displays a description, or help, for that menu item on the line beneath the menu. Each item on your custom menu must have a description, or help, as well. Place these on the row directly beneath the menu options, like this:

MainMenu	Print	Graph	Save	Return
	Print Worksheet	View Graph	Save Data	Exit Menu

The descriptions in the example are brief, so they'll fit on the page. Your descriptions can be much longer, but they must fit on a single line in the control panel.

Beneath the menu descriptions, place the macro commands and keystrokes that the menu option is to perform. These can be of any complexity, from a few keystrokes to a whole series of submenus and subroutines. In this example, each menu item performs a few simple keystrokes:

MainMenu	Print	Graph	Save	Return
	Print Worksheet	View Graph	Save Data	Exit Menu
	/PPGQ	{GRAPH}	/FS ˜ R	{QUIT}

Once you have an idea of what options, descriptions, and tasks your menu is going to perform, you need to access it with one of the menu commands, either MENUBRANCH or MENUCALL. MENUBRANCH works like the BRANCH command in that it passes control to the menu only once. MENUCALL is more like a call to a subroutine; it displays the menu, and after the user selects an option, returns control to the line beneath the MENUCALL command. A couple of examples will demonstrate this.

The MENUBRANCH Command

Figure 11.1 shows a simple menu accessed by the MENU-BRANCH command. The custom menu, activated by typing Alt-m, is displayed in the control panel. As usual, labels in column Z need to be made into range names with the Range Name Labels Right options.

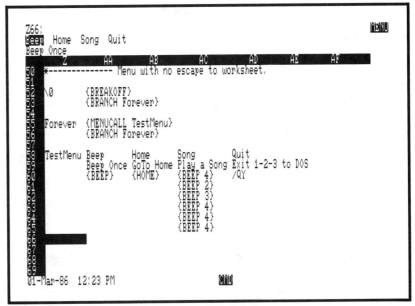

Figure 11.1: Menu called by the MENUBRANCH command

The first command line in the macro calls the menu named TestMenu when the user types Alt-m:

\m   {MENUBRANCH TestMenu}

The TestMenu subroutine displays the menu

Beep   Home   Song   Quit
Beep Once

in the control panel at the top of the screen. Moving the highlighter to the Home, Song, or Quit options makes their descriptions replace the "Beep Once" description on the screen.

Selecting Beep causes 1-2-3 to beep once. Selecting Home makes 1-2-3 home the cell pointer. Selecting Song makes 1-2-3 play several tones. Selecting Quit makes nothing happen, because there are no macro commands or keystrokes associated with the option.

Once an item is selected and performs its task (if any), the macro is finished and 1-2-3 returns to the READY mode.

The MENUCALL Command

The MENUCALL command works differently, as we'll see now. Figure 11.2 shows a sample menu that uses the MENUCALL command. Cells Z52..Z55 contain range name labels.

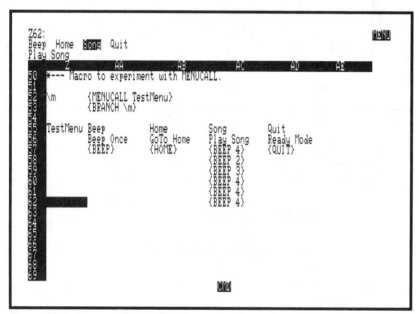

Figure 11.2: Menu with MENUCALL command

The first line causes the macro to display the menu named TestMenu when the user types Alt-m. Since MENUCALL will return control to the first line beneath the menu call, the {BRANCH \m} command will immediately redisplay the menu. Therefore, the menu does not just disappear after a single menu item is selected:

```
\m      {MENUCALL TestMenu}
        {BRANCH \m}
```

The menu displays the same options as the menu in Figure 11.1. In this example, however, the Quit option contains the {QUIT} macro command. The {QUIT} command is necessary in this example, because without it the macro would never end (except with a press on the BREAK key), and therefore the menu would never leave the control panel.

MENUCALL is usually the preferred method for displaying menus, because it keeps you from having to type an Alt-key sequence every time you wish to access the menu. However, there should be a Quit option on the menu with an associated {QUIT} command. Otherwise, there will be no way back to the worksheet, other than to press the BREAK key. MENUCALL is much simpler to understand if you give it a try. If you've never created a 1-2-3 custom menu before, take a moment to type in and try the macros in Figures 11.1 and 11.2. Menus are much easier to understand and master after a little hands-on experience.

A Worksheet Menu

Our sample menus demonstrate basic menu techniques, but they are not too practical. Figure 11.3 shows another worksheet. This worksheet has one named graph associated with it. Notice the custom menu displayed at the top of the worksheet. Figure 11.4 shows the macro in this same worksheet that displays the custom menu. Cells Z52..Z55 contain range name labels.

Let's discuss what the macro does. The first lines display the MainMenu menu when the user types Alt-m. Since MENUCALL is used, and since the line beneath MENUCALL branches back to the start of the macro, the menu is redisplayed after each selection:

*---------------- Macro to display menu for worksheet.

\m   {MENUCALL MainMenu}
**   {BRANCH \m}**

The macro displays the options (and appropriate descriptions) at the top of the screen as shown.

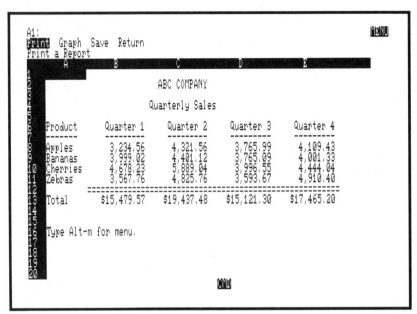

Figure 11.3: Worksheet with custom menu

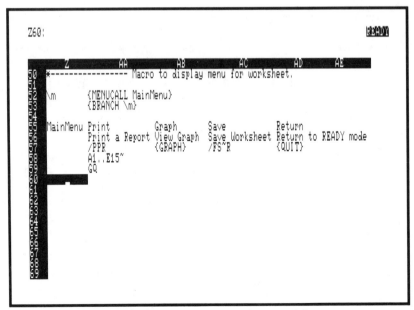

Figure 11.4: Macro to display a custom menu in a worksheet

Print	Graph	Save	Return
Print a Report	View Graph	Save Worksheet	Return to READY mode

If the user selects Print, the macro prints the range A1..E15 on the worksheet and quits the Print menu:

/PPR
A1..E15 ~
GQ

If the user selects the Graph option, the macro displays the one named graph:

{GRAPH}

If the user selects Save, the macro saves the worksheet under the previously assigned file name:

/FS ~ R

If the user selects Quit, the macro quits. This is the only option that does not redisplay the custom menu:

{QUIT}

For the macro to work properly, there must be at least one graph associated with the worksheet, and the worksheet must have already been saved under some file name.

Submenus

The 1-2-3 Main menu has many *submenus* beneath it. For example the options /Worksheet Global Default Other each display their own submenu. You can build submenus into your custom menu system as well.

Suppose that your custom menu displays these options:

Print   Graph   Save   Return
Print a Report

When the user selects Print, you'd like to give these options:

Align   New-Page   Print-It   Return
Set top-of-page

Furthermore, you'd like this menu to stay on the screen until the user selects Return. That way, the user could align, page, and print the report as necessary, then return to the Main menu when convenient. Figure 11.5 shows a macro that displays the menu and submenu. Cells Z52..Z65 contain range name labels.

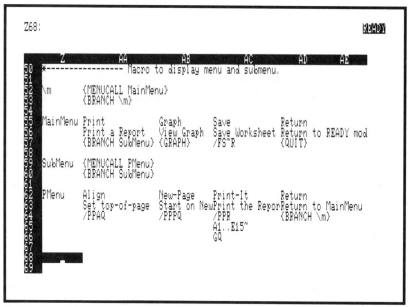

Figure 11.5: Macro to display a custom menu and submenu

At first glance the macro may look a little complicated. In reality, it is simply two menus on a single worksheet. The first macro, Alt-m, calls the MainMenu macro, which displays the Print, Graph, Save, and Return options. Unlike previous macros in this chapter, the Print option, in turn, passes control to a cell named SubMenu:

```
*----------------- Macro to display menu and submenu.
\m          {MENUCALL MainMenu}
            {BRANCH \m}

MainMenu    Print
            Print a Report
            {BRANCH SubMenu}
```

The cell named SubMenu contains a MENUCALL to a menu named PMenu. It also includes a BRANCH back to itself:

```
SubMenu {MENUCALL PMenu}
        {BRANCH SubMenu}
```

The PMenu submenu displays options for printing and performs these tasks when selected, using options from the Print menu:

```
PMenu    Align              New-Page              Print-It
         Set top-of-page    Start on New Page     Print the Report
         /PPAQ              /PPPQ                 /PPR
                                                  A1..E15 ~
                                                  GQ
```

(Portions of the menu descriptions are hidden in the figure but displayed here.)

The Return option passes control all the way back to the \m macro, which redisplays the Main menu, and thereby exits the submenu:

```
Return
Return to MainMenu
{BRANCH \m}
```

As you may have guessed, you can have your submenu call another submenu, and so on. Just be sure to include a Quit or Return option on submenus so the user can branch back to the previous menu (or back to the custom main menu if you prefer).

You can branch to any MENUCALL command simply by using its name in the BRANCH command.

Subroutines and Menus

Back in Chapter 9, we developed a macro to display a graphics slide show of four named graphs. Suppose you wish to include this capability in one of your macros. Do you need to squeeze the entire slide-show macro in under the menu option? Fortunately, no. You can simply assign a range name to the slide-show macro, such as Slides, and call the subroutine from the menu using the {Slides} command. Figure 11.6 shows an example.

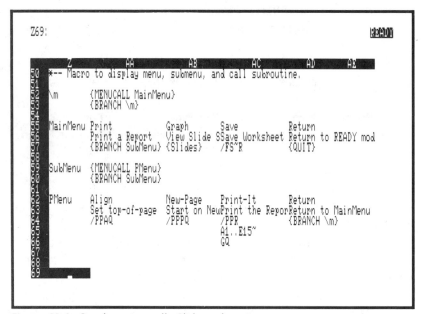

Figure 11.6: Graph option calls Slides subroutine

Though part of the menu description is obscured, the Graph option from the menu contains these three simple lines:

Graph
View Slide Show
{Slides}

To keep the menu macro from becoming unduly cluttered and complicated, the macro to display the slide-show macro is neatly tucked away in cell Z70, as Figure 11.7 shows. The cells Z52..Z78 are range name labels.

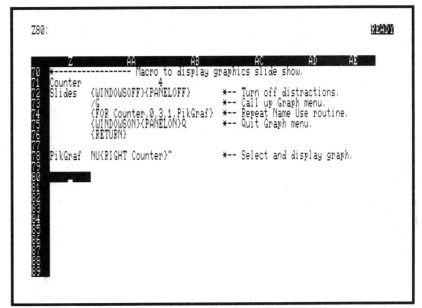

Figure 11.7: The slide-show subroutine

This subroutine is very similar to the slide show macro we developed in Chapter 9. The primary difference is that it is no longer activated with an Alt-key combination. The original macro name, \s, has been changed to Slides, so that the menu command, {Slides}, now activates the macro.

Your menus can be kept very neat and tidy by using subroutine calls for all menu options. For example, this menu

MainMenu	Add	Find	Print	Return
	New Date	Look Up	Report	Exit to READY
	{AddNew}	{LookUp}	{Report}	{QUIT}

is much cleaner and less confusing than this one:

```
MainMenu    Add          Find          Print         Return
            New Date     Look Up       Report        Exit to READY
            {HOME}       {HOME}{RI{LET Reco{QUIT}
            {LET A20,{BLANK B1{GOTO}Input ~
            /RUA30..J{LET B12,/RNCLabels ~{BS}.
            /RUB1..B1{LET B13,{END}{RIGHT}{END}{DOWN}
            /WGPE                      /PPCAQ
            {HOME}{RI{BLANK B1{FOR Counter,1,@ROWS(La
            {IF @CELL{GOTO}Input ~
            {?}{DOWN}/DQI{BS}.{LET Line1,@INDEX(Label
            {IF B1 ="Q{END}{DOW{IF @ISSTRING(@INDEX(La
            {IF @CELL{GOTO}Cri{LET Line1,Line1&" "&@I
            {BRANCH G{DOWN} {IF @ISSTRING(@INDEX(La
```

The second example is a big mess because too many large macros are crammed into the single columns under the menu items. The first example can accomplish exactly the same task simply by calling each macro by name at its named location on the worksheet, as in the {Slides} example.

Menus with No Escape

If you want to develop a particularly sensitive worksheet that users can access only through your custom menus, you can create a no-escape menu that is displayed immediately when the worksheet is retrieved, and that cannot be exited from without leaving 1-2-3. This means that unauthorized users cannot get to the worksheet READY mode and play around with your worksheet. Figure 11.8 shows an example of a no-escape menu. Cells Z52..Z58 are range name labels.

The name \0 (zero) forces the macro to be executed the moment the worksheet is loaded into 1-2-3. The BREAKOFF command disables the BREAK key, so that not even BREAK will disrupt the macro. Then, {BRANCH Forever} passes control to the subroutine that displays the menu. Each item in the menu redisplays the menu, except for Quit. Quit exits 1-2-3 all the way

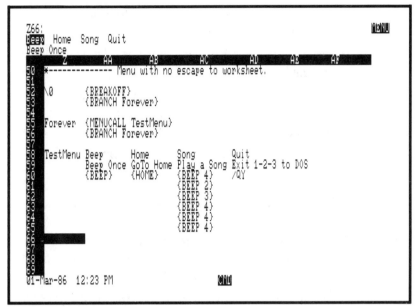

Figure 11.8: Menu with no escape to READY mode

back to the DOS prompt (Quit Yes). Therefore, the user's only options are to select items from your custom menu, or to return to the DOS prompt.

The technique isn't entirely foolproof. A sophisticated user could use File Combine to pull the No-Escape menu into an empty worksheet. Since File Combine does not read range names, the \0 macro will not execute, so the entire worksheet will be in READY mode. Unfortunately, password protection won't work here, because anyone who uses the worksheet at all will probably need to know the password. Nevertheless, a no-escape menu will keep unsophisticated 1-2-3 users from modifying or accidentally damaging your worksheet.

Summary

In this chapter we've discussed the basics of creating custom menus. Here is a summary of the structure of the menus we've developed.

- A menu consists of several options in contiguous cells across a single row.

- A description or help message must be placed in the cell beneath each menu option.

- The tasks that a menu option is to perform (or a branch to another menu or subroutine) begin in the cell immediately beneath the option description (or help message).

- Menu options can call subroutines by name, which allows you to develop neater, less cluttered menus.

Here is a summary of the new commands we've discussed:

- The MENUBRANCH command passes control to a named cell on the menu. The menu disappears from the control panel after the user makes a single selection.

- The MENUCALL command acts like the MENUBRANCH command, except that it acts as a subroutine call and can therefore be used to create menus that reappear after the user makes a selection.

- Menu options can call submenus with a BRANCH command and another MENUCALL command.

- You can create menus from which there is no escape with a combination of the autoexecute macro name (\0), the BREAKOFF command, and the /QY (Quit Yes) menu options.

12

A MENU-DRIVEN DATABASE

IN THIS CHAPTER WE'LL pull together all of the techniques we've discussed throughout the book to create a menu-driven database management system for managing a mailing list. Most of the routines in this system are similar to the database macros in Chapter 10. However, they are all linked together through menus, and some new features have been added.

Using the Mailing System

When the user types Alt-m, the main menu appears at the top of the screen:

Add   Sort   Query   Print   Keep   Worksheet

The Add option allows the user to add new names and addresses through a data entry form, like the one in Chapter 10. To quit entering data, the user enters the letter Q in the Mr/Mrs field and presses Return. This brings back the main menu.

The Sort option displays this submenu:

Zip Code   Alphabetical

Selecting the Zip Code option sorts the records into zip-code order. Selecting the Alphabetical option sorts the records into alphabetical order by last and first name.

The Query option filters the database for mailing labels and form letters. This option presents a query form, as discussed in Chapter 10. The user fills in search criteria, then types Alt-c to continue. For example, if the user fills in the query form like this

Mr/Mrs:

Last Name: Smith

First Name:

Company:
Address:
City:
State: **CA**
Zip Code:
Phone:

then form letters and labels will be printed for Smiths in California only. If the user fills in the query form like this

Mr/Mrs:
Last Name:
First Name:
Company:
Address:
City:
State:
Zip Code: **'92???**
Phone:

then letters and labels will be printed only for people in the 92000 through 92999 zip-code areas.

Selecting the Print option displays this submenu:

Labels   Directory   Form-Letter   Exit

Selecting the Directory option from the submenu prints a listing of the entire database. Selecting Exit returns the user to the main menu. Selecting Labels prints mailing labels. Selecting Form-Letter gives the user a chance to create or edit a form letter, followed by typing Alt-d when done. Both the Form-Letter and Labels options present this menu:

(A)ll, last (Q)uery, or (N)one : _

Entering A prints labels or letters for everyone on the database. Entering Q prints labels or letters only for those individuals who meet the criteria of the most recent query (for example, everyone in the 92000 through 92999 zip-code areas). Selecting None branches back to the main menu without printing anything.

The Keep option from the main menu saves the entire database. The Worksheet option returns to the worksheet READY mode.

The Database

The database consists of the usual Input, Criterion, and Output ranges, as well as a data entry form. Cells A1..A10 contain prompts for the data entry and query forms:

	A	**B**	**C**
1	Mr/Mrs:		
2	Last Name:		
3	First Name:		
4	M.I.:		
5	Company:		
6	Address:		
7	City:		
8	State:		
9	Zip:		
10	Phone:		

Cell A20 contains the label

Type Alt-m for menu

The ranges A25..J25, A30..J30, and L30..U30 contain the Criterion, Input, and Output ranges. Each of these ranges contains these field names:

Mr:Mrs LName Fname MI Company Address City State Zip Phone

Be sure to put each of the ten field names into separate but adjacent cells on the same row.

You'll need to type at least one record of data into the first row of the Input range (A31..J31). Be sure to put data into each field, particularly the Mr:Mrs and Phone fields. (The macros need at least one record to start with.)

Use Range Name Create to assign the range name Input to the range A30..J30. Assign the range name Criterion to the range A25..J26. Assign the range name Output to the range L30..U30. (See Figure 12.12 at the end of the chapter for a complete list of named ranges.)

The Menus

There are three menus in the database system. These are named MainMenu, SubMenu1, and SubMenu2, as shown in Figure 12.1.

```
             Z          AA        AB        AC        AD        AE
 1  *----------- Menus for the menu-driven database management system.
 2  \m         {MENUCALL MainMenu}
 3             {BRANCH \m}
 4
 5  MainMenu Add       Sort      Query     Print     Keep      Worksheet
 6             Add new nSort into Filter DaPrint labelsSave all Return to 1-2-3 READY mode
 7             {DEntry} {SMenu}   {QForm}  {PMenu}   /FS~R     {QUIT}
 8
 9  SMenu      {MENUBRANCH SubMenu1}
10
11  SubMenu1 Zip Code Alphabetical
12             Put into Put into alphabetical order by name
13             {ZSort}  {ASort}
14
15  PMenu      {MENUCALL SubMenu2}
16             {BRANCH PMenu}
17
18  SubMenu2 Labels    Directory Form-LettExit
19             Print MaiPrint DireEdit/PrinReturn to main menu
20             {LabSet} {Direct}  {PrepLet}{BRANCH \m}
```

Figure 12.1: The database system menus

It's impossible to see all the menu descriptions on the screen because they are much too long. Figure 12.13 at the end of the chapter displays the contents of all the cells in the database system. Refer to it for more explicit information.

Note that most menu selections branch to subroutines. These subroutines are similar to the macros discussed in Chapter 10, so you can refer back to Chapter 10 for more technical detail if necessary.

Data Entry

The Add option from the main menu branches to the DEntry subroutine, shown in Figure 12.2. This subroutine is similar to the data entry macro in Chapter 10.

```
         Z        AA        AB        AC        AD        AE
25
26             *---------- Data entry form.
27 DEntry      {HOME}
28             {LET A17,"In Data Entry Mode: Enter Q <--' to Quit"}~
29             /RUA30..J1030~                           *-- Create Unprotect ranges
30             /RUB1..B11~
31             /REB1..B11~
32             /WGPE                                    *-- Global Protection on
33             {HOME}{RIGHT}
34 GetEntry    {IF @CELLPOINTER("ROW")=6#OR#@CELLPOINTER("ROW")>8#AND#@CELLPOINTER("TYPE")="b"}'
35             {?}{DOWN}
36             {IF B1="Q"}{BRANCH Done}
37             {IF @CELLPOINTER("ROW")>10}{TransRec}
38             {BRANCH GetEntry}              *-- GetEntry gets 1 record
39
40 TransRec    {GOTO}Input~                   *-- Transpose form data
41             {END}{DOWN}{DOWN}              *-- onto a database record
42             /RTB1..B10~~
43             /REB1..B10~                    *--Blank the form
44             {HOME}{RIGHT}
45             {RETURN}
46
47 Done        /WGPD                          *-- Turn off protection
48             {BLANK B1}~{BEEP 2}
49             /RPA30..J1030~
50             /RPB1..B11~                    *-- Unprotect ranges.
51             {BLANK A17}~
52             {HOME}{RETURN}
53
```

Figure 12.2: The DEntry subroutine for data entry

Sorting

The Sort option from the main menu branches to SubMenu1, which displays these options:

Zip Code   Alphabetical

SubMenu1, in turn, branches to either the ZSort (zip code) or ASort (alphabetical sort) subroutines shown in Figure 12.3. Both subroutines use the Data Sort options from the menu to sort records.

```
          Z          AA        AB        AC        AD          AE

54                   *-------- Alphabetical Sort.
55  ASort            {GOTO}Input~                    *-- Position cell pointer
56                   /DSD{BS}.                        *-- Highlight data range
57                   {END}{RIGHT}{END}{DOWN}
58                   ..{DOWN}~
59                   PB30~A~SC30~A~G                  *-- Primary, Secondary, Go
60
61                   *-------- Zip Code Sort.
62  ZSort            {GOTO}Input~                    *-- Position cell pointer
63                   /DSD{BS}.                        *-- Highlight data range
64                   {END}{RIGHT}{END}{DOWN}
65                   ..{DOWN}~
66                   PI30~A~SB30~A~G                  *-- Primary, Secondary, Go
```

Figure 12.3: Subroutines for sorting records

Queries

The Query option from the main menu branches to the QForm subroutine to present a query form similar to the one in Chapter 10. The QForm subroutine allows the user to fill in the query form, then type Alt-c to continue. At that point, the Alt-c macro takes over and extracts records that match the criterion (using Data Query Extract) from the Input range into the Output range. This macro is similar to the query form macro in Chapter 10, except that it uses Data Query Extract rather than Data Query Find. The \c macro passes control back to the main menu when done. Figure 12.4 shows the QForm subroutine and the \c macro.

Printing

The printing techniques are a little tricky in this macro. Since both the form letter and the mailing labels use such similar techniques, a single *self-modifying* subroutine takes care of both jobs. If the user requests mailing labels, the Print submenu branches to the LetSet subroutine, which sets up printer settings for two cells named PSet and PrintIt in the LabLet subroutine. The LabSet subroutine is shown in Figure 12.5.

```
        Z        AA        AB        AC        AD        AE
67
68              *---- Present form and perform query.
69 QForm        {HOME}{RIGHT}
70              {BLANK B1..B10}~                *-- Blank query form.
71              {LET B12,"Enter values to search for in column B"}
72              {LET B13,"Then press Alt-c to continue..."}~
73              {QUIT}
74
75 \c           {BLANK B12..B13}~               *-- Remove instructions.
76              {GOTO}Input~                    *-- Assign Input range.
77              /DQI{BS}.{END}{RIGHT}
78              {END}{DOWN}~Q
79              {GOTO}Criterion~                *-- Go to Criterion range.
80              {DOWN}
81              /RTB1..B10~~                    *-- Fill in Criterion range.
82              {GOTO}Criterion~
83              /DQC{BS}.{END}{RIGHT}{DOWN}~Q
84              {GOTO}Output~
85              /DQO{BS}.{END}{RIGHT}~
86              EQ{HOME}
87              {BRANCH \m}
88
```

Figure 12.4: The query form subroutine and macro

```
        Z        AA        AB        AC        AD        AE
89 LabSet       {LET PSet,"/PPCAOOUQQ"}~
90              {LET PrintIt,"/PPROneLab~GQ~"}~
91              {BRANCH LabLet}
92
```

Figure 12.5: The LabSet subroutine

If the user requests form letters, the Print submenu branches to the PrepLet subroutine to allow the user to first create or modify the form letter. The PrepLet subroutine is shown in Figure 12.6. Use Range Name Create to name the range AA154..AE159 OneLab for printing labels. Then use Range Name Create to name the range AA153..AG198 Letter for printing form letters. Use /RFD to select a format for the date in cell AA153.

The PrepLet subroutine stops the macro to give the user time to create the form letter (starting at the line that reads "Start letter here..."). The user writes the form letter (and uses Range Justify to format it, if necessary), then types Alt-d. Typing Alt-d calls up the macro that sets up the self-modifying LabLet routine for form letters. The Alt-d macro is shown in Figure 12.7.

```
            Z        AA       AB       AC       AD       AE

150 PrepLet {GOTO}TopLine~{DOWN}{QUIT}
151
152 TopLine                    Type in form letter, then type Alt-d when done...
153          03/01/86
154
155 Line1
156 Line2
157 Line3
158 Line4
159 Line5
160 Line6
161
162          Start letter here......
163
164
165
```

Figure 12.6: The PrepLet subroutine and form letter workspace

```
           Z        AA       AB       AC       AD       AE

93 \d      {LET PSet,"/PPCAQ"}~
94         {LET PrintIt,"/PPRLetter~GPQ~"}~
95         {LabLet}{BRANCH PMenu}
96
```

Figure 12.7: The Alt-d macro to set up form letters

The LabLet subroutine branches to another subroutine named All/Some, which asks if the user wants to print labels or letters for (A)ll, (Q)ueried, or (N)one individuals. The All/Some subroutine also modifies the LabLet subroutine, making it read data from either the Input range (for All records) or the Output range (for Queried records). The None option simply passes control back to the main menu. Figure 12.8 shows the All/Some subroutine, which modifies the cell named Depend in the LabLet subroutine.

```
           Z        AA       AB       AC       AD       AE

128        *-------- Ask about Query, or All records.
129 QAnswer n
130 All/Some {GETLABEL "(A)ll, last (Q)uery, or (N)one ",QAnswer}~
131         {IF QAnswer="N"}{BRANCH \m}
132         {IF QAnswer="A"}{LET Depend,"Input"}~
133         {IF QAnswer="Q"}{LET Depend,"Output"}~
134         {RETURN}
```

Figure 12.8: The All/Some subroutine

The LabLet subroutine is shown in Figure 12.9. Notice that it first branches to the All/Some subroutine, as mentioned, and contains the named cells Depend, PSet, and PrintIt, which are modified by the All/Some, LabSet, and \d routines.

The Directory option from the Print submenu calls the subroutine named Direct. This subroutine prints all of the records in the database. It sets the right margin to 120 (MR120~), which assumes you have a printer with wide paper. You can remove this option, or modify the macro to use compressed print (Option Setup), if you wish. The Direct subroutine also creates the centered heading "Directory of Customers", which you may want to modify. Figure 12.10 shows the Direct subroutine.

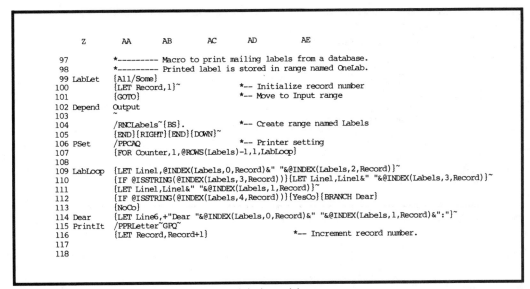

```
           Z        AA       AB       AC       AD       AE

 97               *--------- Macro to print mailing labels from a database.
 98               *--------- Printed label is stored in range named OneLab.
 99 LabLet        {All/Some}
100               {LET Record,1}~            *-- Initialize record number
101               {GOTO}                     *-- Move to Input range
102 Depend        Output
103               ~
104               /RNCLabels~{BS}.           *-- Create range named Labels
105               {END}{RIGHT}{END}{DOWN}~
106 PSet          /PPCAQ                     *-- Printer setting
107               {FOR Counter,1,@ROWS(Labels)-1,1,LabLoop}
108
109 LabLoop       {LET Line1,@INDEX(Labels,0,Record)&" "&@INDEX(Labels,2,Record)}~
110               {IF @ISSTRING(@INDEX(Labels,3,Record))}{LET Line1,Line1&" "&@INDEX(Labels,3,Record)}~
111               {LET Line1,Line1&" "&@INDEX(Labels,1,Record)}~
112               {IF @ISSTRING(@INDEX(Labels,4,Record))}{YesCo}{BRANCH Dear}
113               {NoCo}
114 Dear          {LET Line6,+"Dear "&@INDEX(Labels,0,Record)&" "&@INDEX(Labels,1,Record)&":"}~
115 PrintIt       /PPRLetter~GPQ~
116               {LET Record,Record+1}                   *-- Increment record number.
117
118
```

Figure 12.9: The LabLet subroutine to print labels and letters

```
           Z        AA       AB       AC       AD       AE

119 Direct        {GOTO}Input~
120               /PPCAA
121               OH|Directory of Customers~
122               MR120~QR{BS}.
123               {END}{RIGHT}
124               {END}{DOWN}
125               ..{DOWN}~
126               GCAQ
127
```

Figure 12.10: The Direct subroutine

The YesCo and NoCo subroutines help to format labels and letters. They are similar to the routines in the form letter and mailing labels macros in Chapter 10. Figure 12.11 shows the YesCo and NoCo subroutines.

The menu-driven mailing system is quite large and complex, but it uses techniques that have all been discussed in earlier chapters in this book. Nonetheless, gaining a full understanding of its logic and workings may require some study. For reference, Figure 12.12 lists all the named ranges used in the system, and Figure 12.13 lists the contents of every cell in the system.

```
            Z      AA      AB      AC      AD      AE
      135
      136            *— YesCo routine makes a label with Company name.
      137 YesCo      {LET Line2,@INDEX(Labels,4,Record)}~
      138            {LET Line3,@INDEX(Labels,5,Record)}~
      139            {LET Line4,@INDEX(Labels,6,Record)&", "&@INDEX(Labels,7,Record)&" "&@INDEX(Labels,8,Record)}~
      140
      141            *— NoCo routine makes a label without Company name.
      142 NoCo       {LET Line2,@INDEX(Labels,5,Record)}~
      143            {LET Line3,@INDEX(Labels,6,Record)&", "&@INDEX(Labels,7,Record)&" "&@INDEX(Labels,8,Record)}~
      144            {BLANK Line4}~
      145
      146
      147 Counter
      148 Record
      149
```

Figure 12.11: The YesCo and NoCo subroutines

Summary

In this chapter we've developed a fairly complex custom menu system to drive a mailing list database. The custom menu options and the tasks they perform are summarized here:

- The Add option allows the user to add new data to the database through a form.

- The Sort option allows the user to sort the database into alphabetical order by name, or into zip-code order.

- The Query option allows the user to filter the database through a form.

- The Print option allows the user to print a directory, mailing labels, or form letters.

- The Keep option saves all current changes and additions to the database.

- The Worksheet option removes the menu and returns to the worksheet READY mode.

NAME	CELL(S)	NAME	CELL(S)
All/Some	AA130	MainMenu	AA5
ASort	AA55	NoCo	AA142
Counter	AA147	OneLab	AA154..AE159
Criterion	A25..J26	Output	L30..U30
Dear	AA114	PMenu	AA15
DEntry	AA27	PrepLet	AA150
Depend	AA102	PrintIt	AA115
Direct	AA119	PSet	AA106
Done	AA47	QAnswer	AA129
GetEntry	AA34	QForm	AA69
Input	A30..J30	Record	AA148
Labels	L30..U34	SMenu	AA9
LabLet	AA99	SubMenu1	AA11
LabLoop	AA109	SubMenu2	AA18
LabSet	AA89	TopLine	AA152
Letter	AA153..AG198	TransRec	AA40
Line1	AA155	YesCo	AA137
Line2	AA156	ZSort	AA62
Line3	AA157	\c	AA75
Line4	AA158	\d	AA93
Line5	AA159	\m	AA2
Line6	AA160		

Figure 12.12: Named cells and ranges in the database

Z1:	'*------------ Menus for the menu-driven database
	management system.
Z2:	'\m
AA2:	'{MENUCALL MainMenu}
AA3:	'{BRANCH \m}
Z5:	'MainMenu
AA5:	'Add
AB5:	'Sort
AC5:	'Query
AD5:	'Print
AE5:	'Keep
AF5:	'Worksheet
AA6:	'Add new names and addresses
AB6:	'Sort into alphabetical or zip code order
AC6:	'Filter Database Records
AD6:	'Print labels, directory, or form letter
AE6:	'Save all current data
AF6:	'Return to 1-2-3 READY mode
AA7:	'{DEntry}
AB7:	'{SMenu}
AC7:	'{QForm}
AD7:	'{PMenu}
AE7:	'/FS~R
AF7:	'{QUIT}
Z9:	'SMenu
AA9:	'{MENUBRANCH SubMenu1}
Z11:	'SubMenu1
AA11:	'Zip Code
AB11:	'Alphabetical
AA12:	'Put into zip code order
AB12:	'Put into alphabetical order by name
AA13:	'{ZSort}
AB13:	'{ASort}
Z15:	'PMenu

Figure 12.13: Cell-by-cell contents of the database management system

```
AA15:      '{MENUCALL SubMenu2}
AA16:      '{BRANCH PMenu}
Z18:       'SubMenu2
AA18:      'Labels
AB18:      'Directory
AC18:      'Form-Letter
AD18:      'Exit
AA19:      'Print Mailing Labels
AB19:      'Print Directory
AC19:      'Edit/Print a form letter
AD19:      'Return to main menu
AA20:      '{LabSet}
AB20:      '{Direct}
AC20:      '{PrepLet}
AD20:      '{BRANCH \m}
AA26:      '*---------- Data entry form.
Z27:       'DEntry
AA27:      '{HOME}
AA28:      '{LET A17,"In Data Entry Mode: Enter Q <--'
                to Quit"} ~
AA29:      '/RUA30..J1030 ~
AF29:      '*-- Create Unprotect ranges
AA30:      '/RUB1..B11 ~
AA31:      '/REB1..B11 ~
AA32:      '/WGPE
AF32:      '*-- Global Protection on
AA33:      '{HOME}{RIGHT}
Z34:       'GetEntry
AA34:      '{IF @CELLPOINTER("ROW")=6#OR#@CELLPOINTER
                ("ROW")>8#AND#@CELLPOINTER("TYPE")="b"}'
AA35:      '{?}{DOWN}
AA36:      '{IF B1="Q"}{BRANCH Done}
AA37:      '{IF @CELLPOINTER("ROW")>10}{TransRec}
AA38:      '{BRANCH GetEntry}
AE38:      '*-- GetEntry gets 1 record
```

Figure 12.13: (continued)

Z40:	'TransRec
AA40:	'{GOTO}Input ~
AE40:	'*-- Transpose form data
AA41:	'{END}{DOWN}{DOWN}
AE41:	'*-- onto a database record
AA42:	'/RTB1..B10 ~ ~
AA43:	'/REB1..B10 ~
AE43:	'*--Blank the form
AA44:	'{HOME}{RIGHT}
AA45:	'{RETURN}
Z47:	'Done
AA47:	'/WGPD
AE47:	'*-- Turn off protection
AA48:	'{BLANK B1} ~ {BEEP 2}
AA49:	'/RPA30..J1030 ~
AA50:	'/RPB1..B11 ~
AE50:	'*-- Unprotect ranges.
AA51:	'{BLANK A17} ~
AA52:	'{HOME}{RETURN}
AA54:	'*-------- Alphabetical Sort.
Z55:	'ASort
AA55:	'{GOTO}Input ~
AE55:	'*-- Position cell pointer
AA56:	'/DSD{BS}.
AE56:	'*-- Highlight data range
AA57:	'{END}{RIGHT}{END}{DOWN}
AA58:	'..{DOWN} ~
AA59:	'PB30 ~ A ~ SC30 ~ A ~ G
AE59:	'*-- Primary, Secondary, Go
AA61:	'*-------- Zip Code Sort.
Z62:	'ZSort
AA62:	'{GOTO}Input ~
AE62:	'*-- Position cell pointer
AA63:	'/DSD{BS}.
AE63:	'*-- Highlight data range

Figure 12.13: (continued)

```
AA64:    '{END}{RIGHT}{END}{DOWN}
AA65:    '..{DOWN} ~
AA66:    'PI30 ~ A ~ SB30 ~ A ~ G
AE66:    '*-- Primary, Secondary, Go
AA68:    '*---- Present form and perform query.
Z69:     'QForm
AA69:    '{HOME}{RIGHT}
AA70:    '{BLANK B1..B10} ~
AD70:    '*-- Blank query form.
AA71:    '{LET B12,"Enter values to search for in column B"}
AA72:    '{LET B13,"Then press Alt-c to continue..."} ~
AA73:    '{QUIT}
Z75:     '\c
AA75:    '{BLANK B12..B13} ~
AD75:    '*--- Remove instructions.
AA76:    '{GOTO}Input ~
AD76:    '*-- Assign Input range.
AA77:    '/DQI{BS}.{END}{RIGHT}
AA78:    '{END}{DOWN} ~ Q
AA79:    '{GOTO}Criterion ~
AD79:    '*-- Go to Criterion range.
AA80:    '{DOWN}
AA81:    '/RTB1..B10 ~ ~
AD81:    '*-- Fill in Criterion range.
AA82:    '{GOTO}Criterion ~
AA83:    '/DQC{BS}.{END}{RIGHT}{DOWN} ~ Q
AA84:    '{GOTO}Output ~
AA85:    '/DQO{BS}.{END}{RIGHT} ~
AA86:    'EQ{HOME}
AA87:    '{BRANCH \m}
Z89:     'LabSet
AA89:    '{LET PSet,"/PPCAOOUQQ"} ~
AA90:    '{LET PrintIt,"/PPROneLab ~ GQ ~ "} ~
AA91:    '{BRANCH LabLet}
```

Figure 12.13: (continued)

Z93:	`'\d`
AA93:	`'{LET PSet,"/PPCAQ"} ~`
AA94:	`'{LET PrintIt,"/PPRLetter ~ GPQ ~ "} ~`
AA95:	`'{LabLet}{BRANCH PMenu}`
AA97:	`'*--------- Macro to print mailing labels from a database.`
AA98:	`'*--------- Printed label is stored in range named OneLab.`
Z99:	`'LabLet`
AA99:	`'{All/Some}`
AA100:	`'{LET Record,1} ~`
AD100:	`'*-- Initialize record number`
AA101:	`'{GOTO}`
AD101:	`'*-- Move to Input range`
Z102:	`'Depend`
AA102:	`'Output`
AA103:	`' ~`
AA104:	`' /RNCLabels ~ {BS}.`
AD104:	`'*-- Create range named Labels`
AA105:	`'{END}{RIGHT}{END}{DOWN} ~`
Z106:	`'PSet`
AA106:	`'/PPCAQ`
AD106:	`'*-- Printer setting`
AA107:	`'{FOR Counter,1,@ROWS(Labels)-1,1,LabLoop}`
Z109:	`'LabLoop`
AA109:	`'{LET Line1,@INDEX(Labels,0,Record)&" "&@INDEX (Labels,2,Record)} ~`
AA110:	`'{IF @ISSTRING(@INDEX(Labels,3,Record))}{LET Line1,Line1&" "&@INDEX(Labels,3,Record)} ~`
AA111:	`'{LET Line1,Line1&" "&@INDEX(Labels,1,Record)} ~`
AA112:	`'{IF @ISSTRING(@INDEX(Labels,4,Record))}{YesCo} {BRANCH Dear}`
AA113:	`'{NoCo}`
Z114:	`'Dear`

Figure 12.13: (continued)

```
AA114:      '{LET Line6, + "Dear "&@INDEX
                (Labels,0,Record)&" "&@INDEX
                (Labels,1,Record)&":"} ~
Z115:       'PrintIt
AA115:      '/PPRLetter ~ GPQ ~
AA116:      '{LET Record,Record + 1}
AE116:      '*-- Increment record number.
Z119:       'Direct
AA119:      '{GOTO}Input ~
AA120:      '/PPCAA
AA121:      'OH ┊ Directory of Customers ~
AA122:      'MR120 ~ QR{BS}.
AA123:      '{END}{RIGHT}
AA124:      '{END}{DOWN}
AA125:      '..{DOWN} ~
AA126:      'GCAQ
AA128:      '*-------- Ask about Query, or All records.
Z129:       'QAnswer
AA129:      'n
Z130:       'All/Some
AA130:      '{GETLABEL "(A)ll, last (Q)uery, or (N)one ",
                QAnswer} ~
AA131:      '{IF QAnswer = "N"}{BRANCH \m}
AA132:      '{IF QAnswer = "A"}{LET Depend,"Input"} ~
AA133:      '{IF QAnswer = "Q"}{LET Depend,"Output"} ~
AA134:      '{RETURN}
AA136:      '*-- YesCo routine makes a label with Company
                name.
Z137:       'YesCo
AA137:      '{LET Line2,@INDEX(Labels,4,Record)} ~
AA138:      '{LET Line3,@INDEX(Labels,5,Record)} ~
AA139:      '{LET Line4,@INDEX(Labels,6,Record)&", "&@INDEX
                (Labels,7,Record)&"
                "&@INDEX(Labels,8,Record)} ~
```

Figure 12.13: (continued)

AA141:	**'+-- NoCo routine makes a label without Company name.**
Z142:	**'NoCo**
AA142:	**'{LET Line2,@INDEX(Labels,5,Record)} ~**
AA143:	**'{LET Line3,@INDEX(Labels,6,Record)&", "& @INDEX(Labels,7,Record)&" "&@INDEX (Labels,8,Record)} ~**
AA144:	**'{BLANK Line4} ~**
Z147:	**'Counter**
Z148:	**'Record**
Z150:	**'PrepLet**
AA150:	**'{GOTO}TopLine ~ {DOWN}{QUIT}**
Z152:	**'TopLine**
AC152:	**'Type in form letter, then type Alt-d when done...**
AA153:	**@NOW**
Z155:	**'Line1**
Z156:	**'Line2**
Z157:	**'Line3**
Z158:	**'Line4**
Z159:	**'Line5**
Z160:	**'Line6**
AA162:	**'Start letter here......**

Figure 12.13: (continued)

13

INTERFACING WITH OTHER SOFTWARE SYSTEMS

Microcomputer Interfacing

VERSION 2.0 OF 1-2-3 offers many options for translating files between popular microcomputer software systems. Some transfers, particularly those involving mainframes, require a bit more work. In this chapter, we'll briefly discuss techniques for the simpler file translations, then we'll develop a couple of macros for the more difficult ones.

Microcomputer Interfacing

The Translate utility from the LOTUS menu offers this menu of formats for selecting a file to be translated:

What do you want to translate FROM?

1-2-3, release 1A

1-2-3, release 2

dBase II

dBase III

DIF

Jazz

SYMPHONY, release 1.0

SYMPHONY, release 1.1

VISICALC

When you select an option, the screen presents a menu of formats for translating the selected file:

What do you want to translate TO?

1-2-3, release 1A

dBase II

dBase III

DIF

SYMPHONY, release 1.0

SYMPHONY, release 1.1

You simply select an option, and 1-2-3 finishes the job.

If your translation does not fall under one of the Translate options, you'll probably need to use one of the "mainframe" techniques below, even if the transferred file is coming from, or going to, another microcomputer file.

Mainframe Interfacing

The chances are that when a file is transferred from a mainframe to a microcomputer, it will be an ASCII file in either *structured* (random access) or *delimited* (sequential) data file format. We'll discuss techniques for reading and writing each type of file in this chapter.

Reading Structured Data Files

A structured file stores data in evenly spaced columns, as shown in Figure 13.1. You can use the File Import Text options from the Main menu to read a structured file directly into your worksheet. Although the file will look as if data are already placed in individual cells, this is not the case. Each line of data on the worksheet is actually a long label that needs to be converted into individual columns.

```
1000  Turbo Board       1      555.00 19860401 T
1000  Ram Disk          1     1100.00 19860418 T
1001  Floppy Disks     10        2.11 19860312 T
1001  Color Card        1      101.00 19860331 T
1001  Video Cable       2       16.00 19860615 F
1001  8 Mhz Clock       2       16.39 19860515 F
1001  Ram Disk          1     1100.00 19860518 F
1002  8 Mhz Clock       2       16.39 19860315 T
1002  Ram Disk          1     1100.00 19860411 T
1003  8 Mhz Clock       1       16.39 19860415 T
1003  Tape Backup       1     1250.00 19860420 T
1003  40 Meg. Disk      1      450.00 19860420 T
1003  Floppy Disks      5        2.11 19860512 F
1003  Color Card        1      101.00 19860531 F
1004  Video Cable      10       16.00 19860415 F
1004  8 Mhz Clock       1       16.39 19860515 F
1004  Tape Backup       2     1250.00 19860620 F
```

Figure 13.1: Structured data file

To convert the labels into even columns, place the cell pointer in the upper-left corner of the imported file, and select the Data Parse Format-Line Create options. 1-2-3 will create a "best-guess" format line as shown below:

L≫≫≫≫ **∗L**≫≫ **∗ ∗ ∗ ∗ ∗ ∗ ∗V∗ ∗ ∗ ∗ ∗ ∗L**≫≫≫≫≫≫≫

1000Turbo Board   1   550.0019860401T

1000Ram Disk   1   1100.0019860418T

The ∗ symbols in the format line represent undefined blank spaces. You can replace these symbols by selecting Format-Line Edit and identifying columns using any of these symbols:

L	First character of a Label column
V	First character of a Value column
D	First character of a Date column
T	First character of a Time column
S	Skip the character below
>	Continuation of this column

Figure 13.2 shows an imported file with the format line properly edited to convert labels to columns.

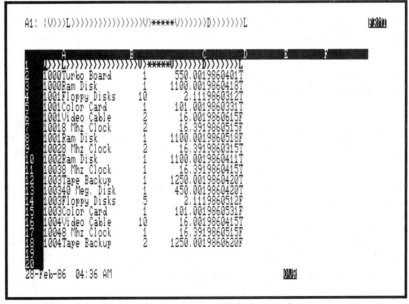

Figure 13.2: Format line edited to convert labels to columns

Once the format line specifies the columns you want, select Input Column and highlight the entire leftmost column of the data to be analyzed, including the format line. (In this example, you would highlight A1..A18.) Then select Output-Range, move the cell pointer to a place on the worksheet that has enough rows and columns to accommodate the entire converted file, and select Go. The Output range will contain the long labels converted to individual columns.

For tips on converting imported dates, like 19860301, to 1-2-3 serial dates, see Chapter 6.

Writing Structured Data Files

To create a structured data file from a 1-2-3 worksheet or database, move the cell pointer to the upper-left corner of the range of cells to be exported. Select the Print File options, and assign a name to the exported file. (If you do not include an extension, 1-2-3 will add the extension .PRN.) Select Range, and highlight the range of cells to export.

Next, select Options from the menu, and set Margin Left to 0 and Margin Right to 240. Select Other from the menu and Unformatted from the submenu. These steps ensure that the printed file does not have page breaks or wrapped-around rows. Select Quit to get back to the main Print menu and then select Go.

Reading Delimited Files

Delimited files are a bit trickier to work with, because there are no evenly-spaced columns. If you use the DOS TYPE command or the 1-2-3 File Import Text options to view a delimited file, you'll probably see that each field is separated by a comma (or some other character) and that character strings are enclosed in quotation marks (or some other character). Figure 13.3 shows a typical delimited ASCII file.

Figure 13.4 shows a macro that can read a delimited file into a 1-2-3 worksheet. Type it in exactly as shown in the figure, then use the usual File Save options to save the macro under a file name, such as DelimIn.

```
1000,"Tape Backup",1,1250.00,19860401,T
1000,"Ram Disk",1,1100.00,19860418,T
1001,"Floppy Disks",10,2.11,19860312,T
1001,"Color Card",1,101.00,19860331,T
1001,"Video Cable",2,16.00,19860615,F
1001,"8 Mhz Clock",2,16.39,19860515,F
1001,"Ram Disk",1,1100.00,19860518,F
1002,"8 Mhz Clock",2,16.39,19860315,T
1002,"Ram Disk",1,1100.00,19860411,T
1003,"8 Mhz Clock",1,16.39,19860415,T
1003,"Tape Backup",1,1250.00,19860420,T
1003,"40 Meg. Disk",1,450.00,19860420,T
1003,"Floppy Disks",5,2.11,19860512,F
1003,"Color Card",1,101.00,19860531,F
1004,"Video Cable",10,16.00,19860415,T
1004,"8 Mhz Clock",1,16.39,19860515,F
1004,"Tape Backup",2,1250.00,19860620,F
```

Figure 13.3: Delimited ASCII data file

```
            Z          AA        AB        AC        AD        AE        AF
50 *---- Macro to read in a delimited ASCII file.
51
52 FileName
53 Size
54 FilePos
55 .Start
56 Stop
57 WorkArea
58
59 \t         {HOME}{CLOSE}
60            {GETLABEL "Enter File Name: ",FileName}~
61            {OPEN FileName,R}{NameErr}
62            {LET FilePos,0}~
63            {FILESIZE Size}
64 ReadRec    {READLN WorkArea}
65            {LET Start,0}
66            {LET Stop,@FIND(",",WorkArea,0):value}
67            {IF FilePos<Size}{Parser}
68            {CLOSE}
69
70 Parser     {LET Chunk,@MID(WorkArea,Start,Stop-Start)}
71            {IF @MID(Chunk,0,1)=@CHAR(34)}{PeelOut}
72 Chunk
73            ~{RIGHT}
74            {LET Start,Stop+1}
75            {LET Stop,@FIND(",",WorkArea,Start+1):value}
76            {IF Stop>0}{BRANCH Parser}
77            {LET Chunk2,@MID(WorkArea,Start,240)}
78 Chunk2
79            ~{DOWN}{END}{LEFT}
80            {LET Start,0}
81            {LET FilePos,FilePos+@LENGTH(WorkArea)+2}
82            {BRANCH ReadRec}
83
84 PeelOut    {IF @LENGTH(Chunk)<=2}{RETURN}
85            {LET Chunk,+"'"&@MID(Chunk,1,@LENGTH(Chunk)-2)}
86            {RETURN}
87
88 NameErr    {BEEP 3}{BEEP 4}
89            {BLANK A1..H2}
90            No such file on disk!~
91            {QUIT}
92
```

Figure 13.4: Macro to read in a delimited ASCII file

To use the macro, make sure that both the DelimIn work-sheet and the delimited ASCII file are available on the same disk. Retrieve the DelimIn worksheet, and press Alt-t. When the screen asks for the name of the file to read in, enter the file name with the extension (e.g., CustList.TXT). If the macro cannot find the file name you entered, it displays the error message "No such file on disk!", and returns to the READY mode. You'll have to try again, starting with Alt-t.

When the transfer is complete the worksheet READY indicator will reappear. To avoid confusion later, you might want to store the imported data in a separate worksheet (not the same worksheet as the macro), using File Xtract.

We need to discuss this macro in some detail, partly because it uses new commands, and partly because there is no room for comments in the macro. As usual, labels in column Z are range names. The top lines in the macro store information used during macro execution:

FileName

Size

FilePos

Start

Stop

WorkArea

The macro first moves the cell pointer to the home position and closes any open ASCII file ({CLOSE}). Then the macro asks the user for the name of the file to import and stores the response in the cell named FileName:

\t   {HOME}{CLOSE}
       {GETLABEL "Enter File Name: ",FileName} ~

Next the macro attempts to open the requested file for reading (R). (Other OPEN options are writing (W) and modifying (M).) If the requested file cannot be opened, the macro branches control to the subroutine named NameErr:

{OPEN FileName,R}{NameErr}

The macro initializes the FilePos (file position) variable to zero, then it records the size of the file in a cell named Size:

```
{LET FilePos,0} ~
{FILESIZE Size}
```

It is important to record the size of the open file in this macro, because the only way to detect when the macro has translated the entire file is to compare the current pointer position in the file with the total size of the file. (We'll see how the macro makes the comparison momentarily.)

Next, the macro reads one line (record) from the open file and stores it in the cell named WorkArea. A single line or record is defined as all characters up to the CRLF (Carriage Return Line Feed) that marks the end of a record in a delimited file. The CRLF is invisible to the eye, but it causes each record to appear on a separate line when the file is displayed on the screen or printer:

```
ReadRec {READLN WorkArea}
```

Now the macro has to break the WorkArea cell into separate columns, based on the comma delimiters and the data types. The first column begins at the first character (0) and extends to the first comma in the WorkArea (@FIND(",",WorkArea,0)). The lines below store, in the cells named Start and Stop, the appropriate coordinates for isolating the field:

```
{LET Start,0}
{LET Stop,@FIND(",",WorkArea,0):value}
```

The macro checks to make sure that the cell pointer position is not yet beyond the size of the file. If it is not, the macro branches control to the subroutine named Parser. Otherwise, it closes the open ASCII file and quits processing:

```
{IF FilePos<Size}{Parser}
{CLOSE}
```

The Parser subroutine stores a portion of the WorkArea in the cell named Chunk. The portion is calculated as the Start and Stop positions, which are calculated by comma positions in the WorkArea:

Parser   **{LET Chunk,@MID(WorkArea,Start,Stop-Start)}**

If the first character in Chunk begins with double quotation marks (ASCII code 34), the macro passes control to a subroutine named PeelOut, which peels off the leading and trailing quotation marks. Then, the contents of Chunk are typed into the currently highlighted cell, and the macro moves the cell pointer one cell to the right:

{IF @MID(Chunk,0,1) = @CHAR(34)}{PeelOut}

Chunk

~{RIGHT}

The Start and Stop positions for the next field are calculated by making the Start equal to the previous Stop plus one. The new Stop value is the next comma found in the WorkArea, starting at the new Start position:

{LET Start, Stop + 1}
{LET Stop,@FIND(",",WorkArea,Start + 1):value}

In other words, when the macro calculates the Start and Stop positions for the second field being extracted from WorkArea, Start and Stop contain numbers pointing to the locations of the quotation marks.

As long as there are still commas in the WorkArea, the macro passes control back to the subroutine named Parser:

{IF Stop>0}{BRANCH Parser}

If there are no more commas in the WorkArea, then the macro is ready to write the last column for the line. The next subroutine takes care of this last field in WorkArea and moves the cell pointer down to the next row, first column, on the worksheet:

```
                   {LET Chunk2,@MID(WorkArea,Start,240)}
       Chunk2
                   ~{DOWN}{END}{LEFT}
```

At this point, the macro is ready to start work on the next record in the ASCII file. It resets the Start position to zero, and it calculates the current position of the cell pointer in the ASCII file by adding the length of the last WorkArea line to the cell named FilePos. (The +2 is for the CRLF, which is not included in the @LENGTH(WorkArea).) The process continues by passing control back to the ReadRec subroutine, which reads in the next ASCII record:

```
       {LET Start,0}
       {LET FilePos,FilePos + @LENGTH(WorkArea) + 2}
       {BRANCH ReadRec}
```

The PeelOut subroutine removes the double quotation marks from the front and back of the character string in Chunk by placing an apostrophe label prefix into the cell, followed by a substring of the Chunk beginning at the second character and ending at the last character minus 2. (Since @MID starts counting at character 0, the formula

@MID(Chunk,1,@LENGTH(Chunk)-2

turns a string like "Howdy" into Howdy.) If the character string is less than three characters long (e.g., " "), then the subroutine doesn't do anything to it:

```
       PeelOut     {IF @LENGTH(Chunk)<=2}{RETURN}
                   {LET Chunk, +" ' "&@MID(Chunk,1,@LENGTH
                      (Chunk)-2)}
                   {RETURN}
```

The NameErr subroutine is called only if the macro cannot find the file that the user requested. When this occurs, NameErr beeps, clears some room for an error message, displays the error message "No such file on disk!", and terminates macro execution:

```
NameErr     {BEEP 3}{BEEP 4}
            {BLANK A1..H2}
            No such file on disk! ~
            {QUIT}
```

The DelimIn macro will work well with most delimited ASCII files, including those that do not mark character strings with quotation marks, as in this example:

```
1000,Tape Backup,1,1250.00,19860401,T
1000,Ram Disk,1,1100.00,19860418,T
1001,Floppy Disks,10,2.11,19860312,T
```

The macro will need modifications for delimited files that use field or character delimiters other than commas or quotation marks. For example, the delimited file might use apostrophes rather than quotation marks to enclose character strings, as below:

```
1000,'Tape Backup',1,1250.00,19860401,T
1000,'Ram Disk',1,1100.00,19860418,T
1001,'Floppy Disks',10,2.11,19860312,T
```

If this is the case, branching to the PeelOut subroutine will depend on whether an apostrophe (ASCII character 39) appears in the field. Hence, the line that reads

```
{IF @MID(Chunk,0,1) = @CHAR(34)}{PeelOut}
```

needs to be converted to

```
{IF @MID(Chunk,0,1) = @CHAR(39)}{PeelOut}
```

The delimited file might use semicolons rather than commas to delimit fields, as below:

1000;'Tape Backup';1;1250.00;19860401;T
1000;'Ram Disk';1;1100.00;19860418;T
1001;'Floppy Disks';10;2.11;19860312;T

If this is the case, these macro commands

{LET Stop,@FIND(",",WorkArea,0):value}
{LET Stop,@FIND(",",WorkArea,Start + 1):value}

which attempt to find commas will need to find semicolons instead, as below:

{LET Stop,@FIND(";",WorkArea,0):value}
{LET Stop,@FIND(";",WorkArea,Start + 1):value}

A quick look at an ASCII file with the DOS TYPE command or with the 1-2-3 File Import Text options will fill you in on the structure of the file.

As mentioned earlier, Chapter 6 discusses techniques for converting foreign dates, such as 19860401, to 1-2-3 serial dates.

Writing Delimited Files

At some point you may find that you need to convert a 1-2-3 worksheet to a delimited ASCII file for exportation to another computer. A macro can help with this task, but you'll want to take care of date conversions yourself before exporting the file.

Figure 13.5 shows a sample worksheet. The data in column E are serial dates displayed in Long International format. Prior to exporting this worksheet, you should change these dates to labels. Here's how.

Move the cell pointer to an out-of-the-way cell in the same row as the top of the range being exported. Make sure that there are as many blank rows beneath the cell as there are rows in the range. Enter this formula:

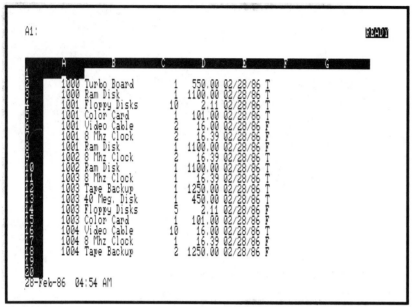

Figure 13.5: Worksheet to be exported

@STRING(@MONTH(E2),0)&"/"& @STRING(@DAY(E2),0)&"/"&
@STRING(YEAR(E2),0)

(The formula is broken into separate lines only to fit in the book.) Put the appropriate cell reference for your worksheet in place of E2 shown in the example.

The formula will display the date in MM/DD/YY format. Copy this formula down for as many rows as there are in the range being exported. Then, convert the entire column of formulas to values by selecting Range Value, highlighting the new formulas, and moving the cell pointer to a new out-of-the-way cell. The new column will contain labels, such as

'02/28/86

Next, replace the serial date column in the range to be exported with the column of label dates. (Select Move, highlight the range of label dates and press Return, move the cell pointer to the top of the column of serial dates and press Return.)

Incidentally, the macro to create delimited files will still work if you do not convert serial dates to labels. However, if you do not convert the dates, the delimited file will have serial dates such as 31470.48, which few software systems can convert. Converting serial dates to labels before the exportation ensures the more common MM/DD/YY format in the delimited file.

Figure 13.6 shows a macro to convert a worksheet file to a delimited ASCII file. As usual, column Z contains range labels. You should create the macro, then save it immediately under a file name such as DelimOut.

```
        Z         AA        AB        AC        AD        AE        AF
50 *---- Macro to create a delimited ASCII file.
51
52 FileName
53 NoCols
54 NoRows
55 Col
56 Row
57 Chunk
58 WorkArea
59
60 \w        {HOME}{CLOSE}
61           /RNCOutGo~{?}~
62           {GETLABEL "Enter Output file name: ",FileName}~
63           {LET NoCols,@COLS(OutGo)}~
64           {LET NoRows,@ROWS(OutGo)}~
65           {OPEN FileName,W}
66           {FOR Row,0,NoRows-1,1,InLoop}
67           {CLOSE}
68
69 InLoop    {LET WorkArea," "}
70           {FOR Col,0,NoCols-1,1,MakeRec}
71           {WRITELN WorkArea}
72           {LET A1,Row+1}~
73
74 MakeRec   {IF @ISSTRING(@INDEX(OutGo,Col,Row))}{Quotes}{BRANCH O
75           {IF @ISNUMBER(@INDEX(OutGo,Col,Row))}{Convert}{BRANCH
76 Ok        {LET WorkArea,@TRIM(WorkArea)&Chunk}
77           {IF Col<NoCols-1}{LET WorkArea,WorkArea&","}
78           {LET Col,Col+1}
79
80 Quotes    {LET Chunk,@CHAR(34)&@INDEX(OutGo,Col,Row)&@CHAR(34)}
81           {RETURN}
82
83 Convert   {LET Chunk,@STRING(@INDEX(OutGo,Col,Row),2)}
84           {RETURN}
85
```

Figure 13.6: Macro to create a delimited ASCII file

To use the macro, retrieve the DelimOut worksheet and home the cursor. Then use File Combine to pull in the worksheet you want to export so it does not overlap cell A1. (If it is a very large worksheet, you may want to use File Xtract to extract a portion of the worksheet to an intermediate file, then use File Combine to pull in the intermediate file.) Convert dates to labels, as discussed earlier.

Type Alt-w to write the delimited file. When the macro creates the range named OutGo, highlight all the data to be exported, as shown in Figure 13.7.

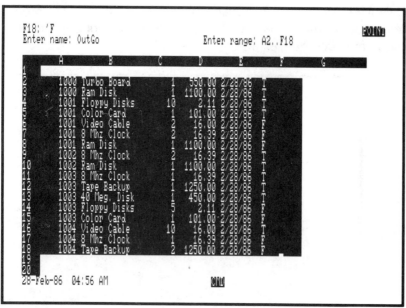

Figure 13.7: Data to be exported is highlighted

When the macro asks for the name of the exported file, enter a legal file name. Include an extension (e.g., Delimit.TXT). The counter in cell A1 will keep you informed of the row number being exported. The READY indicator will appear when the macro is done.

When the exportation is complete, do not save the current worksheet. You can exit 1-2-3 and use the TYPE command to view the delimited file, which will look something like Figure 13.8.

The macro itself begins with several named cells that store data as the macro is executing:

    FileName

    NoCols

    NoRows

```
1000.00,"Turbo Board",1.00,550.00,"2/28/86","T"
1000.00,"Ram Disk",1.00,1100.00,"2/28/86","T"
1001.00,"Floppy Disks",10.00,2.11,"2/28/86","T"
1001.00,"Color Card",1.00,101.00,"2/28/86","T"
1001.00,"Video Cable",2.00,16.00,"2/28/86","F"
1001.00,"8 Mhz Clock",2.00,16.39,"2/28/86","F"
1001.00,"Ram Disk",1.00,1100.00,"2/28/86","F"
1002.00,"8 Mhz Clock",2.00,16.39,"2/28/86","T"
1002.00,"Ram Disk",1.00,1100.00,"2/28/86","T"
1003.00,"8 Mhz Clock",1.00,16.39,"2/28/86","T"
1003.00,"Tape Backup",1.00,1250.00,"2/28/86","T"
1003.00,"40 Meg. Disk",1.00,450.00,"2/28/86","T"
1003.00,"Floppy Disks",5.00,2.11,"2/28/86","T"
1003.00,"Color Card",1.00,101.00,"2/28/86","F"
1004.00,"Video Cable",10.00,16.00,"2/28/86","T"
1004.00,"8 Mhz Clock",1.00,16.39,"2/28/86","F"
1004.00,"Tape Backup",2.00,1250.00,"2/28/86","F"
```

Figure 13.8: Delimited ASCII file from a worksheet

Col

Row

Chunk

WorkArea

The macro homes the cursor, closes any open ASCII file, and helps the user create the OutGo range of data to export. Then the macro asks the user for the name of the output file and stores the answer in the cell named FileName:

\w   {HOME}{CLOSE}
      /RNCOutGo ˜ {?} ˜
      {GETLABEL "Enter Output file name: ",FileName} ˜

The number of columns in the export range is stored in the cell named NoCols. The number of rows in the range is stored in the cell named NoRows:

{LET NoCols,@COLS(OutGo)} ˜
{LET NoRows,@ROWS(OutGo)} ˜

The macro then creates (or opens) the output file in the Write mode. Using OPEN in the Write mode never generates an error, unless you specify a nonexistent drive or directory, because 1-2-3 will just create the file if it cannot find it:

```
{OPEN FileName,W}
```

Next, a loop repeats the subroutine named InLoop for as many times as there are rows in the export range. When all rows have been processed, the macro closes the ASCII file and quits:

```
{FOR Row,0,NoRows-1,1,InLoop}
{CLOSE}
```

Within the InLoop subroutine, the macro stores a blank space in the cell named WorkArea to clear it. Then, for each column in the export range, it repeats the subroutine named MakeRec:

```
InLoop    {LET WorkArea," "}
          {FOR Col,0,NoCols-1,1,MakeRec}
```

After the MakeRec subroutine converts the worksheet row to a delimited ASCII record, the WRITELN command below stores the record on the ASCII file. The LET command increments the visual counter in cell A1 by one:

```
{WRITELN WorkArea}
{LET A1,Row+1} ~
```

The MakeRec subroutine deals with an individual cell item, which becomes an individual field in the ASCII file. The first IF command passes control to a subroutine named Quotes if the cell contains a character string:

```
{IF @ISSTRING(@INDEX(OutGo,Col,Row))}{Quotes}
    {BRANCH Ok}
```

The second IF command passes control to a subroutine named Convert if the cell contains a number:

```
{IF @ISNUMBER(@INDEX(OutGo,Col,Row))}{Convert}
```

Then the macro adds the converted cell contents (stored in the cell named Chunk) to the delimited record stored in the cell named WorkArea:

{LET WorkArea,@TRIM(WorkArea)&Chunk}

If the macro has not reached the last row of the export range, it adds a comma to the end of the delimited record in WorkArea in preparation for the next field:

{IF Col<NoCols-1}{LET WorkArea,WorkArea&","}

The next line increments the Col counter by one to process the next worksheet column for the current row:

{LET Col,Col+1}

The Quotes subroutine adds double quotation marks (ASCII character 34) to the front and back of the cell contents and stores this result in the cell named Chunk:

Quotes   {LET Chunk,@CHAR(34)&@INDEX(OutGo,Col,Row)
&@CHAR(34)}
{RETURN}

The Convert subroutine converts the number in the cell to a character string and stores the result in the cell named Chunk, because numbers must be converted to strings to be concatenated to the record in WorkArea:

Convert   {LET Chunk,@STRING(@INDEX(OutGo,Col,Row),2)}
{RETURN}

The macro is good for general-purpose delimited files and can also be customized for particular applications. For example, you may notice that all the numeric fields in the exported file have two decimal places, while only one column in the actual worksheet has two decimal places. That's because the Convert subroutine in the DelimOut macro rounds all numeric output to two decimal places.

In the the sample worksheet, only the third column (if you start counting from zero) actually has two decimal places. To make the macro follow this same pattern, you need to modify the Convert subroutine so that it calculates the number of decimal places to put into the delimited field. For example, the version below uses the contents of the cell named Dec to determine the number of decimal places to put into the converted number:

81	Z	AA	AB	AC	AD
82					
83	**Dec**				
84	**Convert**	{IF Col=3}{LET Dec,2}{BRANCH Dolt}			
85		{LET Dec,0}			
86	**Dolt**	{LET Chunk,@STRING(@INDEX			
		(OutGo,Col,Row),Dec)}			
87		{RETURN}			

If the macro is processing the third column, the number of decimal places (Dec) is 2. Otherwise, the number of decimal places (Dec) is 0. Dec is then used in the @STRING formula to specify the number of decimal places. Figure 13.9 shows a delimited file created by the modified version of the DelimOut macro.

```
1000,"Turbo Board",1,555.00,"2/28/86","T"
1000,"Ram Disk",1,1100.00,"2/28/86","T"
1001,"Floppy Disks",10,2.11,"2/28/86","T"
1001,"Color Card",1,101.00,"2/28/86","T"
1001,"Video Cable",2,16.00,"2/28/86","F"
1001,"8 Mhz Clock",2,16.39,"2/28/86","F"
1001,"Ram Disk",1,1100.00,"2/28/86","F"
1002,"8 Mhz Clock",2,16.39,"2/28/86","T"
1002,"Ram Disk",1,1100.00,"2/28/86","T"
1003,"8 Mhz Clock",1,16.39,"2/28/86","T"
1003,"Tape Backup",1,1250.00,"2/28/86","T"
1003,"40 Meg. Disk",1,450.00,"2/28/86","T"
1003,"Floppy Disks",5,2.11,"2/28/86","F"
1003,"Color Card",1,101.00,"2/28/86","F"
1004,"Vidio Cable",10,16.00,"2/28/86","T"
1004,"8 Mhz Clock",1,16.39,"2/28/86","F"
1004,"Tape Backup",2,1250.00,"2/28/86","F"
```

Figure 13.9: Output from modified DelimOut macro

Summary

It is virtually impossible to write a single macro to take care of every conceivable data file transfer. However, since most transfers involve either structured or delimited ASCII files, the techniques and macros discussed in this chapter will take care of many situations.

WHAT'S NEW IN VERSION 2

A

THIS **APPENDIX IS** for those readers who have recently upgraded or are contemplating upgrading to version 2.0. The new features are summarized by category.

Worksheet Size

Version 2.0 provides a worksheet with 8,192 rows by 256 columns. A single column can be up to 240 characters wide. Worksheet files are stored with the extension .WK1. The new version supports the 8087 and 80287 math coprocessors for high-speed calculations. Improved memory management allows computers with less RAM to use more of the worksheet. The new version also supports up to four megabytes of RAM.

Worksheet Formats

The Range Format options in version 2.0 provide the following Date and Time formats:

31-Mar-86			
31-Mar		**02:37:15 PM**	
Mar-86		**02:37 PM**	
03/31/86	**(Long Intn'l)**	**14:37:15**	**(Long Intn'l)**
03/31	**(Short Intn'l)**	**14:37**	**(Short Intn'l)**

You can use the Worksheet Global Default Other International options to reconfigure the Long International and Short International dates and times to the formats shown below:

31/03/86	**14.37.15**
31/03	**14.37**

31.03.86	**14,37,15**
31.03	**14,37**
86-03-31	**14h37m15s**
03-31	**14h37m**

You can also specify international number punctuation, as shown below:

12,345.67

12.345,67

12345.67

12345,67

You can use *compose sequences* to specify international currency signs under the Worksheet Global Default Other International options. Once specified, the currency sign is displayed in all Range Format Currency cells.

A compose sequence consists of a press on the Compose key (Alt-F1), followed by a two-digit code. All of the options are listed in Appendix 2 of the *1-2-3 Reference Manual*. A few examples are listed below:

Dutch guilder	{Compose} ff
Cents	{Compose} c¦
British pounds	{Compose} L=
Yen	{Compose} Y=
Pesetas	{Compose} Pt

The older version of 1-2-3 uses the Alt-F1 sequence for STEP. The new version uses Alt-F2 for STEP and Alt-F1 for Compose.

Zero Suppression

The Worksheet Global Zero options allow you to display zeroes either as blanks or as the number 0. This can be especially useful for hiding the results of formulas that evaluate to zero.

Hidden Columns

The Worksheet Column Hide options allow you to hide columns in the worksheet. Hidden columns are invisible to all users. Attempting to move the cell pointer to a hidden column with the GoTo (F5) key results in the error message "Column Hidden." You can conceal macros in hidden columns.

The Worksheet Column Display options show hidden columns with an asterisk next to the column letter and allow you to bring the columns out of hiding.

New Functions

Version 2.0 of 1-2-3 adds many new functions to the worksheet. These are summarized by category in this section.

Financial Functions

@CTERM(*interest,fv,pv*)   @CTERM calculates the number of compounding periods for an investment at present value (*pv*) to reach a future value (*fv*) at a fixed periodic *interest* rate.

@DDB(*cost,salvage,life,period*)   @DDB calculates the double-declining depreciation allowance for an asset at a given *cost,* the predicted *salvage* value, the *life* term, and the depreciation *period.*

@RATE(*fv,pv,terms*)   @RATE calculates the interest rate necessary for an investment of present value (*pv*) to reach a future value (*fv*) over the number of compounding *terms.*

@SLN(*cost,salvage,life*)   @SLN calculates the straight-line depreciation of an asset for a single period given the *cost,* the *salvage* value, and the *life* of the asset.

@SYD(*cost,salvage,life,period*)   @SYD calculates the sum-of-the-years'-digits depreciation allowance of an asset over a *period* of time given the *cost,* the *salvage* value, and the *life* of the asset.

@TERM(*payment,interest,fv*)   @TERM calculates the number of payment periods required for equal *payments* at a given *interest* rate to reach a future value (*fv*).

Logical Functions

@ISNUMBER(*cell*)   @ISNUMBER returns True (1) if the item in *cell* is a number; otherwise, it returns False (0).

@ISSTRING(*cell*)   @ISSTRING returns True (1) if data in *cell* is a character string (label); otherwise, it returns False (0).

Special Functions

@@(*cell*)   @@ returns the contents of the cell address specified in *cell*. Hence, if cell X22 contains 'A1, and cell A1 contains 'Hello, then @@(X22) returns 'Hello.

@CELL(*attribute,range*)   @CELL provides *attribute* information about the cell in the upper-left corner of *range* (see @CELL-POINTER below).

@CELLPOINTER(*attribute*)   @CELLPOINTER displays *attribute* information about the currently highlighted cell. Optional attributes include ADDRESS, ROW, COL, CONTENTS, TYPE, PREFIX, PROTECT, WIDTH, and FORMAT.

@COLS(*range*)   @COLS returns the number of columns in the *range*.

@ROWS(*range*)   @ROWS returns the number of rows in the *range*.

@INDEX(*range,column,row*)   @INDEX returns the value of the cell at the *row* and *column* position in the specified *range*.

Date and Time Functions

In version 2.0, the @NOW function replaces @TODAY. @NOW includes the current time as the decimal portion of the serial date.

@DATEVALUE(*date-string*)   @DATEVALUE returns the serial number of the date specified in *date-string*.

@NOW   @NOW returns the serial number of the current date and time.

@TIME(*hr,min,sec*)   @TIME returns the serial number time of *hr, min, sec.*

@HOUR(*serial date*)   @HOUR displays the hour of the *serial date.*

@MINUTE(*serial date*)   @MINUTE displays the minute of the *serial date.*

@SECOND(*serial date*)   @SECOND displays the second of the *serial date.*

String Functions

The string functions give you control over labels in worksheets and databases.

@CHAR(*x*)   @CHAR returns the ASCII/LICS character of the value of *x.*

@CODE(*string*)   @CODE returns the ASCII/LICS code (number) of the first character in *string.*

@EXACT(*string1,string2*)   @EXACT returns True (1) if *string1* and *string2* are identical. Otherwise, it returns False (0).

@FIND(*portion,string,start number*)   @FIND returns the position at which the smaller *portion* string occurs in the larger *string*. The search begins at the character specified in *start number*.

@LEFT(*string,n*)   @LEFT returns the *n* leftmost characters of *string*.

@LENGTH(*string*)   @LENGTH returns the length of *string*.

@LOWER(*string*)   @LOWER returns *string* converted to lowercase.

@MID(*string,start number,n*)   @MID returns a substring of *string*, starting at the *start number* character, *n* characters long.

@N(*range*)   @N returns the numeric value in the upper-left corner of *range*.

@PROPER(*string*)   @PROPER returns a *string* with the first letter of each word in uppercase and all other letters in lowercase.

@REPEAT(*string,n*)   @REPEAT repeats the character *string n* number of times.

@REPLACE(*original string,start number,n,new string*)   @REPLACE removes *n* number of characters from *original string*, beginning at the *start number* and inserts the characters into *new string*.

@RIGHT(*string,n*)   @RIGHT returns the rightmost *n* characters in *string*.

@S(*range*)   @S returns the character string in the upper-left corner of *range*.

@STRING(*number,dec*)   @STRING converts *number* to a character string with a specified number of decimal places (*dec*).

@TRIM(*string*)   @TRIM removes leading and trailing blanks, if any, from *string*.

@UPPER(*string*)   @UPPER converts *string* to all uppercase letters.

@VALUE(*string*)   @VALUE converts a character *string* with leading numeric characters into a true number (numeric data type).

Character String Lookups

The @VLOOKUP and @HLOOKUP functions can now use character strings as well as numbers. For example, Figure A.1 shows the results of two @VLOOKUP formulas that use a character string argument to look up the customer number and credit limit of an individual named Johnson in the range A1..C8.

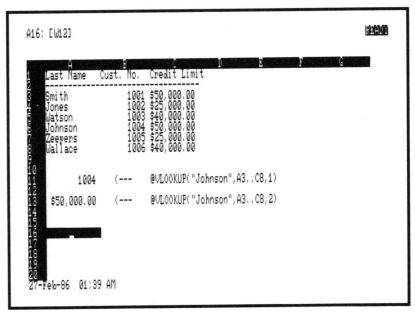

Figure A.1: Results of two @VLOOKUP formulas

Figure A.2 shows how the @HLOOKUP function can determine the column number of a field in a database. This capability is very handy in database management macros, as Chapter 10 of this book demonstrates.

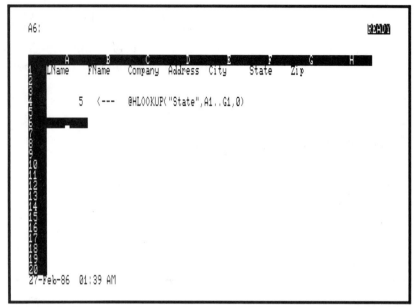

Figure A.2: Column number calculated by @HLOOKUP formula

Range Transposition

The Range Transpose options from the Main menu allow you to transpose columns into rows and rows into columns. For example, you can transpose the range

  Adams
  Baker
  Miller

into the range

  Adams **Baker** **Miller**

and vice versa.

  This capability is especially useful with certain database management macros, as discussed in Chapter 10 of this book.

Range Values

The Range Value options let you copy a range of formulas to a new range, with all formulas converted to their calculated values. This replaces the need to write a macro or to use File Xtract to convert many formulas to their values.

Printing

You can now embed special printer attributes in a worksheet. For example, some portions of your worksheet can be displayed in expanded print, others in compressed print, and others in normal print. To embed a printer attribute in a worksheet, precede the appropriate ASCII code with two ¦ characters. Chapter 5 of this book discusses this topic in more detail.

You can also embed page breaks anywhere in a worksheet by positioning the cell pointer and selecting Page from the Worksheet menu.

Password Protection

Now you can make your worksheets totally inaccessible to unauthorized users. To password-protect a worksheet, use the usual File Save options to save the worksheet. Enter the file name followed by a space and the letter P (or p):

MySheet p

1-2-3 will ask you for the password. Enter a password up to 15 characters in length, then press Return. Make sure you jot down the password and store it in a safe place, because if you forget the password, you'll never be able to access the worksheet yourself! There is no tricky way to sneak in and discover the password.

When you or anybody else attempts to access the worksheet with the File Retrieve or File Combine options, 1-2-3 will ask for the password. If the correct password is not entered, 1-2-3 will display the message "Incorrect password" and will deny access.

New Graphics Features

The Graph Options Scale Indicator options now let you decide whether the scale indicator appears at the left edge of the graph. If you select Yes at this option, a scale indicator, such as (Thousands), will appear at the far-left edge of the graph. If you select No, no indicator will appear.

You can now plot pie charts with an exploded slice and specific hatch marks using codes in the B-Range for the pie chart. Chapter 9 in this book presents instructions and an example. Figure A.3 shows a pie chart with hatch marks and an exploded slice.

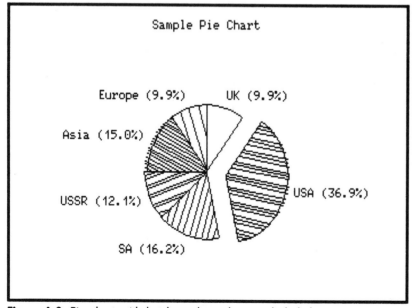

Figure A.3: Pie chart with hatch marks and an exploded slice

New Database Features

A database can now contain up to 8,191 records, with up to 256 fields per record. Also, you can edit records highlighted by a Query Find command.

The 1-2-3 installation program allows you to specify Database Sort sequences, with either numbers before letters (the default sequence) or letters before numbers. Hence a database sort can produce either

> **7-11 Stores**
>
> **Adams**
>
> **Miller**
>
> **Zeepers**

or

> **Adams**
>
> **Miller**
>
> **Zeepers**
>
> **7-11 Stores**

Regression Analysis

Regression analysis lets you view the relationship between a single dependent variable and up to 16 independent variables. You can plot a graph of the results to see the best-fitting straight-line graph among the variables.

For example, suppose you want to predict how well a given stock will perform, and you suspect that the price of gold and silver influence the stock. You have the data in cells B1..D10 of the worksheet shown in Figure A.4. In this example, the stock is the dependent variable (y) and gold and silver are the independent variables (x1 and x2).

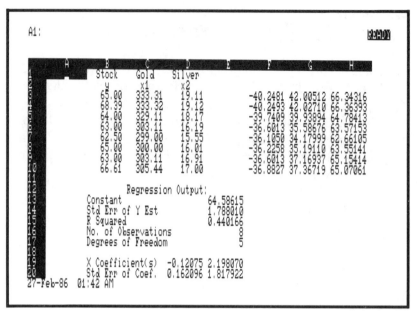

Figure A.4: Regression analysis

To perform a regression analysis, call up the Data menu and select Regression. In this example, you would assign B3..B10 as the Y-Range and C3..D10 as the X-Range of independent variables. The Output range can be any cell on the worksheet that has a few blank columns next to it and a few blank rows beneath it. Cell B12 will do nicely in this example. You can select a Computed or Zero Intercept, the default being Computed. Select Go to see the results.

The Output range (B12) displays lots of numeric results, as you can see in the figure. Unless you happen to be a statistician, the numbers alone probably won't mean much to you.

To see the graph of the relationship, you first need to calculate a Y estimate, which is the sum of the products of the coefficients and independent variables plus the constant. In this example, cell F3 contains the formula D19*C3, the coefficient of X1 times X1. Cell G3 contains the formula E19*D3, the coefficient of X2 times X2. Cell H3 contains the formula

+F3+G3+E13, the sum of the products of the coefficients and x variables plus the constant. All three formulas were copied down seven rows using the usual Copy option from the menu.

Finally, to plot the best-fitting curve, you need to create an XY graph. Be sure to assign the Type XY to the graph. Assign the Y estimate (H3..H10 in this example) to both the X-Range and the A-Range on the graph. The B-Range is the dependent (observed) values; B3..B10 in this example. Set the format for the B-Range to Symbols-only. You might want to make an A-Range legend that reads "Y Estimate" and a B-Range legend that reads "Observed", as in Figure A.5.

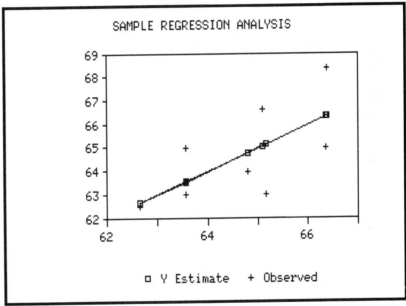

Figure A.5: Graphed results from regression analysis

The + signs show the actual observed stock prices, while the solid line shows the best-fitting curve of the relationship between the stock prices and the prices of gold and silver. As the graph shows, there is a tendency for the stock price to go up as the prices of gold and silver increase.

Matrix Inversion and Multiplication

The Data Matrix options can invert matrices formed by rows and columns of numbers. The range must be a square with a maximum of 90 columns and 90 rows. To invert a range, select Data Matrix Invert, highlight the range to invert, and highlight a range in which to place the results. Figure A.6 shows the initial matrix in cells A1..C3 and the inverted matrix in cells E1..G3.

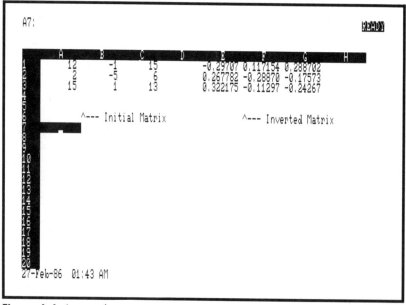

Figure A.6: Inverted matrix

The Data Matrix Multiply options will multiply two matrices of equal size, as long as there are no more than 90 columns and rows in the matrices. Figure A.7 shows the results of multiplying the first matrix (A1..C3) by the second matrix (A5..C7). The result is stored in A10..C12.

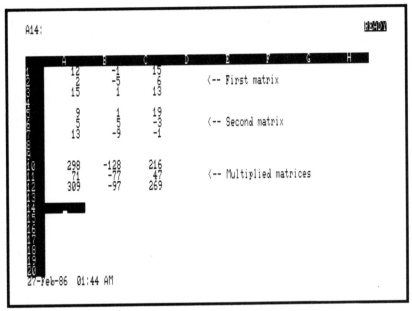

Figure A.7: Multiplied matrices

DOS Access

The System option from the Main menu allows you to temporarily leave 1-2-3 to return to the DOS A> or C> prompt. You can perform any tasks at the DOS prompt, then enter the command EXIT at the DOS prompt to return to your worksheet in 1-2-3. This has some distinct advantages. Before the built-in access to DOS, you needed to save your worksheet then quit 1-2-3 to run an external program. Then you needed to reload 1-2-3 and your worksheet from the DOS prompt, which takes some time.

With the access to DOS built in, you simply select the System option from the menu at any time, and the DOS prompt appears. When you type EXIT at the DOS prompt, 1-2-3 and your currently loaded worksheet appear on the screen immediately, with the cell pointer in its original position.

Interfacing with Other Software

Entering the command LOTUS (as opposed to the old command, ACCESS) brings up options for 1-2-3, PrintGraph, Translate, and so forth. If you select Translate, you'll be given the options below:

What do you want to translate FROM?

> **1-2-3, release 1A**
> **1-2-3, release 2**
> **dBase II**
> **dBase III**
> **DIF**
> **Jazz**
> **SYMPHONY, release 1.0**
> **SYMPHONY, release 1.1**
> **VISICALC**

You can highlight any option and press Return. The Translate utility will then display these options:

What do you want to translate TO?

> **1-2-3, release 2**
> **dBase II**
> **dBase III**
> **DIF**
> **SYMPHONY, release 1.0**
> **SYMPHONY, release 1.1**

Simply select an option, and 1-2-3 takes it from there.

For tricky transfers from mainframes or software systems not included in the Transfer options, the Data Parse options or some macro commands will usually do the trick. Chapter 13 of this book discusses these transfers, and Chapter 6 discusses techniques for converting the many possible date formats from transferred files into 1-2-3 format.

New Macro Commands

Version 2.0 offers the 40 new *macro commands* shown below. Chapter 4 discusses these commands in detail.

{BEEP}	{GETNUMBER}	{QUIT}
{BLANK}	{GETPOS}	{READ}
{BRANCH}	{IF}	{READLN}
{BREAKOFF}	{INDICATE}	{RECALC}
{BREAKON}	{LET}	{RECALCCOL}
{CLOSE}	{LOOK}	{RESTART}
{CONTENTS}	{MENUBRANCH}	{RETURN}
{DEFINE}	{MENUCALL}	{SETPOS}
{DISPATCH}	{ONERROR}	{WAIT}
{FILESIZE}	{OPEN}	{WINDOWSOFF}
{FOR}	{PANELOFF}	{WINDOWSON}
{FORBREAK}	{PANELON}	{WRITE}
{GET}	{PUT}	{WRITELN}
{GETLABEL}		

In addition to the macro commands listed above, version 2.0 supports the original /X commands, so that version 1 macros will function in version 2.0. Since some menus have changed, macros that use the {RIGHT} and {LEFT} arrow keys to make menu selections might need some revision.

Index

Selections from
The SYBEX Library

Integrated Software

MASTERING 1-2-3
by Carolyn Jorgensen
420pp., illustr., Ref. 337-6

This book goes way beyond using 1-2-3, adding powerful business examples and tutorials to thorough explanations of the program's complex features. Detailing multiple functions, powerful commands, graphics and database capabilities, macros, and add-on product support from Report Writer, Spotlight, and The Cambridge Spread-sheet Analyst. Includes Release 2.

ADVANCED BUSINESS MODELS WITH 1-2-3™
by Stanley R. Trost
250 pp., illustr., Ref. 0-159

If you are a business professional using the 1-2-3 software package, you will find the spreadsheet and graphics models provided in this book easy to use "as is" in everyday business situations.

THE ABC'S OF 1-2-3™ (New Ed)
by Chris Gilbert and Laurie Williams
225 pp., illustr., Ref. 0-168

For those new to the LOTUS 1-2-3 program, this book offers step-by-step instructions in mastering its spreadsheet, data base, and graphing capabilities. Features Version 2.

MASTERING SYMPHONY™
by Douglas Cobb (2nd Ed)
763 pp., illustr., Ref. 0-244

This bestselling book has been heralded as the Symphony bible, and provides all the information you will need to put Symphony to work for you right away. Packed with practical models for the business user. Includes Version 1.1.

SYMPHONY™ TIPS & TRICKS
by Dick Andersen
325 pp., illustr. Ref. 0-247

Organized as a reference took, this book gives shortcuts for using Symphony commands and functions, with troubleshooting advice.

BETTER SYMPHONY SPREADSHEETS
by Carl Townsend
287 pp., illustr., Ref. 339-2

For Symphony users who want to gain real expertise in the use of the spreadsheet features, this has hundreds of tips and techniques. There are also instructions on how to implement some of the special features of Excel on Symphony.

MASTERING FRAMEWORK™
by Doug Hergert
450 pp., illustr. Ref. 0-248

This tutorial guides the beginning user through all the functions and features of this integrated software package, geared to the business environment.

JAZZ ON THE MACINTOSH
by Joseph Caggiano/Michael McCarthy
431 pp., illustr., Ref. 0-265

Each chapter features as an example a business report which is built on throughout the book in the first section of each chapter. Chapters then go on to detail each application and special effects in depth.

MASTERING EXCEL
by Carl Townsend
454 pp., illustr., Ref. 0-306

This hands-on tutorial covers all basic operations of Excel plus in-depth coverage of special features, including extensive coverage of macros.

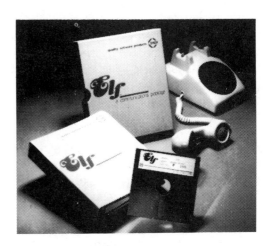

SYBEX Computer Books are different.

Here is why . . .

At SYBEX, each book is designed with you in mind. Every manuscript is carefully selected and supervised by our editors, who are themselves computer experts. We publish the best authors, whose technical expertise is matched by an ability to write clearly and to communicate effectively. Programs are thoroughly tested for accuracy by our technical staff. Our computerized production department goes to great lengths to make sure that each book is well-designed.

In the pursuit of timeliness, SYBEX has achieved many publishing firsts. SYBEX was among the first to integrate personal computers used by authors and staff into the publishing process. SYBEX was the first to publish books on the CP/M operating system, microprocessor interfacing techniques, word processing, and many more topics.

Expertise in computers and dedication to the highest quality product have made SYBEX a world leader in computer book publishing. Translated into fourteen languages, SYBEX books have helped millions of people around the world to get the most from their computers. We hope we have helped you, too.

For a complete catalog of our publications:

SYBEX, Inc. 2344 Sixth Street, Berkeley, California 94710
Tel: (415) 848-8233   Telex: 336311

SIMPSON'S
1-2-3 MACRO
LIBRARY

Available on Disk

If you'd like to use the programs in this book but don't want to type them in yourself, you can send for a disk containing all the macros in the book. To obtain this disk, complete the order form and return it along with a check or money order for $40.00. California residents add sales tax.

SYBEX is not affiliated with SMS Software and assumes no responsibility for any defect in the disk or program.